THE
WORLD'S EVEN DUMBER
CRIMINALS

THE WORLD'S EVEN DUMBER CRIMINALS

UNBELIEVABLE TRUE TALES OF CRIME GONE WRONG

HARPERCOLLINS PUBLISHERS LTD

Published by HarperCollins Publishers Ltd

First edition

HarperCollins Publishers Ltd
Bay Adelaide Centre, East Tower
22 Adelaide Street West, 41st Floor
Toronto, Ontario, Canada
M5H 4E3

www.harpercollins.ca

Library and Archives Canada Cataloguing in Publication

Title: The world's even dumber criminals.
Identifiers: Canadiana (print) 20230148778 | Canadiana (ebook) 20230148816 |
ISBN 9781443468589 (softcover) | ISBN 9781443468596 (EPUB)
Subjects: LCSH: Criminals—Humor. | LCSH: Crime—Humor. | LCSH: Criminals—
Case studies. | LCGFT: Humor. | LCGFT: Case studies.
Classification: LCC PN6231.C73 W67 2023 | DDC 364.102/07—dc23

Printed and bound in the United States of America
23 24 25 26 27 LBC 5 4 3 2 1

CONTENTS

Think of how stupid the average person is,
and then realize half of them are stupider than that.
—GEORGE CARLIN

AUTHOR'S NOTE

Pseudonyms have been used to protect the identities of various individuals mentioned in this book where warranted or deemed appropriate in the circumstances. Any name that appears in quotation marks the first time it appears in the book is a pseudonym and not, as far as we are aware, the real name of the person so identified.

PREFACE

People don't always commit crimes because they're dumb. Some people become criminals out of necessity—they steal to eat. Some become criminals for political reasons, breaking laws deliberately to highlight an injustice.

But then there are the other kind—the egotistical, overconfident criminals. These men and women (apparently a lot more men than women) think they are above the rules. When they look at society, they don't see people doing their best to coexist and collaborate. They view the rest of us as plump sheep they can fleece. They see the laws we live by as a game for fools—a game they aspire to beat.

Deciding to go it alone as an enemy of millions seems like a dumb choice, but that's the choice these criminals make. It rarely ends well, and the outcome of their misplaced ambition is often as funny as it is inevitable. Instead of reaching for the sky, they grab for the gutter—and miss.

Some of the criminals in these pages are drawn to schemes where the flaw should be obvious, but they are too stubborn to see it and too arrogant to recognize their own deficiencies. They bumble through their inept plans and are quickly caught.

Others display a grander scale of sociopathic "dumb." These criminals possess real skill and even show remarkable talent in some areas, but it's all wasted on small-minded criminal endeavors. Their carefully planned frauds and heists often come crashing down when professional crime solvers enter the picture.

We hope you enjoy this selection of bungling burglars, failed fraudsters, and addled assassins.

Just one word of warning—as you read these stories, you may find yourself thinking, *I know what they should have done. I know what I would do* . . . If that happens, don't follow that train of thought too far. You don't want to end up in a sequel to this book.

I THINK I FORGOT SOMETHING

GIBB GLUB GLUB

It isn't always personal items that criminals forget. Sometimes, they forget to do something important.

"Clyde" was a criminal with a special interest in Andy Gibb. Remember him? His three older brothers formed the Bee Gees, and Andy was a big name in music during the disco boom of the late 1970s, with eight top-twenty hits.

But while most fans were interested in Gibb's music, Clyde was more interested in the star's fifty-eight-foot luxury yacht. According to a tantalizingly brief report in the *Colorado Springs Gazette-Telegraph*, it seems that in the summer of 1978, the thief decided to make his move. While the boat lay unattended in Miami, Clyde shifted it from its berth into the water then made a swift getaway across the bay.

If you don't know much about boats, one surprising fact is that most of them have a hole in the bottom. The hole is stoppered with a drain plug, which is like a sturdier version of the plug in your bathtub. When the boat is being stored, the plug is removed from the drain. That way, if the boat gets rained on, the water just drains out through the hole. Boat owners will tell you that the very first thing you want to do before putting the vessel in the water is to make sure the drain plug is installed. Otherwise, your boat has a hole in it—and, well, you don't need to be a boat expert to know what happens then.

Clyde knew enough about boats to get this one into the water, but as the boat left the marina, the criminal skipper skipped a vital step—he forgot to install the drain plug.

Clyde sailed on, but he soon noticed that water was rapidly filling his newly acquired yacht, and the further he traveled, the lower the boat sat in the water. Soon, the engine was submerged and packed in, and

Clyde found himself stranded in the middle of the bay. A short time later, police picked him up—wet, miserable, and still clinging to the half-sunk vessel.

His lapse in memory had pulled the plug on his career as a boat thief.

COLD CASE

In 2003, "Gavin" lived and worked in Fort Yukon, Alaska, a small community on the edge of the Arctic Circle.

Gavin owned a big green duffel bag and didn't want it stolen by thieves, so he wrote his name on the side in giant, bold letters. He knew this would make the bag a less appealing target for criminals. One of the reasons Gavin knew this was that he was himself a small-time burglar. He used the bag to hold the loot and the tools of his trade.

Robbing a house isn't easy during an Arctic summer. A thief can't use the cover of night to move undetected because it doesn't get dark—in Fort Yukon, the sun doesn't set at all during the month of June. Still, Gavin tried to make the best of it, wandering the sunlit streets late at night.

By the small hours of a Saturday morning, he had discovered a house that appeared empty. Using all his finely honed burglar skills, he pulled a hammer from his duffel bag and smashed his way inside.

According to a report in the *Fairbanks Daily News-Miner*, Gavin searched the house for valuables. But as he was exploring one of the bedrooms, he froze. He heard the rattle of keys in the lock. He heard the front door open and people talking. The homeowner, "Wendy," had returned, along with a couple of friends.

Gavin knew he couldn't get out past the new arrivals, so he hid in the bedroom closet.

We don't know exactly what it was that gave away Gavin's location. Perhaps it was the trail of ransacked drawers and cupboards. Perhaps it was the noise he made closing the squeaky closet door. Or perhaps his silhouette was just easy to see through the closet slats in a room well lit by sunlight. Whatever the reason, Gavin was quickly discovered, and he found himself facing Wendy and her two male friends.

Gavin made a run for it. The three tried to stop him, but he fought his way past them and escaped into the night—the sunlit Arctic night.

We're guessing he wouldn't have been difficult for the trio to chase, but they seem to have had their fill of fighting with the crook. Besides, there was no need to chase him. They knew who he was because he'd left his green duffel bag behind—yes, the one with his name on it, in giant letters.

In a town of under 600 people, it wasn't hard for police to track down the thief. Gavin was taken in and charged with burglary, assault, and criminal mischief.

CASH IN POCKET

Thieves are not usually the brightest lights on the tree, and important details have been slipping their criminal minds throughout history. One curious tale comes from a 1911 edition of the *Newark Evening Star and Newark Advertiser*.

A burglar we'll call "Lou" was operating in Newark, New Jersey. He had his sights set on the big house of a local businessman, Herbert Eddy. Lou watched the place, and one evening, when he saw the home-owner heading out for the evening, he seized his chance and broke in.

Lou moved quickly through the house, checking the contents. In one room, he found a suit hanging up. The suit looked new. On a hunch, Lou searched the pockets and hit the jackpot: a wad of bills totaling $38. That may not sound like much, but in those days, when a can of soup was ten cents, it was a lot of money.

Lou stuffed the cash into one the pockets of his own garments. He was about to leave the house when an idea occurred to him. His own clothes were old and worn, but the suit he was looking at on the hanger was smart and new—and, what's more, it looked to be about his size. Although he'd come here looking for cash and valuables, why shouldn't he take the fancy suit, too?

Lou undressed, put his clothes on the hanger, and tried on the new suit. He liked what he saw. He left the house, pleased with his fashion upgrade.

Later that evening, Herbert Eddy returned home. He realized he'd had a break-in. One of his suits was gone, and he was alarmed as he remembered that there had been a large sum of money in the pocket. Then Herbert noticed an unfamiliar set of clothes hanging in the wardrobe, obviously left by the suit thief. He examined the outfit, looking for a clue to the criminal's identity. He didn't find any identification, but he was pleased to discover, in one of the pockets, the sum of $38.

I'LL NEVER FORGET WHAT'S-HIS-NAME

With their trails of phones and personal property, criminals seem to be a forgetful crowd. But the first prize for criminal absent-mindedness must go to a shoplifter in Germany.

"Klaus" was a twenty-nine-year-old man who, in 2020, decided to steal some food from a supermarket in the German town of Bautzen. He walked into the store and calmly lifted a few dollars' worth of groceries, then tried to look nonchalant when he walked out. According to an Associated Press report, he set off the alarm when he went through the doorway. Klaus was startled and made a run for it, but he stumbled and fell hard. Before anyone could grab him, he managed to scramble to his feet again and escape with the stolen goods.

Unfortunately, he'd left behind a vital clue to his identity: his eight-year-old son!

Perhaps it's understandable that, in the heat of the moment, Klaus panicked and ran off alone—but why did he take his son along on his supermarket heist in the first place? Was he trying to give lessons in shoplifting? Did he think a child would give him an innocent, wholesome, "family guy" look? Whatever the reason, leaving the boy behind was a big mistake. The police chatted with the lad and found him very helpful. He told them his name and where he lived, so they had no difficulty tracking down his dad.

The cops took Klaus into custody. He must have been feeling very sorry for himself, fretting about his lost boy, and nursing some injuries he'd received when he tripped and fell. Klaus ended his crime spree by getting treated in hospital.

DON'T FORGET TO CALL

A lapse of memory can incriminate a thief.

In 2019, "Matt" and "Ruth" of Abbotsford, British Columbia, discovered that their garage had been broken into. The garage door was wide open, and so was the door to the family car. According to Global News, Matt's papers were scattered around the car interior, and his wallet and ID were missing—Matt had made the mistake of leaving them in the vehicle.

Ruth phoned the police while Matt set to work tidying up the car. After the papers were put away, he found a mobile phone on the passenger seat. The wallpaper photo showed an unfamiliar face. In the excitement of stealing Matt's personal possessions, the thief must have forgotten his own.

Matt called some of the contacts on the phone, trying to get more information about the thief. Presumably, some of the friends got in touch with the thief, asking what was going on. Before long, the thief phoned Matt, looking to make a deal. Matt made him a reasonable offer:

he'd return the phone if the thief gave him back his property. The thief agreed to the plan. Problem solved.

Unfortunately, the thief must have thought better of it later, because the meeting never happened. What's worse, Matt discovered that his stolen credit cards had been used to make purchases.

The RCMP showed up at the house and began their investigation, taking the phone as evidence. But Matt's wife, Ruth, hadn't given up on the do-it-yourself approach to law enforcement. Before handing over the phone, she had copied the desktop picture. Now she shared the photo on social media, along with the story of how their garage had been broken into and the thief had left the phone in the car.

Ruth's post was shared hundreds of times by readers who were amused or concerned. Some people said they recognized the face in the photo, and passed the information back to Ruth, who sent it on to the police.

Meanwhile, the police were also on the lookout. After spotting a vehicle that had been registered as stolen, the police pulled it over. The driver's face matched the one on the lost mobile phone. They arrested the thief and were able to return most of the property stolen from Matt and Ruth.

There are two morals here: If you're a car owner leaving your vehicle, don't forget your wallet. And if you're a thief breaking into a vehicle, don't forget your phone.

STEALING THROUGH THE CEILING

OCEANS ZERO

Most of us love a good heist movie, and bank robbers are no exception. Perhaps a desire to reenact these Hollywood movie heists explains one strange incident.

In January 2022, in Newcastle, Washington, bank employees noticed a drip from the ceiling. According to NBC News, workers checked the building and found the problem: the bank's roof had a three-foot-square hole cut out of it. Obviously, some thief had tried to get in.

The police were called. They examined the roof, filled out a burglary report, then left the workers to patch the roof. It was soon as good as new. Meanwhile, the bank employees carried on with their work in the branch.

Around 5:30 p.m., the bank had closed its doors and the tellers were doing their end-of-day paperwork. Suddenly, a masked man dropped through the ceiling. He had been waiting in the gap below the roof, hiding among beams and insulation for at least twelve hours. He must have kept very still, because none of the bank staff had heard a thing.

The crook pulled a gun on the terrified employees and took three hostages, tying them to the furniture with zip ties. He demanded money from the vault. The other bank staff explained to him that the bank's security system prevented them from opening the safe. He argued and threatened. He tried to open the vault himself. Finally, he gave up and left the bank through the front door.

As far as we know, the failed bank robber still hasn't been caught.

But when you think about it, his method of robbery doesn't make a whole lot of sense. Why go to the trouble of climbing onto a bank building, cutting a hole in its roof, and waiting there motionless for half a day just to pull a gun on bank staff? You could do that just as easily by walking through the door on a slow afternoon. Did he imagine that, after banking hours, the vault would be open wide, a glittering array of cash, gold, and jewels?

It's possible the thief had intended a Hollywood-style nighttime heist, but things went wrong. He might have entered the roof hoping to drop inside the vault from above, like Tom Cruise in *Mission: Impossible*. Once he'd cut his way under the roof, he looked for a position where he could drop through into the vault below. There was no easy access to the bank vault—because, well, it's a bank vault and they think of things like that—but he took so long looking that he was interrupted by the workers who had been brought in to fix the roof. At that point, he had no choice but to hide out of sight in a corner of the roof space as the workers and then the police did their checks. To his dismay, he found that the workers were fixing the roof, sealing him inside. After twelve hours, and perhaps feeling the need for a washroom, he decided to cut his way through the ceiling of the bank and improvise.

This is just speculation, of course. The true explanation remains a mystery.

But the police are sure that the criminal must have told some people what happened. As one detective said, "It is too bizarre a story for someone to keep to themselves."

THE BINGO HAUL

You've seen the "ceiling crawl" in the movies a thousand times. The hero creeps through the enemy building in the ceiling or air duct, stopping occasionally to peer down through a vent and overhear important conversations by the bad guys.

"Chip" was a middle-aged man who was perhaps inspired by these movie adventures and figured he could use the technique for criminal purposes at a bingo hall in Edmonton. His activities were reported in the *Globe and Mail* in 2006.

It appears Chip's intention was to move through the building using the ducts until he found a room he imagined held huge piles of bingo cash and gold ingots. Then he could fill his pockets and leave silently by the same route.

On a December evening in 2006, he put his plan into action. He entered the building and asked to use the washroom. Once locked inside, he removed a ceiling panel and hoisted himself into the space above, then crawled on his way.

It wasn't quite like the movies, though. The big stars always find themselves in a sturdy ceiling space or gigantic air duct. But Chip was trying to crawl over tiles in a flimsy false ceiling. These tiles are not meant to support a person's weight—and they don't! Feeling the ceiling straining and crumbling beneath him, Chip grabbed tight to a power cable and put some of his weight on that as he shuffled and scraped his way forward.

In the kitchen, a cook was frying burgers on a grill. The cook heard a noise above him—obviously someone was crawling through the ceiling. Moments later, the ceiling collapsed, and Chip fell through. No, he didn't land on the hot grill—that sort of thing only happens in the movies. Instead, he landed on the extractor hood above the oven.

At this point, a less determined—or wiser—thief might have dropped to the floor and run from the kitchen. But Chip was no quitter. His covert mission must continue. As the cook watched in astonishment, he climbed back into the ceiling and continued his slow crawl.

Moments later, the tiles cracked again. This time, Chip's legs went through the kitchen ceiling, but he was still clinging to an electrical cord, so he was dangling several feet from the ground.

The cook had had his fill of Chip's nonsense. He grabbed the intruder's feet and called for help. Then, assisted by some restaurant patrons, he pulled Chip down and pinned him to the ground until the police arrived.

SCHOOL SUSPENSION

A teenage thief was suspended from school. Or rather, suspended *in* school.

"Logan" was a nineteen-year-old who worked at a local construction company. He knew there was a stash of money stored in an elementary school in Natchez, Mississippi, according to *Newsweek*. He wanted that money and he figured he would get it the way he had seen it done in movies—go in through the roof and lower himself on a rope.

On a Sunday night in March 2021, he got through the roof and made his way into the ceiling above the cafeteria. He lowered himself a few feet, then ran into a problem. He couldn't get himself any lower, and he couldn't climb back up. He was just hanging in midair.

None of Logan's attempts to get free worked. He was trapped.

In the end, he had to give up. Fortunately, he was able to reach his mobile phone. He called 911.

The Natchez fire department and police turned up to rescue him. He was then checked out at the hospital before being sent to jail, charged with felony burglary.

THE CREEPING PEEPING TOM

Criminals who climb into ceilings aren't always doing it as part of a burglary. Sometimes their motives are more unsavory.

A Virginia man we'll call "Chris" was a Peeping Tom. The forty-two-year-old had previously been caught in the act and convicted of misdemeanors. He'd also been convicted of a couple of burglary charges. But none of this deterred him from a life of smutty crime.

Chris joined a fitness club and looked for ways to spy on women in the locker rooms. The facility had a suspended ceiling—which, as we've seen, won't support a person's weight. He went into the ceiling and figured out the weight problem. His solution was to set up a series of clips and straps so that most of his weight was borne by the beams above him. Now he could move through the ceiling unseen without cracking the tiles.

Chris was a highly organized pervert. According to a 2022 report in the *Free Lance-Star* newspaper in Fredericksburg, Virginia, he cut holes in the ceiling so that he could peer down into the women's locker rooms. He also set up cameras in the ceiling. He seems to have made voyeurism a full-time job. He spent hours up in the ceiling, spying on people below. He imagined he could maintain his activities without ever being detected.

In January 2021, his world came crashing down—literally. One of his support straps gave way, and Chris fell through the ceiling tiles above the women's locker room. Now it was his turn to be exposed—he still had one limb through another strap, so he dangled in midair, in front of two shocked women who were in the room at the time. He managed to cut himself down, but other gym members heard the commotion from the locker room and ran to help. They grabbed Chris and held him down until the police arrived.

While Chris waited in jail, police investigated the ceiling. They soon discovered how much planning had gone into Chris's creepy interests. Police found the network of straps he'd fixed to the beams, and his cameras. His routine was to go into a washroom, lock the door, and then access the ceiling area by pulling down a hidden rope ladder.

In court, the women from the locker room and the manager of the facility testified how uneasy the experience had made them feel.

The judge agreed. The maximum recommended sentence for this crime is six months, but the judge was so appalled by Chris's crimes that he sentenced him to a whopping nineteen years in prison. To be more precise, the sentence was fifty-nine years, but forty years were (like Chris in the ceiling) suspended. He'll find those prison ceilings more difficult to access.

TWO-FOR-ONE DEAL

Thirty-one-year-old "Carlos" was a violent guy from Norwich, Connecticut. He had previously served prison terms for armed home invasions. In June 2020, he shot and killed his cousin. Now he was wanted for murder.

According to the *Westerly Sun* newspaper, police had chased Carlos, but he had managed to escape into a wooded area where they lost track of him.

Carlos hid in an apartment complex, but a woman living in the building recognized the wanted man and called 911. When police arrived, Carlos escaped into an attic area that ran over five apartments. He tried to avoid detection by lying flat between rafters on foam insulation and drywall. If you know anything about ceilings, you'll know that you want to put your weight on the wooden joists, not the areas in between.

The police were in one of the apartment bedrooms below his hiding place when suddenly the ceiling collapsed, and Carlos fell in front of them. They seized him and put him under arrest.

But he wasn't the only person they caught in the search. Another criminal happened to be hiding in the building. This man was wanted for failing to appear in court. When he saw the building teeming with police, he assumed they had come for him. He panicked, made a run for it, and the police grabbed him without even knowing why he was running. It was only after checking his ID that they discovered they'd caught a second fugitive—albeit a minor one. Don't run if nobody's chasing you.

But Carlos was the most important catch. He was arrested on murder charges as well as first-degree criminal mischief and interfering with a police officer. He was held on $1 million bail.

Carlos's mother proclaimed her son's innocence in the media and started an online crowdfunding campaign to raise money for his legal fees. At last count, only $5 had been donated.

CLIMB-UP IN AISLE TWO

Some criminals have tried to use those lightweight suspended ceilings as an escape route. That doesn't work well, either.

In Edmonton, in the summer of 2018, a criminal couple we'll call "Shane" and "Olivia" were trying to turn a stolen credit card into cash. According to a report on CBC News, they dropped by a local convenience store, and Shane went inside to give the card a try. He bought a can of pop and tried tapping the card to pay for it. The transaction was rejected. He tried again. Rejected again.

The store owner helpfully suggested that Shane could insert the card and enter the PIN. Shane hedged—he couldn't do that because . . . uh . . . it was his girlfriend's card . . . and she was at work. Sure . . .

Shane left the store, but the owner was suspicious of his lame excuse, and became more suspicious when he looked outside the store and saw Shane with Olivia. From the way they were acting, it seemed Olivia must be his girlfriend, but Shane had just said his girlfriend was at work.

The store owner called the RCMP to report what he suspected was a stolen credit card. The couple were still outside the store when the police pulled up a few minutes later. The couple went into the store, but the police followed. As an officer approached Shane, he shoved Olivia into the police officer and jumped away. The officer tried to hold on to Olivia while the store owner grabbed at Shane, but he made a break for it, running through the store, hoping to escape through the back.

In the backroom, Shane tried the door—it was locked. He ran back into the store and dashed up and down the aisles like a rat in a maze.

The officer now had his weapon out, but Shane wasn't giving up. He grabbed a bag of chewy candies and brandished them—it's not clear what he was threatening. Insulin shock, perhaps?

While the officer was preoccupied with Shane, Olivia looked for a way to get out of this mess. More police cars were on their way, but the store owner stood near the main door, preventing her escape through that route.

She ran to the rear of the store and tried the back door. As her boy-friend had done moments earlier, she found it locked. She checked out the washroom, but it didn't seem to offer a good hiding place. Then Olivia spotted a ladder. She climbed up and squeezed into the space above the ceiling. It might have worked as a hiding place, but Olivia was more ambitious than that. She started inching her way across the store, trying once again to get out through the front entrance.

Shane was still putting up a fight, but more officers arrived on the scene, and Shane was finally overpowered. One of the officers went looking for Olivia.

Suddenly, in the center of the store, the ceiling gave way in a shower of broken tiles. Olivia came crashing down, hitting a row of shelves. The police arrested her. The painful fall had taken the fight out of her, and she didn't give the officers any further trouble.

After the arrest, the RCMP gave special thanks to the store owner, whose action "was instrumental in helping with the apprehension of both suspects." Nobody was seriously hurt. Shane and Olivia were charged with using a stolen credit card, resisting arrest, assaulting a police officer, attempting to disarm a police officer, and resisting arrest from someone aiding the police.

Their movements were captured on the store cameras and later became a popular video on YouTube, accompanied by slapstick music. It's an appropriate soundtrack for two criminal clowns.

PLAYER SUSPENDED

One unusual ceiling crime involved major league baseball players carrying out a robbery in the middle of a game.

It was all about a baseball bat.

In professional baseball, bats must meet official standards—they need to be a certain size and weight. Some players try to dodge the rules and use a "corked bat," which is made by hollowing out the middle of a wooden bat, then replacing the wood, usually maple, with cork, which weighs much less. The bat looks normal from the outside, but because the corked bat is lighter, the batter can swing it faster, hitting the ball with more power.

As it happens, these beliefs about corked bats are mostly wrong—scientists have tested bats with and without cork, and there doesn't seem to be much advantage to the corked version. The faster bat speed is offset by the lower weight, which prevents the bat from driving the ball any harder; in fact, in some ways, a corked bat performs less well than a legitimate one. But what mattered was that players *believed* in the corked bat. And what mattered more was that officials would punish players caught using one.

In July 1994, the Cleveland Indians (now the Cleveland Guardians) played the Chicago White Sox in Chicago. The manager of the White Sox got a tip that a Cleveland outfielder, Albert Belle, was using a corked bat. The manager went to the umpire and challenged the bat. The umpire confiscated it, and it was locked in the umpires' dressing room so that it could be inspected later.

Belle's teammates were worried. They knew the bat Belle had been using that day was corked—because all of Belle's bats were corked. If the secret were to be discovered, they could lose one of their best players. The team couldn't afford to have the bat examined.

A relief pitcher, Jason Grimsley, had an idea. He had noticed that the players' dressing room and the umpires' room both had false ceilings.

Although there were solid walls between the rooms, he figured it might be possible to go from one room to the other via the ceiling. It seemed worth a try, so the team sent Grimsley on a secret mission—to steal the corked bat and replace it with a normal one. They handed him a replacement bat to use in the switch; it belonged to first baseman Paul Sorrento and was legitimate.

While the game continued on the field, Grimsley went to the dressing room, put a flashlight in his mouth, and crawled into the ceiling. As we've seen, this is never as easy as it looks in the movies, but Grimsley successfully made it to the umpire's room and replaced the confiscated bat with the substitute. Meanwhile, his teammates won the game, beating the White Sox, 3–2.

Unfortunately, the substitution of Belle's corked bat with Sorrento's regular one was easy to detect. For one thing, the crawl through the space above the ceiling had left a trail of broken tile pieces and bent metal supports. For another, the switched bat had Sorrento's name on it. If you think thieves are dumb, try sports stars trying to be thieves.

The matter now became criminal. The White Sox called in the police and said they would charge the burglar. They soon figured out the route the intruder had taken—a trail that led back to the Cleveland dressing room.

The American League demanded that Cleveland provide Belle's original bat. If they refused, the league would bring in the FBI to investigate the theft and substitution. The team had no choice: they handed over one of Belle's actual bats. With great ceremony, the bat was X-rayed and sawed in half to reveal a cork interior. Belle was suspended for seven games. Sadly, his rule-breaking wasn't limited to baseball. In the years that followed, he had a few other run-ins with the law, and spent some time in prison.

And the team thief? Grimsley confessed to the crime years later in an interview with the *New York Times*. The former relief pitcher wasn't punished. Which made him a relieved pitcher.

THE ART OF CRIME

ONE STEP A-HEAD OF THE LAW

One of the risks of burglary is that you never know what kind of person lives in the home you're breaking into. There's always the possibility that the homeowner could be someone dangerous.

"Casey" was a small-time crook living in Liverpool, England. According to the *Guardian*, in 2003, he broke into an apartment while the owner was away. He searched the place and grabbed a few hundred pounds' worth of electronics. But his search stopped when he came across something truly horrific—a human head, stripped of its skin, and preserved in a large jar. Casey was shocked, nauseated, and terrified. What kind of psychotic monster lived here? Where was the rest of the body? How many other people had he killed? What would he do to keep his dark secrets? Was he coming back? Casey wasn't taking any chances. He quickly left the apartment.

Back at his own home, Casey agonized over what to do next. Of course, the easiest thing would be to put the terrible experience behind him. If he went to the police, he'd have to explain how he came to be in the apartment, and he would be arrested. On the other hand, if he didn't say something, the killer might strike again—more innocent lives could be lost. Perhaps it was worth taking a burglary rap to save a human life. He even talked to his mother about his dilemma, admitting his criminal activities and asking for her advice.

While Casey was still wrestling with his conscience, he got picked up on an unrelated matter. At this point, he seems to have figured he had nothing to lose—the arrest was clearly fate. He told the detectives about the burglary and about the grisly discovery he had made. They believed Casey and took the matter very seriously.

The police went to the apartment. Nobody was home and the door was locked, as Casey had left it. The cops broke down the door and searched the place. Sure enough, there was the head in a jar—although on closer examination it wasn't quite what it had appeared to be. Inside the formaldehyde-filled jar was a metal frame, molded in the shape of a head, and covered in bacon.

It turned out that the owner of the apartment was a conceptual artist named Richard Morrison. When he returned from his time away, he discovered that his apartment had been broken into twice, once by Casey and once by the police.

He explained that he had created this object as an artwork—the frame was based on his own head. He was amazed to hear what had happened in his absence. Artists are used to getting a wide range of responses from the public, but Morrison said, "I never expected to get this reaction."

As for Casey, the police said that after the shock of finding the bacon head, he vowed to give up crime for good. That's the restorative power of art.

IT'S IN THE BAG

Sometimes a dumb approach to an art heist can actually work.

A young Greek man we'll call "Nico" seems to have had a strong interest in paintings. In 2012, a new gallery had just opened in New York. The gallery, Venus Over Manhattan, had an exhibition of art titled *À Rebours*, meaning "against the grain." It included works by a range of artists from the 1700s to the 1970s. The newer art included pieces by Andy Warhol and a 1949 drawing by Salvador Dalí.

Nico wanted that Dalí, but it wouldn't be easy. The drawing was worth $150,000. Naturally, the gallery had security cameras and a guard.

Nico assembled his equipment: an empty shopping bag ... and nothing else. He walked into the exhibition, a nervous kid in a checkered shirt, and walked past the security guard. The guard noticed Nico but didn't take much interest—perhaps he just didn't see Nico as a threat.

After spending a quarter of an hour in the gallery, Nico walked over to the Dalí, removed it from the wall, and put it into his shopping bag. Then he walked out again.

The security video showed the moment the drawing was stolen, with the security guard standing nearby. But while the camera caught the thief, nobody else did. By the time the theft was noticed, the valuable drawing was gone.

Talking to the *New York Times*, the owner of the gallery was flabbergasted that a robbery like this was possible. Suspicion fell on the security guard—was he in on it? No, it seemed he was just bad at his job.

Many people wondered how the thief would be able to profit from this crime, since it's very difficult to sell a stolen painting.

However, Nico didn't even try to sell it. In fact, soon after carrying out the robbery and flying to Greece, he seems to have been filled with remorse. He sent the drawing back to the gallery anonymously by express mail and sent the gallery an email with the tracking number for the package. The artwork was safely returned.

But police weren't going to drop the investigation just because the stolen art had been recovered. They analyzed the mailing tube the drawing was shipped in. It had a fingerprint. They matched it to a print in their records from a supermarket shoplifter and identified Nico. He was still in Greece, so they sent him a fake job offer to lure him back to the United States. When he arrived in New York, he was arrested. Nico pleaded guilty in court. He got off lightly—he spent two weeks in jail and had to pay $9,100 in fines before being deported.

DOUBLE YOUR MONET

The problem with forging high-value art is that most buyers won't pay top dollar unless the art is accompanied by certificates of authenticity, and those certificates need to be verified by independent experts. But one art dealer found a unique way around all that.

"Farid" was an Iranian-born engineer who became interested in art as a profitable investment. He owned several galleries in Manhattan, and he also invested in art for himself. He owned paintings by many important artists, including Gauguin, Monet, and Renoir.

According to the *New York Times*, his stroke of criminal insight was to hire artists to make plausible copies of some of his valuable artworks, then sell the copies as the originals, along with the certificates from the original works. That way, he could keep the valuable art he collected while collecting the money it would be worth if he sold it.

For this scam to work, he needed to ensure the new owners didn't have the paintings authenticated. He'd previously found that buyers in Asia were particularly trusting—if the paperwork looked right, they would accept it, rather than go through the fuss of hiring a European expert to assess it. Farid hired some low-paid artists, gave them a space to work above his gallery, and they made forgeries of valuable works of art, painted on old canvases from low-value paintings. He sold those phony works, with the genuine certificates, and made a huge profit.

Years later, Farid had another idea—and this is where things get *really* dumb. He decided to sell his own real paintings. He no longer had their certificates of authenticity, but he figured that was not a problem; it had been years since he had sold the fake paintings. He brought in experts to examine the real ones. They confirmed that his genuine paintings were indeed genuine, and they gave him new certificates of authenticity.

Farid might have been tempted to copy the paintings a second time and make more sales to the Asian market, but that seemed too risky—after all, Japanese art enthusiasts talk to each other. Instead, he sold the genuine paintings to buyers in New York and London.

He was racking up millions with this scheme, but the risks were obvious. What happens when someone realizes that their valuable, one-of-a-kind painting is also owned by someone else? And that's exactly what happened in May 2000. The auction house Christie's was selling a Gauguin painting, *Vase de fleurs*, which shows a vase of flowers. The painting included its certificates of authenticity. At the same time, Farid was selling the real painting, also with its certificates, at another big auction house, Sotheby's.

It was pure coincidence that both the original and the copy happened to end up being auctioned at the same time, but the timing couldn't have been worse for Farid. It didn't take a genius to see that something was very wrong here. Of course, the Christie's version was the fake, while the one Farid was selling at Sotheby's was real.

Farid denied any knowledge of how a second painting had appeared, and he pocketed $310,000 on the Gauguin; however, it didn't take long for people to become suspicious of Farid's involvement. Other art buyers started checking their records of items sold by Farid. There were two identical Chagalls and two identical Monets. In total, he'd duplicated at least twenty-five paintings and made an estimated profit of $25 million.

Farid was arrested by the FBI and charged with fraud. He was sentenced to forty-one months in prison, fined $12.5 million, and had to surrender eleven other works of art. After he got out of prison, he went back to running a New York art gallery. You can visit it today. But if you see a painting you want to buy there, you might want to check to see if it's available for less in Tokyo.

THERE'S NO MONEY IN ART

Sometimes there's a fuzzy boundary between crime and art. For example, it would be a crime to destroy a valuable artwork, but in a famous incident in 2018, the artist Banksy sold an image of a girl with a balloon, and as the auction closed with a final bid of $1.4 million, a hidden shredder destroyed most of the artwork. The fame of this self-destructing artwork made it even more valuable as a new piece (including a free shredder!), and three years later, the shredded picture was resold for eighteen times the original sale price.

A Danish artist named Jens Haaning tried a variation on this crime-as-art theme. He was hired by the Kunsten Museum of Modern Art to re-create one of his earlier artworks. The original piece was made of piles of genuine banknotes. The money was arranged on a large canvas and a smaller canvas, showing the stark difference between the annual incomes of Danes and Austrians.

The museum provided the artist with the appropriate banknotes—enough to represent a year's salary in Danish kroner and Austrian euros; however, instead of re-creating his earlier work, the artist gave the museum two blank canvases. The artist said that this was his new work, and its title was *Take the Money and Run*.

The museum officials were amused at Haaning's little joke, but then responded, "Seriously, though, where's that money? We need it back."

Haaning cheerfully refused to return the cash. In an interview with the Danish morning radio show *P1 Morgen*, he said, "The work is that I have taken their money."

If an artist is given money to make an artwork, and instead he just walks off with it, is that really art? Isn't it just theft? Haaning was asked that question in the interview with *P1 Morgen*. He said no. "It's not theft. It is a breach of contract, and breach of contract is part of the work."

He encouraged other workers who didn't like their working conditions to follow his example.

The stunt received worldwide publicity, so the museum displayed the blank canvases as part of an exhibition about artists in the workplace. The exhibition is titled *Work It Out*. Visitors might try to work out whether they're looking at an artwork or a con job.

After the exhibition was over in 2022, the museum still hadn't got its money back, so it announced plans to take legal action. But they say they won't go to the police. If their response seems half-hearted, perhaps that's because they have had more attention from this stunt than they could ever have received from the work they first commissioned.

As of this writing, the artist remains defiant, saying, "This is only a piece of art if I don't return the money."

So, is it a dumb crime? Is it a brilliant crime? Is it a crime at all? That's another situation where the rest of us may just have to "work it out."

SHEIKH-DOWN ARTIST

Two brothers, "Mateo" and "Daniel," from Catalonia in Spain, had an interest in art. They were offered a good deal on a painting by one of the most famous Spanish painters in history, Francisco Goya.

The painting showed Antonio María Esquivel, a bearded Spanish artist in aristocratic clothing, and it came with certificates of authenticity. According to a report on Artnet.com, the seller was asking 270,000 euros. The brothers put down a deposit of 20,000 euros, intending to pay the rest on a payment plan.

But when the painting was examined, the experts noticed that one of the details was wrong: the portrait was missing a medal that should have been present. The painting was a forgery, a skillful fake from the 1800s, and it had fooled the earlier experts. The sellers demanded the full sale price, but when the case went to court, the transaction was halted. The court ruled that the brothers could keep the painting for the amount they'd already paid.

So, now the brothers had a Goya that was realistic but fake. But they also had a certificate of authenticity saying it was a real Goya. They figured *they'd* been conned, so why shouldn't they con the next guy? Maybe their fake Goya could be turned into real moolah.

After sitting on the painting for a few years, the brothers looked around for a sucker to buy it. In 2015, they connected with an Italian broker, "Rocco." He said he was interested in acquiring the painting. Rocco was part of the entourage of a fabulously wealthy Arab sheikh. The sheikh wanted to invest in quality artworks and would love to own a genuine Goya. Rocco suggested that he might be able to get the sheikh to pay as much as four million euros for such a fine painting.

The deal sounded pretty good to Mateo and Daniel, but before things went any further, Rocco wanted to make sure he got his cut—he asked for a broker's fee of 300,000 euros, to be paid privately to him in exchange for arranging the sale to the sheikh. There was no risk: when they met, the brothers could hand Rocco his fee, and Rocco would give them the first payment from the sheikh.

The brothers scrambled to find the cash for Rocco's fee. They ended up borrowing it from a friend. It was small potatoes compared to the huge sum they'd make when they sold their fake Goya.

They traveled to Turin, in Italy, to exchange the funds. Rocco handed over the first installment for the painting—1.7 million Swiss francs. He asked for his payment. But Mateo and Daniel were no fools. Before proceeding any further, they wanted to check the bills at a bank machine. Rocco had no issue with that—he even helped them with the process. Yes, the bills were indeed genuine. Satisfied, they took the bag of Swiss francs and handed over the 300,000-euro commission to Rocco. They each went their separate ways.

The brothers were overjoyed. It was happening. Their scheme was working. They were rich, and once they unloaded the Goya onto the sucker sheikh and got the remaining payments, they would be even richer. The pair traveled on to Switzerland, where they could put their newfound wealth into a Swiss bank account. It would be safe there from prying eyes. Only fools pay taxes.

But when they tried to deposit the money, the bank rejected it. It seemed that the money in their bag was all fake—all of it. Just photocopies of Swiss francs. Apparently, when Rocco helped them check the money, he performed a switch, perhaps handing them the same bills over and over. The money they had carefully checked in the machine wasn't the same as the money they took away.

If Mateo and Daniel had been smarter, they might have wondered why they had to pay cash to Rocco in the first place, when he was already carrying cash for them. Why not just take a few handfuls from the sheikh's "payment" and give that money to Rocco? Of course, the reason was that Rocco wanted their real cash, not his "funny money."

The brothers made some phone calls but were unable to get hold of Rocco or the sheikh. With growing horror, they realized there was no sheikh and no art deal. They had just paid a mysterious stranger 300,000 euros for nothing and come away with a bag full of worthless paper.

The sorry pair made their way back home. For reasons known only to themselves, they kept the bag of phony cash with them as they crossed the border from Switzerland. Bad idea. The French authorities examined the money and realized it was counterfeit. They sent a message to their Spanish counterparts. When the brothers rolled into Spain, they were arrested by the Spanish police for trying to smuggle 1.7 million in counterfeit Swiss francs into Spain. The brothers were charged with fraud, and the fake money was confiscated. The police also searched the brothers' homes and found the fake Goya, which they also confiscated.

Their attempts to sell a fake Goya had earned them only fake cash and left them 300,000 euros in debt.

FIT TO BE COUNTERFEITED

AND HERE'S THE BILL

Technology has made it much easier for a criminal to print low-grade counterfeit currency—but being dumb can make the process harder again.

"Perry" needed a way to make money, so he decided to take the term literally. In 2013, he bought himself an inkjet printer and started printing sheets of hundred-dollar bills, two bills on each sheet of paper. They were about as convincing as you'd expect from money printed on regular paper with a cheap printer. Perry was disappointed with the results. What had happened to quality, to craftsmanship, to the days when a $60 inkjet printer could knock off a passable fake banknote?

Disgusted with the disposable world he was living in, Perry put the printer back in its box and marched into his local Walmart in the Wisconsin village of Lake Hallie. Perry wanted his money back.

According to the *Chippewa Herald*, the Walmart staff were happy to help. They asked for his receipt. Perry didn't have a receipt. (That might be because he didn't buy the printer from Walmart in the first place.) But that didn't matter to Perry—the printer was there, and it was in its box. That should be enough for him to get a refund.

The clerk dutifully checked the contents of the box. It contained a printer, but the paper tray was missing. So was the installer CD. One surprising thing that *was* present was Perry's handiwork—a sheet of paper with prints of hundred-dollar bills. The employee presented this to Perry.

Unfazed by the incriminating discovery, Perry crumpled the page and threw it aside. He decided to negotiate with the Walmart clerk. He'd accept half the price. Come on! It was a good deal! A printer, with most of its parts, in its original box. How could they turn that down?

The Walmart staff declined his offer and said he'd have to leave the store. Perry was having none of it. He wasn't leaving until the matter was settled to his satisfaction. He stayed there, insisting on his refund until the store called the police.

Perry refused to talk to the officers. He warned them not to bother him, or he would hurt them. Unsurprisingly, instead of being intimidated by Perry's threats, the cops grabbed him and arrested him. When they searched his pockets, they found another $300 of Perry's special home-brew cash.

A check of the records showed that Perry was already wanted by the police for burglary and armed robbery. He now had some new charges added: forgery, attempted theft by fraud, and resisting arrest. And he made his next set of digital prints by rolling his fingers on an ink pad.

D-I-Y MONEY

It is risky trying to spend counterfeit currency. Some criminals get around that by passing the problem on to someone else.

"Warren" worked as a vault associate at a Home Depot store in Tempe, Arizona. His job involved taking the money from the store's cash registers, then counting and bagging it so it could be sent to the bank. Warren knew he couldn't steal the store's money outright—the discrepancy would be quickly traced back to him—but a more subtle approach crossed his mind. What if he took a few juicy hundreds from each stack of bills and replaced them with fake money? Nobody could fault him. It would look as if a careless cashier had made the mistake.

According to ABC News, Warren bought some "prop money" online. The bills could pass for real currency if you didn't look too closely. Only a few small details were different. A real hundred-dollar bill has the text "This note is legal tender for all debts, public and private." On the fake notes, the fine print reads, "This note is not legal. It is original to be used for motion pictures." And where the real bill had the name "Franklin" below the figure of Benjamin Franklin, the fake had "Best Prop Money." But anyone not looking at these details might be fooled. Warren began substituting fake hundreds for the real thing. Nobody seemed to notice, so he kept at it and was making a pretty good income for what he figured was an undetectable crime.

Warren was living in a fool's paradise. He hadn't been at it long before accountants at Home Depot noticed that their store in Tempe was losing much more than usual on counterfeit currency. Suspicion quickly fell on Warren, but his guilt was difficult to prove. The management wanted a conviction, so they took a slow and careful approach. They brought in their own security personnel, security people from the bank, and the US Secret Service. Many agents watched Warren on security cameras, hoping to catch those moments when he took money from the bank deposits and discreetly substituted it with bills from his wallet.

A search of his online activity showed that Warren had purchased fake currency at least twenty times. It was estimated that he'd used his substitute money to steal nearly $400,000 from the store between 2018 and 2022.

By January 2022, the investigation had collected enough information to make a move. Warren was arrested. He admitted his guilt and agreed to repay the money. But he didn't get off that lightly. He was also charged with "uttering of counterfeit US currency," which can mean up to twenty years in prison. A police search of his house turned up $5,000 in counterfeit currency, and over $27,000 in real—presumably stolen—cash.

THE MILLION-DOLLAR BILL

Why try to pass twenties and fifties in counterfeit currency? What if you could pass a million at a time?

In 1988, the American Bank Note Company printed a novelty million-dollar bill. The front shows the Statue of Liberty, while on the reverse is an image of Mount Rushmore. The bill has a serial number (unique to each bill), is printed on security paper, and includes fluorescent highlights and microprinting. It is meticulously printed and looks quite real.

The United States has never issued a million-dollar bill. The highest-value bill ever circulated to the public in the United States was a paltry $10,000, and even that was discontinued in 1969. The most valuable bill currently circulating is the hundred.

Because a million-dollar bill has never existed, printing a pretend one isn't against the law—as long as it's just for fun and you don't try to pass it off as real. To make sure nobody gets fooled, the American Bank Note Company included fine print on their bill saying that it is not negotiable.

A few other companies have copied this idea, printing their own versions of the million-dollar bill, although not to the high standard of the American Bank Note Company's offering.

The bill is an entertaining gift, and most recipients laugh and perhaps imagine what it would be like to spend it. But you won't be surprised to learn that some dumb criminals have tried it for real.

In 2004, "Cherie" put three of these bills in her purse, then went shopping at Walmart, that well-known millionaire's playground. NBC News reported that she put more than $1,600 worth of goods in her trolley and pulled out a million-dollar bill to pay for it.

She was immediately arrested. She claimed she had thought the bill was legitimate. "You just can't keep up with the US Treasury," she told NBC News from jail. Yes, Cherie, in these fast-changing times, it's a mistake anyone can make. Her real millions were probably in her other purse.

In 2012, "Stevie" also decided to spend his million-dollar bill at Walmart, according to the *Winston-Salem Journal*. This fifty-three-year-old dim-crim-wit heaped more than $400 in goods into his shopping cart, including a vacuum cleaner and a microwave oven. Did he leave the store with the merchandise, a parade of eager helpers, and an attaché case holding his change in hundreds? No. He left in police custody and was charged with "attempting to obtain property by false pretense" and "uttering a forged instrument."

That's usually how it goes. But one woman got further than most. "Sue" had one of those million-dollar bills and perhaps spent a little too much time fantasizing about spending it. In 2001, according to an Associated Press report, she walked into a bank in Newport, Pennsylvania, and asked to open a new account. The teller politely filled out the paperwork, then asked for the funds Sue intended to deposit. Sue presented her million-dollar banknote.

Most bank employees are trained to know what money looks like, but the one across from Sue was even less on the ball than she was. Perhaps the teller was impressed by Sue's confidence, or just assumed it was a denomination they hadn't heard about in banking class, because, you know, "you just can't keep up with the US Treasury." After a moment's hesitation, the bill was accepted and deposited, and Sue's new bank account showed a healthy million-dollar balance.

Sue went home and waited, nervously checking her bank account. Surely the bank would discover their error. But no, it was still there. As the days passed, Sue's excitement grew as she found the fortune still sitting in her account. Doing her best to stay cool, she transferred a portion of the funds to her husband's account. The transaction went through. She'd done it! She was rich!

Unfortunately for Sue, bank errors like this don't go unrecognized for long. At some point, another bank employee—presumably someone who had received a passing grade in Money Recognition 101—queried the vast sum in Sue's account and the novelty paper backing it. We can only imagine the corporate panic that followed. What we do know is that the police were summoned and Sue was arrested and jailed, charged with sixteen counts of theft by deception.

CAN YOU SPLIT A TWENTY?

In 2015, England's *Daily Mirror* reported a fake bill that one police officer said was "probably the worst forgery we've ever seen."

When he said "worst," he didn't mean it was a threat to the money system. He meant it was unbelievably badly executed. The fake in question consisted of a twenty-pound note reproduced on a photocopier. The counterfeiter's copier clearly didn't do double-sided printing, so they had printed the note on two separate sheets and attached them—with staples.

Incredibly, when this note was offered as payment at a bar in Manchester, the bartender accepted it. Later, when the unusual bill was discovered in the cash drawer, management suspected that something was wrong and took it to the police station.

Fake notes like this are sometimes used as a practical joke. The joker may leave the fake on the ground, then watch as a sucker runs to claim it. In this case, it's possible that a joker pulled the follow-up gag of using the bill to buy drinks, not expecting it to be accepted (although that wouldn't be a good excuse in court).

A police spokesman reminded business owners to look at the money they receive. He added, "We want to make it clear that we are not trying to embarrass anyone for accepting this as legal tender." Apparently, he managed to keep a straight face as he spoke.

ACE IN THE HOLE

We associate counterfeiters with banknotes, but there have been many other profitable ways to counterfeit valuable papers. One of the more unusual crimes was forging playing cards.

In the 1700s, playing cards in England were subject to a large tax. To prove the tax had been paid, a stamp would be placed on the outside of the pack. A second mark was also placed on the ace of spades—a card that was printed only on government presses, and whose design had the sort of intricacy you'd see on a banknote.

In those days, ninety-five percent of the price of a pack of cards was tax. Predictably, the people who made and sold these decks of cards wondered if there was a way to game the system and keep more of the price for themselves.

Richard Harding was a playing card manufacturer in the early 1800s. Harding ran two shops selling cards in London, and like all his colleagues, he purchased "duty cards"—the licensed aces—from the government printers. His shops did a brisk trade, but government agents noticed he wasn't buying as many aces as they expected. They investigated his business and examined his cards more closely. His aces were forged. After searching the properties of his associates, they discovered the printing plates he'd used to make the fake cards.

In 1805, Harding was tried for counterfeiting and selling the cards, found guilty, and sentenced to death. The government took this crime very seriously. Despite calls for him to be spared, he was hanged at Newgate prison. The case had been in all the papers, and a huge crowd turned out for the execution.

Despite the fearsome penalties, Harding wasn't the only one trying to get around the card duty. Around the same time, a twenty-eight-year-old printer named John Blacklin figured he had found a safer way to avoid the tax. He sold bargain-priced decks of fifty-one playing cards—all the cards except the expensive ace of spades. And if you happened to be one of those picky players who wanted to complete the set, he also sold packets with a dozen not-entirely-official aces of spades. With one ace-of-spades set and a stack of incomplete decks, you could buy a lot of cards without paying any tax.

The way Blacklin saw it, the scheme was pure genius.

Or maybe not.

When agents got wind of the scheme, Blacklin was arrested and hauled before a judge. His lawyers argued that the aces weren't taxable on their own, and neither were the incomplete decks. The court was not convinced; as far as they were concerned, the aces were forged. Blacklin was convicted of "feloniously vending playing cards." He was also sentenced to death.

The tax on cards continued in the UK until 1960, although by then nobody was being hanged for violations. The amount of the tax hadn't kept up with inflation, and when someone calculated that the cost of collecting the tax was more than the money the government was making from it, the card tax was dropped for good.

Despite the disappearance of the tax, the laws influence the design of playing cards even today. In many packs, the most ornate card in the pack is still the ace of spades.

THE BICYCLE THIEVES

TAKEN FOR A RIDE

In 2013, "Ashley" worked as a bartender in downtown Vancouver. She had spent some of her hard-earned tips on a good bicycle worth over a thousand dollars. According to a report in the *Globe and Mail*, she went to visit a friend, and carefully locked up her prized bike with a high-security lock.

Ashley hadn't accounted for Vancouver's high level of bike theft. Criminals are brazen, knowing that the police don't usually spend much time chasing down stolen bikes, even expensive ones. When Ashley came back to where she'd locked her bike, it was gone. She was devastated. She reported the theft to police but knew the odds of getting it back were small.

But shortly afterward, one of her friends, who knew about the theft, drew her attention to a new ad on Craigslist. "Doesn't that look like your bike?"

Ashley checked out the ad, and it certainly did look like her bike—the same make and model, and a bargain at $300.

Ashley decided to take the matter into her own hands. She called the seller, "Joshua," and pretended to be an interested buyer. She suggested that they meet so that she could look at the bike, as she just happened to have the day off. Joshua was taken in by her act, and maybe a little charmed. He said sure, he'd meet her.

She met Joshua in the parking lot of a local McDonald's. As soon as she saw him with the bike, she could tell it was hers: it had the same custom brakes and the same stickers she had put on it. Working hard to maintain her composure, she kept playing the interested customer. She asked Joshua if she could possibly take the bike for a test ride.

"OK," said the bike thief—adding, with a laugh, "Don't ride away!" He knew a thing or two about that!

Ashley hopped on the bike, and she did ride away, not stopping until she'd found a spot where she was out of his sight but could still watch him. At first, Joshua was puzzled and confused. Then, it seemed, he realized something was seriously wrong. He ran off.

The police don't recommend this kind of strategy with thieves—it makes it harder for them to get an arrest and can be very dangerous for the vigilante. Ashley would have been better off letting the police know about the planned meeting, so that they could have officers ready on the scene. This criminal seems to have got away with his bike theft for now, but police said they were glad to learn Ashley had recovered her bike safely.

The story made headlines internationally and was even turned into an illustrated children's book.

BIKE THIEF RE-CYCLED TO PRISON

The COVID pandemic saw a surge in demand for bicycles, as people looked for safe ways to exercise. This, in turn, led to a rise in bike crime.

In the city of Newcastle, in the north of England, twenty-five-year-old "Blake" was well aware of the high prices used bikes were fetching. He also knew a thing or two about bike crime—he had been released from prison just four weeks earlier, after serving a sentence for stealing a bicycle. But in March of 2021, he was out on the street again, carrying a bag with some clothes, his wallet and ID—and the large bolt cutters he used to cut through bicycle locks. Some people don't learn.

As Blake passed a local hospital, he saw a bike locked up. It was a tempting target. He put down his bag, pulled out his bolt cutters, and set to work. A short time later, he had stolen the bike and was wheeling it along the street.

Things started to go wrong for Blake when a police officer caught sight of him. Blake got nervous and the officer became suspicious.

When Blake saw he was being watched attentively, he became still more nervous. And the officer became more interested. Finally, Blake panicked and ran, letting the bike fall to the ground and making an escape.

As reported in the *Metro* newspaper, the officer recovered the bicycle, then, acting on a hunch, tried to retrace the fugitive's path—perhaps he could find a cut chain, which would show where the bike had been stolen from.

The bobby found the remains of the lock, but he did one better: he also found Blake's bag, with his wallet and ID still inside.

The bicycle was given back to its owner, who was very grateful. She was a local mother and needed the bike to transport her small children to school.

With Blake's ID in hand, the police had no difficulty finding and arresting him. In court, he pleaded guilty to the offense. He received a ten-week prison sentence.

Blake's story made the papers, but it turns out this wasn't the first time Blake's absent-minded crimes had won him media attention. A year earlier, he'd broken into a school and stolen several laptops. On that occasion, he had left his phone behind. The phone was locked, but police got a lucky break when it rang. They answered, and Blake's mother asked for her son by name.

Blake seems to have left a trail of personal belongings whenever he went out on a job. He might have been better off financially if he'd given up the thieving and stayed at home.

STAY IN YOUR LANE

Sadly, bicycle theft is one of those crimes that crooks often get away with. But some criminals work extra hard to get caught.

On an evening in June 2022, a tough guy we'll call "Hunter" was throwing his weight around in Seattle. According to a report on

KIRO-TV, he used strong-arm tactics to take a bicycle from its owner, then cycled away.

Police turned up to talk to the victim, but even as they were investigating, they got news that a man who matched the description of the thief had been spotted by a police helicopter. He was pedaling along Interstate 5.

This is a busy highway, and it seems crazy that any cyclist would want to take a trip along it, sharing the road with fast-moving eighteen-wheelers. But surprisingly, cycling on this highway is perfectly legal, providing the cyclist keeps to the shoulder. Hunter was not keeping to the shoulder. He was in the southbound lanes and causing a huge traffic backup. It was a bad choice for a cyclist who had just stolen a bicycle and might have wanted to keep a low profile.

Washington State Patrol troopers sped to the scene to arrest the bicycle thief. But Hunter wasn't going down easily. When the troopers approached him, he punched one and kicked another. They stunned him with a Taser, but he kept fighting, then spitting at the cops.

The troopers put a "spit sock" on Hunter (it seems they have equipment for every situation), and more police arrived to help with the arrest. Somehow, even with the spit sock in place, Hunter managed to spit at the new arrivals.

Finally, Hunter was subdued and taken to jail, facing multiple accounts of assault and robbery.

THE POST-APOCALYPSE BIKE LORD

Sometimes, police will turn a blind eye to a criminal. And sometimes, the criminal responds by pushing things further and further, until police are forced to act.

"Anton" may have been the most prolific bicycle thief in the world. According to CTV News, he ran a bike repair shop in Toronto, but it was well known in the cycling community that stolen bicycles were likely to end up in his shop. If a theft victim went to the police, they'd suggest trying Anton's store. If the bike was there, he'd return it to its owner—for a fee.

Anton claimed he was opposed to bike theft, and that he merely bought or collected discarded bikes for repair. He said the destitute men he hired were just fixing bikes, but the word on the street was that his people were paid to steal bikes rather than fix them.

He had a "second-hand license" to acquire bicycles, which meant that any bike he took possession of became legally his after fifteen days. So the presence of stolen bikes in his storage areas couldn't be used against him.

But the longer Anton got away with stealing bikes, the more frequent and brazen his crimes became. The police found themselves facing a surge in bicycle theft, as well as mounting outrage from Toronto's cyclists. The police planted bikes around the city and kept an eye on them. They were soon stolen—by Anton himself and one of his assistants.

Finally, in July 2008, Anton was arrested. Cyclists watched and cheered as he was taken away. He was charged with the theft of fifty-eight bicycles, but this was just a drop in the bucket. A search of his properties turned up more than three thousand bikes. In fact, his own shop had so many bicycles squeezed inside it that the fire department declared it too dangerous for the police to enter, and the bikes had to be removed by crane through a window.

Anton was an odd guy who harbored some strange ideas. He believed the world was facing global economic collapse caused by a shortage of fossil fuels. When the collapse came, everyone would ride bicycles, and then he, Anton, would emerge with his huge stash of bikes. He would be one of the rulers of this new bike world. He had come from Slovenia, where he sometimes claimed he had been a police officer, and sometimes claimed he was a KGB agent. Given his bizarre views about the world, it might not come as a surprise that he was also charged with multiple drug offenses.

Anton pleaded guilty to the charges against him. He was sentenced to thirty months in prison. When released, he left Canada and settled in Switzerland. If you find yourself in the Swiss Alps, watch where you leave your mountain bike.

SADDLED WITH GUILT

"Fujita" was a sixty-one-year-old man from Tokyo.

His life of bicycle crime began in 2018, when he returned to his bicycle only to find that a thief had stolen the saddle. Fujita was shocked by this crime, and disappointed in humanity.

He didn't want to report it to the police—he doubted they would take the crime seriously. And there was no use trying to track down the criminal, who had surely vanished into Tokyo's criminal underground. Instead, Fujita vowed revenge against an indifferent society. He embarked on a campaign to raise awareness of bike-seat theft—by stealing saddles himself. He would teach them all a lesson. The cyclists of Japan would feel the pain he had felt.

And so, Fujita began his career as an infamous serial saddle-snatcher. According to the *Tokyo Reporter*, he patrolled the city, searching for untended bicycles and swooping down on their saddles like an avenging eagle. After removing each victim's saddle, Fujita put it into his bike basket and pedaled away, leaving pain and mystery in his wake.

One of his victims was annoyed enough to go to the police. Surprisingly, the cops took the crime seriously and launched an investigation. They checked surveillance videos and identified Fujita as the thief. In August 2019, the police arrested Fujita for the petty theft. When they went to his apartment, they were amazed to find a collection of 159 bicycle seats.

But in 2020, an even more serious case of saddle theft was uncovered. Kyodo News reported that a fifty-seven-year-old truck driver,

"Daichi," was arrested after being caught on video stealing two saddles from parked bicycles. He confessed to the crime and admitted that this was not his first offense. He had started stealing bike seats more than twenty-five years earlier. At first, he said, the thefts helped relieve stress at work, and, as he continued, "It turned out to be fun." His total haul eclipsed Fujita's efforts—he had stolen somewhere in the region of 5,800 saddles.

Daichi targeted bikes in the places he drove for work—Osaka and Tokyo. Is it possible that the saddle theft that started Fujita's reign of terror was one of Daichi's thefts?

FRUIT LOOTS

SEATING ORANGE-MENTS

In 2018, a small gang of thieves robbed a warehouse in the Spanish town of Carmona, stealing the oranges stored in the warehouse. There was a problem, though. There were four tons of the fruit, and the gang hadn't really thought about how they were going to move such a large quantity.

They had brought a van to the fruit heist, so they filled it with as many oranges as it would hold. When the van was full, they set up their cars as auxiliary fruit trucks. They placed cardboard behind the front seats of a four-door sedan, creating a compartment in the back, then they started throwing the extra oranges in—so many that oranges covered the back seat and literally filled the car from floor to ceiling.

They drove away from the warehouse without being nabbed, their cars straining under the huge weight of fresh fruit. According to a report by Europa Press, the robbers formed a tight convoy as they made their way down the highway. When they spotted a police patrol, they carried out what they probably imagined was an evasive maneuver. To the eyes of the police officers, the sudden movement just looked strange and suspicious. The police gave chase. The orange convoy took a detour down a dirt road. The police followed and soon caught up. The van sped away, but police stopped the two cars and questioned five members of the gang.

When police officers opened the rear door of the car, a mass of oranges tumbled down onto the road. They asked the cars' occupants where they had acquired this fruit.

One thief claimed they'd picked them up off the ground. Another added they had driven here from far away, and just . . . kind of . . . collected the oranges on their travels. The way you do. The police asked what they intended to do with so many oranges. The gang members said they were just going to eat them. They were massive fans of oranges.

In the meantime, more police cars arrived on the scene and started searching the area. They found the third vehicle—the van. Its occupants had escaped, but its cargo of oranges remained.

The story the gang members gave to police was obviously nonsense, and the gang had no paperwork for such a large amount of fruit, so they were detained. The police put out queries and soon learned of the warehouse break-in. We're wondering if the gang were still orange enthusiasts after spending some time in orange jumpsuits.

NOT USING THE OLD MELON

Two young criminals in Virginia were planning to rob a local convenience store in 2020. But how do you carry off a crime like that without being identified? Disguises, that's how. And what disguise could be better than a hollowed-out watermelon? It's cheap, it hides your face and hair, it blocks your vision, and it leaves your head smelling of watermelon. Come to think of it, a lot of disguises are better than a hollowed-out watermelon, but criminals don't usually think an idea through.

The pair got two watermelons and spent some time cutting eyeholes and carving out the interior with a spoon—a process they videotaped for TikTok. In the video, their faces are visible, and their truck can also be seen—a distinctive black Toyota Tacoma pickup with raised wheels. The video even shows the license plates.

The two criminal masterminds visited a supermarket and took selfies in their melon-head disguises. But if images on CNN are anything to go by, carving the headwear seemed to have exhausted their creative abilities—the rest of their outfits appeared to be their day clothes. One wore a blue-and-white checkered shirt, while the other sported a grey hoodie.

After their photo session, they drove to a convenience store and carried out their robbery. While they were careful to wear their disguises, they drove to the scene in the same black Toyota truck that had been captured so well in the TikTok video.

Police soon caught up with one of the criminals, and we can assume it didn't take long to catch his friend. According to news reports, the twenty-year-old was charged with wearing a mask in public while committing larceny, underage possession of alcohol, and "petit larceny" of alcohol.

HANDS UP—I HAVE A NECTARINE

Monty Python once performed a comedy sketch about a self-defense trainer who teaches people to protect themselves from attack by fresh fruit. Outside the world of comedy, fresh fruit isn't normally considered much of a weapon, but that hasn't stopped some criminals from trying.

Take the case of "Pierre." In 1985, the thirty-four-year-old had been convicted of attempted murder and bank robbery and was doing eighteen years in a Paris prison. But Pierre vowed that no prison could hold him. He made four attempts to escape, none successful.

But his fifth attempt, in 1986, was spectacular, and it involved his wife, "Marie." United Press International reported that she was no stranger to crime—she'd been convicted of many offenses herself, and the two had married while in prison. Pierre's escape plan involved breaking out of his cell and getting to a clear area of the prison. Marie would then fly her helicopter down next to him so he could jump on and escape.

There were some snags. One was that Pierre didn't have a way to get out of the prison building to a clear area. The other was that Marie didn't own a helicopter and didn't know how to fly one. But it could all be worked out.

Marie's efforts were extraordinary. She signed up for helicopter flying lessons. She was a good student: she learned about navigation, operational procedures, communications, principles of flight, what to do in a crash. The classes cost plenty and took hundreds of hours, but after several months, she managed to get her helicopter pilot license.

In the meantime, Pierre had decided that the best location for hitching a helicopter ride was the prison roof. He would have to find a way to get there without being stopped by guards. He needed weapons—guns, perhaps, or even a bomb—but he had no way to get these things.

He decided to improvise. Nectarines were available at the prison cafeteria. He would use those and pretend they were grenades. True, a nectarine doesn't look all that much like a grenade, and would land with an unconvincing splat if you threw it or dropped it, but Pierre was an optimist—maybe if they were painted green, they could pass for grenades, from a distance . . .

The day of the breakout arrived. Pierre produced a box of nectarine-grenades. He had brought on a partner, "Lucien," who was waiting to be tried for armed robbery. Lucien agreed to help Pierre get to the roof in exchange for a ticket to fly away on the chopper.

The men brandished their painted nectarines, threatening to unleash an explosion of fruit flavor on the guards. Incredibly, the threat worked. The guards were convinced the nectarines were real grenades. Meanwhile, Marie had rented an Alouette II helicopter and, ignoring radio warnings about flying over a restricted zone, she brought it down over the roof and threw down a rope. Pierre climbed into the helicopter. Lucien was grabbed by the guards before he could reach the rope, so the helicopter flew off without him.

Marie landed the helicopter in a nearby athletic field a few miles away. The couple abandoned it and ran for a car she had arranged to have waiting. They made a clean getaway.

It was an audacious escape, and Pierre might have remained free if he'd left the country and stayed hidden for a few years. Instead, he remained in Paris, and the couple embarked on a series of bank robberies. They were both arrested within the year.

BANANA SLIPUP

In June 2022, a Colombian drug smuggler had a simple idea for smuggling cocaine from Colombia to Europe: just hide the drugs inside banana shipments. Bananas are a leading Colombian export, so customs officials wouldn't be surprised to see crates of bananas entering Europe and heading for the supermarkets.

The smugglers had the cocaine molded into blocks and wrapped in green plastic, then placed the drugs in the middle of boxes of bananas. According to the *Guardian*, the boxes were marked for shipment to supermarkets in Prague and other Czech cities. Of course, that was just a ruse. Once the boxes were inside Europe, it would be easy to redirect them to the smugglers' European contacts.

The boxes arrived in Hamburg and went through customs without a problem. But then they hit a glitch. Instead of going to the drug dealers' confederates, the boxes were shipped on to their destination supermarkets in Czechia. When they arrived, supermarket workers opened the boxes so they could put the fruit in the produce aisle. They were surprised to find mysterious green blocks stacked in among the ripe bananas.

The supermarket staff reported their find, and the police seized nearly a ton of cocaine, with a street value of over $80 million.

So, what went wrong? It's possible the banana boxes were supposed to be intercepted at the port, and someone didn't get to them in time. Or perhaps two different shipments had their labels mixed up? If so, it's likely that, while the supermarket staff made their discovery, criminals across Europe were searching through boxes of bananas and peeling the contents, desperately trying to figure out where the drugs were hidden.

Drug dealing isn't a glamorous business, but when these dealers ended up as peelers, knee-deep in bananas, some of them must have been thinking it was time to split.

LEMONADING AND ABETTING

In the summer of 1903, a thief named Frank Lowman was attempting to pick the lock of a Chicago building using a long, narrow knife, according to an article in the archives of the *New York Times*.

Unfortunately, someone spotted him at work, and as he looked up, he saw the janitor of the building heading his way, accompanied by a police detective. Frank ran, and they ran after him. He spent a few frantic minutes dashing through streets and alleyways.

He found himself on a residential street a couple of miles from where he'd started. He was exhausted and covered in sweat, but he had shaken his pursuers.

Nearby was a seven-year-old girl, Margaret Evans, selling lemonade. He asked for a drink.

Margaret poured him a glass, and he gulped it down.

She asked, "Have you been running a race?"

He told her yes. Yes, he had.

He took a second glass of lemonade and stirred it with his long knife. She asked if he'd won his race.

He glanced around. No sign of them. He smiled and said yes again. He'd won his race, all right.

"You're awful hot, ain't you?" said the girl, evidently doing her best to engage with the customer. "Did you run far? Is the lemonade cold enough?"

At that moment, Frank saw his two pursuers come into view. He left his knife at the lemonade stand and started to run.

Moments later, he realized he hadn't paid for his drink. He couldn't do it. He just couldn't! It was one thing to break into a building, but no way was he going to steal lemonade from this sweet little girl.

Even as the detective was closing in, Frank ran back, fished out some coins from his pocket, and dropped them on Margaret's lemonade stand. Then he was off like a shot, through a vacant lot, jumping a fence, and down an alley. But his delay meant his pursuers were close behind him, and they were soon joined by another detective. They grabbed him and took him in. He was caught by a janitor, two detectives, and a brief burst of integrity.

Further details on this case are long lost, but if it went to court, we hope Frank called young Margaret as a character witness.

CAUGHT BY THE FUZZ

Ray Bradbury wrote a short story titled "The Fruit at the Bottom of the Bowl," in which a murderer worries about removing all fingerprints from the scene of his crime. At first, he remembers objects he's touched around the house, and wipes his fingerprints off them, but as his paranoia builds, he starts wiping imagined fingerprints from everything. When police arrive, they find him obsessively polishing the fruit at the bottom of a fruit bowl.

In October 2019, Newcastle's *Evening Chronicle* described how an English burglar took a more laid-back approach to the fruit in the bowl. "Isaac" had broken into a home in Ashington, in the northeast of England, around fifteen miles from Newcastle. While he was collecting valuables from around the house, the twenty-seven-year-old snacked on the homeowner's candies and chocolates. He also grabbed a peach. He ate part of the peach, but then, instead of obsessively polishing away all traces from it, he just left it behind—a half-eaten peach with his teeth marks.

When police were called to the scene of the crime, they found the partially eaten fruit. Of course, they passed it to the forensics team, who set to work analyzing the DNA; impressively, they managed to identify Isaac as the person who had eaten it.

Isaac was arrested and charged. Or is it impeached? At Newcastle Crown Court, he pleaded guilty, and was sentenced to pay a victim surcharge of £181 (around $250) and serve 876 days in prison.

LAWN ORDER

DRUNK IN CHARGE OF A LAWN MOWER

In 2005, in Springfield, Illinois, "Dylan" had been convicted of theft and given a two-year sentence. He was on parole and confined to his home with an ankle monitor. But parole or no parole, a fella can still enjoy some drinks, can't he? That's how the forty-five-year-old Dylan saw it, and he enjoyed quite a few.

A number of bottles later, he was in a free and easy mood. With alcohol now guiding his reason, he figured it would be a fine idea to climb onto his ride-on lawn mower and take it for a test drive—put it through its paces. He set out across the local landscape, presumably leaving a neatly shorn path behind him. The rogue mower was quickly reported, and it wasn't hard to figure out which way he'd gone.

According to an Associated Press report, the police caught up with Dylan as he was crossing a cornfield.

The police set up a perimeter preventing Dylan's escape, and one cruiser drove alongside him and asked him to please stop the mower and get off. Dylan eyed the big police cruiser, then looked at his little mower—and figured, sure, he could make a break for it. Kicking his mower into overdrive, he trundled into the field at a little over four miles per hour.

The police officers were surprised by this reaction—it wasn't as though Dylan was going to get away. Chasing him in the car seemed like overkill, so one of the officers stepped out of the car and ran up to Dylan, then jogged along beside him, avoiding a spray of cuttings and little stones as he tried to persuade him to stop.

Dylan had no intention of stopping. No cop could catch him. His ponytail was blowing in the breeze. He was the Easy Rider of lawn-mower operators.

It was obvious to the police officer that negotiations were going nowhere, so he had to get serious. He advised Dylan that if he didn't stop, *now*, the officer would stun him with a Taser. This made Dylan think twice. Unable to push his mower's engine faster than the officer's slow jog, even the drunken Dylan could see that his freewheeling, corn-mulching ride was all over.

Dylan stopped the mower and was taken in. The law might have turned a blind eye to the grass-cutting adventure, but not to the parole violation. His lawn-mower ride meant he would serve out the rest of his two-year sentence in prison.

DRINK YOUR LAWN CARES AWAY

In the summer of 2020, in the town of Ear Falls, in Northern Ontario, not far from the Manitoba border, a forty-eight-year-old man was suspected of drunk driving of a lawn mower. The main clue to his state was that he was driving the mower down the main street, although he did occasionally veer off to randomly cut—or cut across—the lawns of the town's residents.

CTV News reported that the Ontario Provincial Police found him, arrested him, and tested his blood alcohol levels.

In Canada, not everyone realizes that the crime of impaired driving applies not only to operating cars, but also to boats (including kayaks and canoes), planes, Jet Skis, snowmobiles, and, yes, ride-on lawn mowers. It doesn't matter whether you're driving on a public road or on your own property.

It's rare for police to charge someone with impaired driving of a lawn mower, but if the drunk driver is causing a problem, they have that option.

This driver had been causing a commotion and was over the limit. He was charged with operation while impaired, *and* operation while impaired with a blood-alcohol concentration over eighty (that's more than eighty milligrams of alcohol per hundred milliliters of blood).

There have been similar cases in Canada. In 2016, the *Sudbury Star* reported a drunk-mowing arrest near the city of Niagara Falls, Ontario. Thirty-four-year-old "Willis" was sitting on his ride-on mower with a case of beer between his knees. He drove the mower into a ditch, where a neighbor tried to help him. Police arrived on the scene and found him displaying "extreme signs of impairment." When they took Breathalyzer samples, he was over four times the limit. The case went to court, and Willis received a $2,000 fine and was prohibited from driving for a year.

Drunken mower drivers: they fought the lawn and the law won.

BUT FIRST, A SPOT OF GARDENING

The choices criminals make can be very strange. Take, for example, a theft that occurred in the town of Port Arthur, Texas.

On an April evening in 2022, a homeowner heard a noise from outside. According to CBS News, he looked through the window and saw someone mowing the lawn. That wasn't so unusual, except that it was the homeowner's own lawn, and his own lawn mower, and he didn't recognize the person pushing the mower. He called the police to report the event.

Security video would later show that the burglar had illegally entered a shed on the property. He moved a bicycle to one side and pulled out a red gas-powered lawn mower. He returned to the shed and found gasoline for the mower. He filled the tank, then put the gas away. Starting the mower, he set to work mowing the backyard. It was a small patch of grass, and once it was mowed, he moved to the front.

The police arrived on the scene while the mystery mower was working. He fled, dragging the lawn mower behind him.

It's not known why he spent so much time mowing. Perhaps he felt guilty that he was about to steal the mower and wanted to make sure the lawn was presentable before he removed it. Or perhaps he was a picky mower thief and needed to fully test the mower before stealing it.

The mower was later found abandoned in an alley and returned to its owners, but the thief escaped, and when we last checked, he was still at large. The Port Arthur police department have appealed to the public for any leads that will help them catch the criminal, a man who will stop at nothing to provide free lawn care for residents.

MOW THE MAN DOWN

Lawn mowers are not only objects of criminal desire. They can sometimes be deadly weapons.

In May 2020, Global News reported on a feud between two suburban neighbors in Guelph, Ontario, that got one of them so worked up that he used his ride-on mower in anger, driving at his enemy again and again. Fortunately, the other neighbor was able to avoid injury by stepping out of the way, but the driver was still charged with assault with a weapon.

But some lawn mower crimes are more serious and more bizarre. In October 2018, in Bristol, Tennessee, a father and son owned adjoining properties. The seventy-six-year-old father had a history of disputes with family members and neighbors, insisting that their property was actually his own. According to WKYC-TV, while the son was mowing the lawn on a ride-on mower, the old man came up behind him and tried to kill him with a chainsaw. Witnesses said the son became aware of the father's attack at the last minute, wheeled the mower around, and the father fell under it, into the blades.

The father was rushed to hospital, and one of his legs was amputated. Once he'd recovered from his injuries, the police charged him with attempted second-degree murder.

In court, the father claimed he was just using the chainsaw to trim his bushes, and the mower had struck him out of the blue. He also continued to insist that other people's property belonged to him. He received a five-year prison sentence. He didn't have a leg to stand on.

NOISY NEIGHBOR

A fifty-seven-year-old Florida man, "Jackson," was the neighborhood eccentric. His property was covered with junk and "No Trespassing" signs. According to a report in the *Washington Post*, when the homeowners association ordered the mess to be cleared from Jackson's yard, he responded by putting up signs complaining about the homeowners association.

But what upset his neighbors the most was the constant noise coming from Jackson's direction. Sometimes it was loud music; the rest of the time, it was Jackson's lawn mower—he owned a ride-on mower and rode it at all hours, revving the engine and even using it as his transportation.

One neighbor complained that the mower wasn't even capable of cutting grass, but its sound could certainly cut through the still of the evening. "He'll run that tractor all night, and it echoes all over the neighborhood."

Jackson's activities generated more than a hundred complaints to the police. Some neighbors were reaching the point where they simply couldn't stand it anymore.

A police officer showed up to talk to the problem neighbor. The officer approached the property and called out to Jackson, but the homeowner responded by revving the engine of his mower to drown out the calls. Not the smartest move. Things went downhill from there. The officer tried to tell Jackson about the complaints over his behavior. Jackson didn't care and revved his mower. The officer warned him that he could be arrested for disturbing the peace. Jackson ignored him, then went indoors. Jackson was ultimately arrested for refusing to stop his disturbing behavior and not complying with a law enforcement officer's command.

Jackson spent the next little while in jail. And Jackson's neighbors finally got a quiet night.

EAT, DRINK, AND BE MOW-EY

Sometimes the motives of criminals are difficult to understand—and some of those mysteries spin around lawn mowers.

The *Glasgow Times* tells of a drug dealer in Glasgow who was arrested after a police raid in 2020. Police searched his place and found a range of illegal drugs and more than £100,000 in cash. The money was hidden in a lawn mower in his bedroom.

What person in their right mind hides their money in a lawn mower, then hides the lawn mower in a bedroom? Wouldn't it be the most suspicious object in the room? And what happens if some joker starts the mower? Shredded money everywhere!

Then there's the mystery of the Maidenhead Mower Celebration.

Maidenhead, near Windsor, is an affluent English town, with big houses on country lanes. According to a report in the *Windsor Express*, a police patrol discovered a discarded lawn mower. Checking nearby houses, they noticed one for sale that had been broken into. The criminals were long gone, but it was clear they had stolen the lawn mower—and drunk two bottles of champagne.

How do you put these clues together? What were they celebrating with the champagne? Was it the successful theft of the lawn mower? If it was, why didn't they keep the mower? These questions, too, remain unanswered.

And how do you explain the actions of the couple in Missouri who stole a lawn mower and rode it along the street? The man was fifty-five and the woman was forty. Their actions attracted some attention as they were both stark naked at the time.

The *Joplin Globe* reported that the police had found the stolen mower in front of the couple's house and confronted them. They had an excuse—they said they had been skinny-dipping at a local creek when thieves had stolen their clothes. What else could they do but borrow a mower and ride home naked? (How about borrow some garments and walk home clothed?)

The police were not impressed by the story and arrested the couple on suspicion of stealing.

But the mystery remains: Why did they take this naked lawn-mower ride in the first place? If you want to steal a lawn mower, why be naked? If you want to flaunt your nakedness, why ride a stolen mower? What were they thinking? With this, as with many other mower mysteries, we may never know.

THE HEIST AND THE LOWST

A TASTE FOR THE FINER THINGS

"Angus" was a thirty-one-year-old thief in Perth, Scotland, who stole to support a drug habit. On a winter night in 2001, he went off to collect more money. According to BBC News, he broke into one house and had just found three expensive rings when he was interrupted by the arrival of the homeowner. Angus knew he had to escape fast, and he decided on the direct route. He climbed out of the second-floor window and jumped from the icy window ledge down to the ground. He landed badly on the patio below and hurt himself.

The police were soon on the scene and found Angus. Despite his injuries, he made a run for it, and even managed to climb a wall in his effort to escape, but the pain of the injuries soon got the better of him and he was caught. The homeowner told the police that the rings were missing, and that they were worth thousands. The police searched Angus, but there was no sign of the jewelry.

Angus was in pain from his fall, so the police took the burglar to the hospital and explained what had happened. The doctors took X-rays to assess the extent of his injuries. The X-rays showed he'd broken his hip and one of his vertebrae, but the doctors were amused by another discovery: three metal circles in his stomach. They had solved the mystery of the missing rings: Angus had obviously swallowed them before his escape.

Police put a twenty-four-hour guard on the patient and waited for the rings to make an appearance. After nine days, they finally emerged.

In court, Angus claimed that, because of all the drugs he had taken, he had no memory of stealing the rings and didn't know how they'd ended up inside him. The judge was unimpressed and gave Angus an eleven-month jail sentence.

The rings were returned to their owner. But strangely, the owner chose to sell them rather than keep them. A diamond is forever, but so is the memory that your ring has spent nine days in a drug addict's digestive tract.

THE DRILL-A-HOLE-IN-THE-WALL GANG

The Hatton Garden robbery was an audacious heist carried out in 2015. The gang were all career criminals from London, most of them in their sixties and seventies, aided by a few young whippersnappers in their forties and fifties. Their target was the Hatton Garden Safe Deposit facility. The firm's wealthy clients used the safety deposit boxes in its basement vault to store their valuables. The vault had a huge steel door and was surrounded by walls more than a foot and a half thick.

The gang knew of a disused elevator shaft that would get them to the outside of the vault. The main door was virtually impregnable, but there was another way in. Over the four-day Easter holiday, they used a big diamond-tipped industrial drill to bore a ten-inch hole through the concrete walls of the company's vault.

They made a few mistakes. They had tried to disable the alarm system, but left some parts working. The alarm went off and a security officer rushed to the building—but everything looked OK from the outside, and he'd been instructed not to enter without the police. When the police didn't show, he just went home again.

The gang weren't aware of how narrowly they'd escaped. They were busy drilling through the wall below ground level even as the security guard stood on the street just a few feet above them.

They bored a second and a third hole, until the row of holes was just big enough for a man to get through. But although they'd penetrated the wall, their route into the vault was blocked by the backs of the safety deposit cabinets. They hoped to push the cabinets over, but the heavy units wouldn't budge, and they had to leave without a penny.

However, it was a long weekend, so the next day, the gang came back with more tools, including a heavy ram. After many attempts, they finally managed to dislodge and push over the cabinets, clearing their way into the vault. The geriatric thieves then squeezed their way down the narrow hole.

Once inside, they set to work on the safety deposit boxes, opening seventy-two of them and scooping up the contents. They took mostly diamonds, gold, jewelry, and cash—in total, around £14 million in valuables. They threw the loot into wheeled trash bins and trundled them out of the building, pretending to be garbage collectors.

This step was their biggest mistake. The movements of the gang on the street were caught on camera, and one of the gang members had used his own car to get to the scene. It was easy for police to trace this car's owner—he was a thief with a long criminal record. With one man identified, detectives put a watch on him to see who his contacts were.

The investigation went quickly because this gang seemed to have no sense of modern police methods. One lawyer described them as "a 1980s team taking on twenty-first-century law enforcement." They used their regular phones to call each other and met at the pub to brag about the heist and discuss their next job. Meanwhile, the police were busy collecting information. Not only were they listening in on the phone calls, they had also bugged the vehicles of the suspects.

The gang seemed surprisingly naive in other ways, too. One thief had taken the bus to the scene of the crime, using his senior's discount. The men doing the drilling had no idea how to operate the device—they learned by watching YouTube videos.

When the police had enough evidence, they moved in. Most of the gang were quickly caught, although it took another four years to catch the final member, their bungling alarm expert. Most received sentences of six or seven years.

The events fascinated the public and were the inspiration for at least three different feature films. The films were true to the original in one respect—the unsuccessful robbery produced unsuccessful movies.

STUCK WITH IT

Committing crimes costs money, and some criminals think they should be allowed to deduct their costs.

"Jean-Claude" had pulled off an unusual heist that made headlines worldwide. In 2012, working with a team of others, he stole 9,500 barrels of maple syrup. According to the Canadian Press, the syrup was collected from producers all over Quebec and stored at a central facility. Sticky-fingered Jean-Claude tapped this rich source with enthusiasm. He distributed the syrup in small batches and sold it to unsuspecting buyers. The amount stolen was worth over $18 million, but if you are dealing in stolen goods, you don't usually sell it for the full value, so Jean-Claude raked in $10 million for himself. At first, the warehouse barrels were drained of syrup, then carefully refilled with water. Later, the crooks became less careful—they just left the barrels empty. Their laziness eventually led to the discovery of the theft: an inspector tried to climb what he thought were heavy barrels, only to lose his balance when the lightweight barrels shifted.

Jean-Claude was caught and sentenced to seven years and ten months in prison. He was also ordered to pay a huge fine of $9 million to compensate producers for the syrup he'd stolen. And the judge warned him that if he hadn't paid the fine by the time his sentence was up, he'd be in the slammer for another six years.

Jean-Claude complained that this deal was unfair. Sure, he'd sold the syrup for $10 million, but that had included many costs—shipping, paperwork, paying henchmen . . . And because he'd flooded the market with cheap syrup, other producers had cut their prices, so he hadn't made as much as he'd hoped. After expenses, he'd walked away with only about a million dollars. The way he saw it, that was what he should repay.

The Quebec Court of Appeal listened to his argument and—surprisingly—decided he had a point. "OK," they said. "We'll reduce your fine to match your profits. A million dollars it is."

The case went to the Supreme Court of Canada, which disagreed with the Quebec court. The way the justices saw it, it would be wrong to treat Jean-Claude's theft like a legitimate business. Sure, the punishment was severe—but that's the point of a penalty. It's supposed to teach criminals that crime doesn't pay, not give them breaks when it doesn't pay enough.

Jean-Claude had been given a huge fine for stealing maple syrup—and he'd have to stick to it.

CAN YOU TRUST A ROBBER WHO ROBS ROBBERS?

The phrase "honor among thieves" doesn't always hold true, as in this startling story of blundering and betrayal from the annals of history. It got wide press coverage, and even spawned a book, *The Great Taxicab Robbery*, by James H. Collins.

In 1912, in New York, a criminal known as "Eddie the Boob" planned to rob money that was being transferred between bank branches. The money was always delivered by two bank tellers: an elderly man and a teenage boy. They always used the same taxi, one that was regularly parked outside the building. Neither teller was armed. They would be easy pickings for Eddie and his gang.

One morning, while the taxi was driving through an alley, one of the gang members drove in front of the taxi to bring it to a halt. Eddie climbed into the front seat and pointed a pistol at the driver, while two other men clambered into the back seat and pummeled the two tellers. The gang forced the cabbie to come with them to their getaway car. They made off with $25,000—a fortune in those days.

Later, the gang went to the back room of a local bar and counted out shares of the loot. A man approached them—he was five foot nothing, and a hundred pounds soaking wet. The man, Matteo, wore glasses with bottle lenses. The gang didn't think much of him until he drew his pistol and demanded that the gang hand over a share of the cash. It seemed Matteo was himself the leader of a gang, known as the "Three Brigands."

Matteo divvied that money up with his two companions, who had been waiting outside. They parted ways, and Matteo took his $3,000 share, boarded a plane, and skipped town.

At a bar in Cuba, Matteo the gang leader tossed back drinks, sharing his tale of brigandry with an alluring woman he had just met. But when Matteo woke up the next morning, the money had vanished. He was left with a single hundred-dollar bill he had hidden in his shoe.

In any case, this was the sorry tale he told police upon returning to New York, and the press ran with it, running headlines like "Robber Robs Robber Who Robbed Robbers."

But as the investigation continued, it seemed like there was a little more to the robbery than a series of incredible coincidences.

In fact, Matteo was probably the one who planned the entire taxicab heist. His gang had found the scheme too risky, so they had hired Eddie the Boob and his friends to take all the chances. The cab driver was likely in on it, too, although he maintained his innocence until the end.

The Three Brigands had always planned to double-cross their co-conspirators when they divided up the loot. They had stolen some of the money, and Eddie had paid more to other collaborators, who had been working for Matteo all along. So, Matteo's gang had taken most of the money for little risk. And as for the money lost in Cuba? Police suspected that Matteo still had it, and the money had actually been hidden away. Still, it was hard to prove anything, and Matteo only got a relatively short jail term of two to four years—while some of the active participants got ten to eighteen.

When a criminal says you can't trust a criminal . . . you can't trust that.

THE LUCK OF THE DRAW

The odds for lotteries are terrible—that's why governments are so fond of running them.

Two Chinese bank employees learned that the hard way.

"Haoran" was a vault manager at a bank in Handan city. Every day, he walked into a safe containing a fortune in cash. He wished the money were his, but obviously he couldn't just steal a stack of hundred-yuan bills—at some point, the money would have to be accounted for, and he would be the obvious culprit.

But as Haoran considered the matter, he saw an interesting loophole. He could only be arrested for theft if the money went missing. But what if he just borrowed the money? After all, that was what banks were all about—helping people borrow money. All he had to do was find a way to multiply the money he took before it was missed, return the original amount, and keep the net profit for himself. The bank lost nothing. There was no crime!

In 2006, Haoran collaborated with a couple of security guards and gave himself a temporary "loan" of 200,000 yuan (worth about US$26,000 at the time).

What scheme did they have in mind? Day trading? Competitive poker? Beanie babies? No, he spent it all on lottery tickets.

Against the odds, he won. He was able to put the borrowed money back into the vault and pocket the profits. It was the worst possible outcome—because now he was hooked.

According to the *Straits Times*, Haoran teamed up with another vault manager, "Zhiming," who was also a friend. Haoran confided to Zhiming about his earlier experiences. He wanted to try it again, but it was too difficult working alone. Zhiming would be the perfect accomplice: the bank relied on both vault managers to watch the money, each keeping an eye on the other. If they were both in on it, it would be much easier to hide their activities.

Haoran and Zhiming started small—they took a mere 50,000 yuan ($6,500). They went to various stores around the city to make many modest purchases of lottery tickets.

They say you'd have to spend thousands on tickets before you ever got one that was a winner, but these two had tens of thousands to spend.

Unfortunately for the itinerant bank managers, the bet didn't pay off. Their winnings were minimal. Fifty thousand yuan down the drain in less than a day.

At this point, some people might call the plan a wash, replace the missing funds with their savings, and live frugally for a while. But these two opted for the strategy of throwing good money after bad. They "borrowed" and gambled even more money from the vault in the hopes of recouping their losses, and with each new loss they became more desperate.

The pair ended up sinking an incredible 47 million yuan (around $6 million) of the bank's money into the scheme. Local store owners must have been surprised to see the men return again and again over the next two weeks, spending a fortune and winning nothing every time. Then again, perhaps they were used to people buying lottery tickets and losing.

Haoran and Zhiming figured that, given enough tickets, they would be bound to win. But they didn't account for the fact that a large chunk of the lottery goes to the government. If someone bought all the tickets on every lottery, they would win every prize and still walk away with far less than they had spent.

The friends were now in big trouble. They had stolen a fortune from the bank, but they had nothing to show for it. They would have been better off just stealing the money and keeping it for themselves.

Haoran and Zhiming might have reached the same conclusion when they finally saw that they had no way to replace the missing money.

In mid-April 2007, the bank discovered that money was missing and reported the theft to the police. Haoran and Zhiming decided to take more money and run. They took a further four million yuan apiece from the vault and fled the city, leaving their friends and families behind.

They didn't get far. The bank soon discovered the crime, and police were alerted across China.

Two days later, Haoran was arrested in Beijing. The next day, Zhiming was tracked to the countryside.

They were charged with embezzlement. That is a capital offense in China. They were found guilty and executed in April 2008.

They had broken all records for money stolen in a Chinese bank robbery.

And they had also broken all records for money lost on a Chinese lottery.

YOU COULD DO BETTER

In December 2016, "Amanda" was checking out the men on an online dating site. She exchanged messages with one of them, "John," and decided to take a chance on seeing him in person. She lived in Massachusetts and he was in Rhode Island, but that was OK. And he was a little younger than her—thirty-three to her forty—but that was OK, too. She didn't even mind that he still lived with his parents. It's nice that a guy gets along with his family.

They arranged a day to meet over the weekend, and she drove to his place to pick him up. It was early afternoon. According to the *Boston Herald*, as they were driving to their next destination, she saw that he was drinking from a bottle of wine. Not classy. It also wasn't legal. This guy might be more of a "fixer-upper."

He asked if they could stop at a bank. She said sure. She parked her Nissan, and he went inside.

But minutes later, John came running out of the bank building. He was wearing a hat and sunglasses that weren't on his head before, and he was carrying a gun and a fistful of money.

He asked her if she would please drive away immediately . . . although in fewer words and with more expletives.

Yes, John had used his first date to carry out a bank heist.

Amanda panicked and did what she was told, but when she saw the flashing lights of police cars in her mirror, she became really scared. She pulled into a donut store parking lot and left the car. The police surrounded John and pulled him from the vehicle, as he struggled and spat at them.

At first, police figured Amanda was an accomplice and arrested her too, but when the bizarre truth came out, the charges were dropped, and she was left with a "date from hell" story to top them all.

As for John, it turned out he had a long criminal record. He was sentenced to three years for armed robbery and another two for assaulting the officers who arrested him. On the plus side, he didn't face any charges for drinking wine in the car.

The couple probably will not have a second date.

HEIST VICTIM AND ACTING COACH

Some heists are "inside jobs," but if you're the insider, you'd better make sure you stick to your assigned role of shocked victim.

According to Australia's ABC News, "Nathan" was a thirty-seven-year-old manager at the Melbourne Gold Company. His friend "Connor" was forty-eight and ran a property company. They decided to expand their business interests—and become robbers. The vaults at Nathan's workplace held large quantities of gold and cash, and if they worked together, it would be easy to steal it—Nathan had it all figured out. There would be no trouble. Connor could be the robber, and Nathan would be a well-behaved employee, doing everything the robber asked.

On the morning of April 27, 2020, Nathan was at the front desk. Connor entered, pushing a cart. He was disguised with a broad-brimmed hat, safety glasses, and a surgical mask, and he held an unloaded pistol.

"This is a robbery," said Connor.

Nathan looked terrified and did his best to continue looking terrified as he led Connor around the premises. The problem was that Connor, who had no experience as a professional stickup artist, lacked the aggression and desperation you'd see in a real robber. At least, that's how Nathan saw it. And, unfortunately, Nathan was one of those actors who can't resist critiquing and directing his fellow cast members. This was a critical error in mid-robbery, when security cameras were recording everything.

After leading Connor to the safes, Nathan signaled to his accomplice, trying to get him to be more threatening with the gun. He also tried to indicate, with gestures, which safes were worth robbing. Connor was slow to pick up on some of these signals. Nathan kicked the floor near one particularly valuable safe, but Connor missed the cue and the safe was left unopened.

Connor and Nathan loaded the valuables onto the cart. Connor then tied Nathan's hands with zip ties and left the premises.

When customers entered the establishment, Nathan told them, "Don't be alarmed, but we've been robbed." After the zip ties were removed, he called the police.

Connor left with around $700,000 in cash and more than sixty pounds of gold. With a total value of more than $3 million, it was one of the largest gold heists in Australian history. But it might have been much larger—the safe Connor had failed to open held more than all the rest—another $4.6 million.

Connor took the haul and buried it on a property owned by his mother. Ironically, it was in a rural community named Dollar.

When police reviewed the security footage, they became suspicious of Nathan's story. His gestures looked like signals. He could also be seen turning off the alarms before Connor appeared on the scene. The helpless victim began to seem more like an accomplice. Nathan denied involvement at first, but finally he cracked and admitted that he was in on it.

Both men were arrested and most of the loot was recovered. In court, the robbers gave a variety of limp excuses for the crime, pleading poverty, diabetes, having to care for three children, the stresses of COVID, and an unpleasant work environment. It was even suggested that the robbery was a sort of joke. None of this washed with the judge. Connor was sentenced to four years in prison, and Nathan got five years and eight months—which should give him plenty of time to refine his role as victim.

DOME AND DUMBER

We've heard many stories of bungled robberies and heists, but what happens if doing wrong is done right? What if the criminals were all professional, worked out a detailed plan, then practiced their methods until they had everything rehearsed perfectly? According to BBC News, that's the way one British gang did things.

In 2000, London's Millennium Dome hosted an exhibition of some of the world's most spectacular diamonds, including rare "blue diamonds" and the Millennium Star, a diamond weighing over two hundred carats and worth hundreds of millions.

Mastermind "Frankie" intended to steal these diamonds. If he pulled it off, it would be one of the biggest robberies in history, but he knew it wouldn't be easy. One problem was that the gems were surrounded by super-strong glass—it was bulletproof, bombproof, and almost impossible to break. But Frankie figured out a way through. If the glass was first weakened with shots from a high-powered nail gun, it could then be smashed with a sledgehammer.

Frankie assembled a gang of professional thieves and carefully worked out all the details of the heist. They would use a backhoe to smash through the perimeter fence and into the dome, then destroy the glass to get the diamonds. But how to escape? Frankie had a perfect solution. The Millennium Dome was situated on the River Thames. While the police were trying to put up roadblocks, they would escape with their loot on the water—roaring away in a powerful speedboat.

It seemed like a good plan, but as a professional thief, Frankie wasn't taking any chances, and he made sure his team practiced every detail. They memorized the layout of the target site. They rehearsed their speedboat escape. They gathered information on high and low tides to work out the perfect time for the raid.

It may sound like a recipe for a successful crime. But in the meantime, the police had received a tip that this gang might be up to something and put a watch on them. Detectives followed the gang members, many of them familiar criminal faces. They saw some members speeding up and down the river on a speedboat, refining their technique. They saw other members of the gang visiting the area around the diamond exhibition, always around high tide. The police guessed that the diamond exhibition was the target, so they made plans of their own.

On November 7, 2000, the gang moved into action. After they donned body armor and gas masks, one gang member smashed the backhoe through the fence and through the wall of the Millennium Dome. Once inside, another robber threw smoke bombs to hide their activity, while a third used the nail gun to weaken the glass, then stepped aside so a fourth could set to work with the sledgehammer. It worked exactly as Frankie had planned. The glass broke and the diamonds were within reach. Outside, the speedboat was waiting, ready for a fast getaway.

What the gang didn't know was that the police were waiting for this moment. The diamonds had been removed and replaced with fakes. The employees, cleaners, and tourists strolling around the area were all armed police officers, and more police in full tactical gear were lying in wait behind a false wall. On a signal, the police emerged. The thieves inside the dome suddenly found they couldn't get out. The building and river area were teeming with police officers. They not only arrested the gang inside the building, but also the speedboat pilot and another gang member whose job was to listen in on police radio chatter. In total, more than two hundred police officers were involved in the operation.

The shocked gang members were whisked off by the police. They ended up getting sentences between five and eighteen years in prison.

Yes, you can plan your crime to the last detail and use only professional criminals—and it's going to attract police attention. In real life, the "professional heist" is just a higher level of dumb.

KIDS GOT NO RESPECT FOR THE LAW

GUARDIANS OF WONDER MOUNTAIN

An adventure involving a group of kids, an abandoned theme park, and a crime-solving dog sounds like the basis for a *Scooby-Doo* episode. This one took a different direction.

In April 2017, a group of teenage boys from Vaughan, Ontario, in the suburbs of Toronto, decided to have a little adventure. According to reports from the Canadian Press, they lived near Canada's Wonderland, an amusement park. In summer, its Wonder Mountain and spectacular roller coasters attracted huge crowds, but this was early April, and the theme park wouldn't be open for business until the end of the month. Under cover of night, the kids snuck onto the site. A store on the premises was stocked with candy, and the kids were peckish, so they broke in and took some candy for themselves. They had put masks over their faces just in case anyone saw them.

Unknown to them, someone had already seen them. As soon as they entered the park, they had been picked up by security cameras. The guard watched the three sinister intruders moving through the park and didn't like the look of it. The guard phoned the police, and they didn't like the look of it, either—mysterious figures entering a popular theme park just weeks before the big opening day? Were they there to sabotage something? Plant a bomb? You don't take chances on something like that.

Meanwhile, the kids munched on their stolen candy, enjoying their nighttime adventure. Suddenly, all hell broke loose. Police officers converged on the scene from many directions. Some had dogs. A helicopter swooped down and started sweeping the area with its spotlight. It seemed that stealing candy was a bigger deal than they'd imagined.

The kids made a run for it. They dashed for cover near some trees and bushes. If they crouched down among the foliage, they thought, they wouldn't be spotted by the cops.

Wrong again.

The helicopter was scanning the ground with a thermal camera. The kids under the tree shone like fireworks in the cool night. While the helicopter gave instructions from above, four officers moved in on their hiding place, including one officer with a police dog.

This was way more than the kids had counted on. As the police approached, they stood and threw their hands in the air. "We surrender!"

They were taken into custody. The police described the attitude of the teenagers as "remorseful"—although perhaps "shocked and terrified" might have been more accurate. They were returned to their parents with a warning and told to take part in a community service program.

This seems like a story that should end with a heavy-handed moral. How about this: "In Canada's theme parks, there's only one theme that really counts: justice!" Too much? OK, let's try: "Canada is a peaceful, law-abiding country, but if you steal a candy bar, you *will* be hunted down with dogs and helicopters."

CAUGHT YOU COZ WE COULD

Young criminals often have a false sense of invulnerability. Many also seem to like the Leonardo DiCaprio movie *Catch Me If You Can*—and some take its message a little too seriously.

"Brandon" was a nineteen-year-old troublemaker in Caerphilly, in South Wales. He attacked someone in the street with a knife. That got him a prison sentence. In 2015, he was released early, on condition that he checked in at intervals with the police.

But once he was out, he didn't report to police at all. The police posted a picture of him on their Facebook page, asking the public for information. Brandon posted an unpunctuated reply underneath it: "Haha catch me if you can wont see me slipping."

If you want police to forget about you, this is not the way to achieve it. And Brandon made things worse for himself when he talked to a newspaper journalist and repeated his challenge. According to the *Daily Mirror* newspaper, the fugitive spoke from "an unknown location," saying, "They are not going to be able to catch me—I won't let them." He went on to mock the police department's sorry efforts so far: "They have been round my mum's house four times a day, but I'll be out for at least a month or two before they get me."

Brandon wasn't quite the brilliant escape artist he imagined himself to be. Police caught him later the same day. There would be no more parole for him: he was sent back to prison to serve out the rest of his sentence.

A similar case occurred in May 2022, in Bedfordshire, UK, probably inspired by the same Leonardo Di Caprio movie.

"Bennett" was eighteen when he threatened two girls with an imitation gun. The next year, he was involved with a burglary. Police posted Bennett's picture on their Facebook page seeking information from the public. Bennett posted a reply: "Catch me if you can." The comment received more than five thousand reactions.

The police were up for the challenge. A short time later, they posted a message of their own underneath. "Guess what happened next? We caught him, obviously." They added that Bennett would now be spending eight years in prison. The police signed off, "Catch ya later."

BABY DRIVER

Younger drivers are statistically more likely to get into car crashes—and the younger they are, the higher the risk.

In March 2022, an eleven-year-old boy, "Ryan," from Whitby, Ontario, decided to take the family Hyundai for a spin. Global News reported that his twelve-year-old friend "Tyler" sat in the passenger seat, giving guidance and support as the two swerved through the town's streets, driving on the wrong side of the road at speeds up to 95 miles per hour.

People were alarmed by the driving and reported the vehicle and its plate number to police. One cruiser was on the way to the owner's address when the car sped by in the other direction. The officer did a U-turn and chased it. The police figured they were chasing a dangerous drunk driver, and more cars joined the chase.

Despite the mass of flashing lights behind them, the kids kept going. At one point, Ryan lost control and the car went off the road, smashing through a fence and into a backyard. But the driver wasn't going to be caught that easily. He drove the car out again, nearly causing a head-on collision with a police cruiser, and sped off, smashing more fences along the way.

Eventually, police managed to block the rogue car, and they moved in to arrest the driver. They were amazed to find two kids in charge of the vehicle. Because of the age of the kids, there were no charges. The boys were returned to their respective parents.

However, if a case in the US is anything to go by, maybe the kids should have received a punishment.

A 2017 report in the *New York Daily News* describes how a ten-year-old boy borrowed the car keys and took his mother's car for a joyride through the city of Cleveland, Ohio. He managed to get three flat tires during the trip, which brought the journey to an end. The boy and the car were returned to his home without any charges.

A week later, the boy was waiting for his older sister to take him to school. She was spending too much time in the washroom, so he took the keys to his mother's boyfriend's car and went for a second drive.

The boy's worried mother called 911, setting off a police chase that lasted an hour. The boy sped along the Ohio Turnpike pursued by cruisers. The police put a spike strip across the road to destroy the tires, but the young driver—who apparently had learned a thing or two about tires from his previous outing—swerved around the strip and kept going.

He was only brought to a halt when one police car smashed into the back of the vehicle, driving it into another. Police officers surrounded the vehicle, shouting orders for the child to roll down the window. (The phrase "disproportionate response" comes to mind.)

The kid put up a fight while being taken in, spitting and kicking, and was sent to a juvenile detention center, charged with fleeing and eluding.

The boy's father didn't approve of the way the mother was raising the child. He was quoted as saying, "He thinks because he got away with it the first time, they ain't going to do nothing to him this time."

But there are younger car thieves. In May 2020, in Utah, a five-year-old boy, "Brayden," was having an argument with his mother because she wouldn't buy him what he wanted. As KSL-TV reports, what Brayden wanted was a real Lamborghini. When the exasperated mother left him alone in the car for a few moments, Brayden took matters into his own hands. He slid into the driver's seat and drove off.

He was a more careful driver than some of the other offenders we've described. There were no high-speed chases here—the car was weaving along the highway at under thirty miles per hour as Brayden perched on the front of the seat, trying to reach the pedals while peering through the windshield.

A state trooper soon spotted the slow-moving vehicle and sounded his siren. The car dutifully pulled over. The officer was shocked when he saw the driver, and helped the little boy shift the car into park. "How old are you? You're five years old?"

Brayden explained that he was on his way to California. First stop: his sister's house. Second stop: the Lamborghini shop. The luxury sports cars usually cost more than $200,000. Brayden was carrying $3.

The boy was returned to his parents, but after the story made headlines, he received a pleasant surprise. A local Lamborghini owner, who could understand Brayden's enthusiasm, showed up at his home and took the boy and his mother for a ride.

Stealing a car at age five is young, but we can go younger. In Minnesota, a four-year-old boy wanted candy, so he took his grandfather's car keys off the hook and got into his Hyundai SUV. He managed to back the vehicle out of the driveway and drive, very slowly, to the local gas station, making his way along a busy road during the morning rush hour.

Along the way, he banged into a tree and knocked over some mailboxes, but he made it. Witnesses called police, who assumed they were chasing a drunk driver. They were astonished to find a small child at the wheel.

But the youngest driver we've heard of didn't make the papers. In a police discussion group on Quora, a police officer describes spotting a woman drive past on a four-lane road. She was focused on tying her child's shoes, while her two-year-old stood in her lap and steered the car. A true baby driver. And yes, Mom got a ticket.

GRILLING THE SUSPECT

Growing up in Dust Bowl–era Kansas, Louise had always been a wild child. She was one of four kids in a single-parent household, and she didn't like her home life. Her first runaway attempt came at the tender age of nine, and by the time she reached her teens, she had escaped all the way to the big city of St. Louis, Missouri. Here she fell in with a young twentysomething named Jim.

As the *Detroit Free Press* told it in 1932, Louise's new beau was self-employed—specifically, in the business of robbing summer homes, with the help of his gang, while the owners were away. At first, Louise didn't want to come along on these ventures.

"What are you, yellow?" Jim mocked. She replied that she wasn't afraid of anything.

She joined Jim and his friends in robbing houses; then came armed robberies of gas stations and even a streetcar. She almost didn't get away from the streetcar robbery after the conductor closed the door on her, but with her diminutive frame, the girl managed to wriggle free.

But it wasn't until the pair robbed a hamburger restaurant that they really caught the attention of police. While Jim held up the proprietor, Louise realized her stomach was growling, and the young accomplice took the opportunity to swipe some lunch from the grill. The press had a field day with this incident, calling her the "Baby-Talk Bandit," the "Baby-Face Bandit," and the "Hamburger Queen."

It wasn't long before Jim and Louise held up another hamburger restaurant. This time, the proprietor had been tipped off about a girl bandit who was fond of hamburgers.

As usual, Jim pointed his gun at the man behind the till, while Louise rifled through the cash register. Then, her eyes alighted on a sizzling sandwich on the counter. At that point, most people would take the money and run, or even take the hamburger and run, but instead, Louise decided to sit down with the patty before it got cold.

Jim was anxious to get away and told her to leave the hamburger this time, but Louise was determined to enjoy the meal, turning the incident into a different kind of holdup. When she was finished, she complimented the chef on a "swell" sandwich, to which the owner asked if she would like another, saying he'd cook one up for her right there. Louise said yes! But by now, Jim had had enough, and he dragged her out of the restaurant before there were any more delays.

The robber duo managed to speed away in Jim's car before the cops arrived, but not fast enough. Bystanders had noted their license plate.

Police caught up with them in Jim's suburban house, where Jim and an accomplice threw down their guns and surrendered. Inside the bedroom, the cops found an unruffled Louise lounging on the bed, reading a romance novel.

Back at the station, Louise was sure that this trouble would all resolve itself soon. But the interviewers explained to her that armed robbery was a very serious crime with a hefty sentence. When she realized the trouble she was in, she broke down.

Louise spun her sob story: She was only seventeen, she said, and she came from a broken home. After the death of her mother, her neglectful father had married a cruel woman. Louise had led a tragic life, bouncing between orphanages and boarding schools. She explained that she and Jim were soon to be married, and swore off her robber ways, so wouldn't they take pity on her?

The officers were deeply moved, but regretfully informed her that seventeen was just old enough to disqualify her from being tried as a minor, and that she was instead looking at a long prison sentence. The girl wailed that she hadn't used a gun, but the law made no exceptions for doe-eyed young accomplices.

Fortunately, Louise was saved at the last minute by a stunning development: the appearance of her mother, who was very much alive. The mother gave the police a different story: Louise was one of four children. There was no stepmother, but there was a stepfather, and he loved her very much. But her most important revelation was that the girl was sixteen, not seventeen.

This meant that Louise was able to escape serious consequences. She was sent to a juvenile correctional school. Meanwhile, her testimony meant that Jim and two of his friends would now stand trial for burglary and armed robbery—all because she stopped for a hamburger.

THE ARTFUL DODGER OF APRICOTS

A life of crime can start young. Very often, parents have no idea that their kids are breaking the law. This was the case with four-year-old "Clare," who accompanied her father to a grocery store in Everett, Washington, in 2011.

Clare looked sweet and innocent, but while her father was getting groceries from the shelves, she was practicing the art of the "five-finger discount." According to a report from KOMO-TV, she opened a bag of dried apricots, removed some fruit from the bag, then returned the bag to the shelf so that the theft wouldn't be spotted.

Her father missed her shoplifting, but Clare hadn't counted on "Ethan," a sharp-eyed security guard. He saw it all—and he had a zero-tolerance policy on crime. Regardless of age, sex, or race, nobody would steal anything from the store he guarded.

When Clare's dad had paid for his groceries and was ready to head out of the store, Ethan barred their way. They would have to stop right there. He ordered father and daughter to accompany him to a private room.

Once they were alone, Ethan confronted Clare and her dad. He'd seen what the little girl had done: the flagrant theft of valuable fruit. He had news for them. The girl was banned from the store. Furthermore, the store would be pressing charges against the pint-sized shoplifter.

Ethan pulled out a form for the girl to sign, saying that she understood she was banned—she would no longer be permitted into the store, or any other branch of the supermarket chain.

The father pointed out that Clare wasn't in school yet and didn't know how to write or sign her name.

Nice try, Dad. But Ethan had an answer. The way he saw it, he didn't need a signature—any mark would stand up in court. He instructed Clare to scribble on the paper, showing she understood the document. Clare dutifully made her best scribble. We assume Ethan added the correct date.

The paperwork completed, Ethan released the young criminal and her inattentive father. He could take pride in the knowledge that, thanks to his firm actions, Clare would not steal from the supermarket while he was on duty there.

After Clare's parents complained about what had happened, and the story hit the news, company officials were appalled at the heavy-handed treatment of this little girl.

"Our policies on shoplifting are intended to protect our customers but built on common sense," said a spokesperson. They apologized to the parents.

And Ethan was right in thinking Clare would never again steal from the store while he was on duty. His duties were brought to an abrupt end when he was fired.

TOO BIG TO STEAL?

BRINGING HOME THE BEACON

A gang of criminals from the English Midlands took a trip to the south-west of the UK—to scenic North Devon—in 2022. BBC News reported that they found plenty of easy pickings in this pretty, rural area. They broke into homes and stole valuables. They stole some vehicles.

They pilfered a few items from a local inn. They also broke into some of the containers at a local self-storage unit and grabbed what they could find. They found a boat engine, fishing tackle, power tools . . . oh, and a lighthouse lantern.

It's hard to understand what motivated them to take the lantern. It can't have been easy to move.

The lighthouse lantern was historic—one of only three in existence, and the last of its kind still in use. It came from the Hartland Point light-house, on the rocky Devon coast, where the Bristol Channel meets the Atlantic Ocean.

It had been put into storage so it could be refurbished. Even in pieces, it's big. The lantern is constructed of twelve huge brass frames, each holding a massive section of curved cut glass. It weighs two tons.

It is thought to be worth around £1 million (US$1.1 million)—that is, for those looking to buy a lighthouse lantern. But the owners feared the brass was probably headed to a scrap-metal dealer, where it might yield a couple of thousand. A reward of £5,000 ($5,700) was offered for the return of the lantern, but so far, there has been no sign of it.

Police said that this seemed to be one of a string of burglaries in the area—but most had involved tools and cars. There had been reports of locks cut on motorcycles at a business nearby, although nothing was stolen.

The thieves who made off with the lantern stole a bicycle at the same time. If you happen to be in Devon and spot a bicycle topped with a giant two-ton flashing light, let someone know. You could make a quick £5,000.

QUEST FOR THE POLE

The confusing period following a natural disaster can be a profitable time for criminals.

In September 2017, Hurricane Irma had done damage all over Florida. The *New York Post* reported that two friends, "Soren" and "Austin," both in their forties, were cruising to see what money they could make from the disaster. Over the past months, they had made dozens of sales of scrap metal they'd acquired "here and there." Now they were looking for more metal they could convert to cash. They found what they wanted on the side of a local bridge—a thirty-foot aluminum light pole.

As Soren and Austin told it, the light pole had been blown down by the hurricane. That's certainly possible. It's also conceivable that they removed it and used the hurricane as an excuse. Whichever it was, the two shirtless men were soon lifting the pole onto the top of their Kia Sorento. The pole stuck way out in front of the car, and just as far behind. As responsible citizens, they tied a rag to the rear of the stolen pole to warn other cars of the long load.

Their actions were spotted by a passerby, who called 911. A police officer drove to the bridge and noted the pole's absence, then went off to look for the thieves. It didn't take long to find them on the highway and pull them over.

He asked them why they had a light pole on their car.

Soren explained that they were just moving the pole, because they'd found it lying on the ground near the road. Someone could hit it.

If that were true, the officer asked, why did they need to drive the pole to a new location? Why didn't they just roll the light pole farther from the road?

Soren and Austin thought hard, but had no answer. A few minutes later, they were sitting at the side of the road with their hands cuffed behind them.

They were arrested and charged with grand theft.

History repeated itself in November of 2020, according to Fox News. Another driver, "Dakota," spotted a fallen pole by Interstate 4. The seventy-one-year-old sensed a scrap-metal opportunity. He pulled over onto the shoulder and, somehow, lifted the huge pole onto the roof his car. Dakota was driving an old Toyota Camry. It had no roof racks—the pole, which was twice as long as his car, was balanced on the car's roof, held in place with telephone wire.

Once again, a good citizen spotted the thief's activities and phoned police. Dakota was pulled over. He claimed he didn't know it was illegal to pick up a city light pole from the side of the road. He then learned that it isn't the same as scooping up a dead deer. Dakota was arrested and taken to jail, charged with grand theft.

What does a criminal do with a stolen light pole if they acquire one? It really is a dumb thing to steal. Scrap metal is a highly regulated industry, and selling items like this requires ID and proof of ownership. Without proper documentation, most scrap metal dealers wouldn't touch the metal with a ten-foot ... well, you know ...

ABRIDGED CRIME STORIES

The American fraudster George Parker was infamous for repeatedly selling the Brooklyn Bridge to gullible buyers. But that was just a con. Some thieves have stolen real bridges.

The two Czech villages of Loket and Horní Slavkov lie about five miles apart, separated by a landscape of forests, meadows, and rolling hills. A pedestrian path runs between the communities. The route includes a steel footbridge, part of a disused railway.

TIME magazine reported that, one day in early 2012, a team of workers descended on the bridge and started dismantling it, cutting the metal into sections and removing them with a crane.

Locals were puzzled by the activity, so police approached the workers and asked what was going on. The workers showed paperwork—the bridge was being replaced by a bicycle path. Their job was to remove the old bridge. Someone would be by later to put in the bike-friendly replacement.

The workers left, taking the ten-ton bridge away with them. As you have already guessed, nobody else arrived to put in a replacement. When the police checked, they discovered that there were no plans for a bicycle path, and no plans to tear the old bridge down. The documents were fake. The workers had simply stolen the bridge for its scrap metal value.

The bridge was worth about $6,300 in scrap. Considering the risk, the fuss of making forged documents, and the heavy equipment needed to remove it, it seemed a lot of trouble for the money. It was certainly an expensive theft for the town. A local expert estimated that the replacement cost would be in the millions.

In 2021, an American man, "Garrett," also stole a bridge. Garrett, sixty-three, lived in rural Ohio. According to *Newsweek*, he spotted a partly disassembled footbridge sitting in a local park. The bridge had once been a pedestrian walkway across a nearby river, but the river area had been repurposed as part of a wetland restoration project, so the bridge had been removed. It was scheduled to be moved to a new site—a women's shelter in Akron—but in the meantime, it was to be stored in a farmer's field.

It was a large object—ten feet wide, six feet tall, and fifty-eight feet long. But Garrett seemed to be one of those people who believe that if a large object is left somewhere for long enough, its ownership falls under the "finders keepers" doctrine. He first removed the deck boards of the bridge. Then he hired a local company with trucks and a crane, and he moved the rest of the structure to his own property.

When city workers came to collect the bridge, it was gone. The police asked the public for help through their Facebook page and received some useful tips that pointed the finger at Garrett. He had a place in the next county.

A few weeks later, armed with a search warrant, police converged on Garrett's property. They found the pieces of the missing bridge and arrested Garrett on a charge of felony theft.

He learned his lesson: if you're tempted to steal a pedestrian bridge—just walkway.

FLYWAY ROBBERY

"Patrick" was an American flight engineer who worked out a plan to steal an airliner in 2003. His dream plane was a Boeing 727. The one he had in mind was an older aircraft, built in 1975, and for the past year, it had been sitting at the airport in Luanda, Angola, on the west coast of Africa, about six hundred miles south of the equator. The owners of the plane had accumulated more than $4 million in airport fees, none of which had been paid. Now the plane was being refurbished for use by another airline—the passenger seats had been removed, and it had been adapted to transport diesel fuel.

Patrick knew he couldn't steal the plane alone, so he enlisted the help of "Noah," a mechanic from the Republic of Congo. Neither man was certified to fly a 727—Patrick only had a private pilot license—and the plane normally required a crew of three, not two, but they figured they could get it in the air somehow.

According to ABC News (Australia), on May 25, 2003, as sunset was approaching, the men boarded the plane and turned on the systems. They were seen, but nobody thought much of it—everyone knew the plane was in the process of being converted, so it wasn't so strange for people to climb aboard. But it certainly got everyone's attention when the airliner started moving. Patrick did his best to taxi the huge aircraft, taking it on a wobbly path across the tarmac.

He ignored the frantic messages from the control tower trying to contact the rogue plane about its unscheduled departure. Lining up the plane on the runway, Patrick gave the engines full throttle. The plane thundered along the runway and soared into the air, heading out across the Atlantic Ocean. The plane's lights were off, and they were heading into a darkening sky. Patrick and Noah were soon beyond the range of the airport's radar.

Patrick had successfully stolen a full-size commercial airliner.

But once you've stolen a plane like that, how do you profit from your crime? After all, a huge jet costs a fortune to run and maintain—it's not a good vehicle for personal joyrides. It's hard to sell, too. The plane would be instantly recognized if it landed at an airport. And he didn't have much time to find a buyer. Patrick's new-to-him 727 had enough fuel to travel about 1,500 miles—not enough to cross the Atlantic, but enough to turn around and reach other parts of Africa.

Unfortunately, we will never know Patrick's plan. The stolen airliner and its crew of two were never seen again. Given the age of the plane and the pilot's lack of qualification in flying planes of this type, it probably crashed. Then again, nobody has found any wreckage, and it's a big planet. It's just possible that the thieves got away with it.

BEASTLY CRIMES

THE CLUMSY CAT BURGLAR

Most people get their rescue pets from the humane society, but in Pennsylvania, "Gilbert" thought of a better option—the local petting zoo. It was early February in 2022, and the facility was closed for the winter, but the security gate hadn't locked properly. Gilbert crept inside to see what animals were available. He peered into a heated building and spotted an attractive cat. It would do nicely. He grabbed the feline and walked out. According to reports on WBRE and WYOU-TV, he left a $50 bill in the cat's place.

But this was no regular tabby. In fact, Gilbert had stolen one of the center's best-loved animals, a North American bobcat named Blanche. She was twenty-two years old and had several medical issues, including arthritis. She was normally gentle, but she was still a wild animal.

Blanche allowed Gilbert to carry her out, cradling her in his arms, but as he kept walking away from her warm home and out into the winter air, she started to struggle, and then she put up a fight. Gilbert dropped her a couple of times, but managed to grab her again before she could run off. Blanche decided she didn't like this man. She fought harder, twisting and scratching. By the time they'd reached the parking lot, Gilbert was having a hard time controlling the animal—and his own temper. He was seen holding Blanche by the scruff of the neck, yelling and swearing at her. He finally got into his car and drove off with the bobcat.

A few minutes later, the zoo's owners discovered Blanche's absence and were alarmed to find the money left in her place. Fortunately, the thief had been captured on their security cameras. The zoo contacted the police and posted images of the theft on social media. The response was huge, and some people were able to identify Gilbert.

State police spotted Gilbert's car. They followed him down the highway and were surprised when he pulled into the petting zoo grounds. It's not clear whether he was going after more animals, returning the one he had, or just wanted his fifty bucks back. The police pulled him over. They found Blanche hidden in the trunk. Gilbert was arrested on multiple charges, including burglary and animal cruelty.

As for Blanche, she had only a minor injury to a claw—from her fight with her catnapper—and was reportedly happy to be returned to her home.

COWBOYS ON THE TRAILER

Thieves in the city might steal high-value items like smartphones and computers. In Oklahoma, the easiest thing to steal is cattle. There are two cattle for every person, and livestock farmers can't watch all their animals all the time. The crime rate in the state is low, and most farmers in the state are trusting, so they don't usually brand their animals or spend money on fancy electronic ID tags—but this means that, when thieves do show up, livestock is an easy target. A single calf could be worth $1,500 or more.

"Jesse" and his friend "Bryce" were two Oklahoman twentysomethings in search of easy money so that they could buy marijuana. The pair dressed in an odd combination of sweatshirts, baggy pants, and cowboy boots. One wore spurs.

According to a report on NPR, in September 2014, the two ganja gauchos were driving around in a pickup truck with a livestock trailer, looking for livestock to snatch. They found a pasture with six cows. The animals weren't branded, so they were perfect targets for the thieves. After checking that nobody was around, the pair walked into the pasture with food in a bucket. The cows ambled over, looking for a treat. Jesse and Bryce lured the cows into the trailer, then backed up their truck. Before long, the six cows were on their way to the auction house.

Oklahoma auction house staff are as trusting as the state's farmers, so when Jesse showed up with six cows, nobody raised an eyebrow. No paperwork was required, or proof of ownership. The animals were passed over on a handshake. After they were sold, Jesse and Bryce collected their money and went off to invest it in more drugs. It would have been the perfect crime—except for the fact that Jesse had been rustling for a while, and some people were starting to get suspicious.

The agriculture department has agents who investigate these kinds of crimes, and one of them had recently received a tip that Jesse might be stealing cattle. When the report came in that six cows had just been stolen, the agent checked auction records to see what Jesse had been up to. He discovered that, not long after the theft, Jesse had sold six cows of the same breed at the auction house. The agent placed a special watch on Jesse and Bryce.

The thieves had soon burned through their money and once more heard the call of the herd. On their next foray, the thieves loaded another three cows into their livestock trailer and dropped them off at the auction house. Another perfect crime, it seemed. After the auction was over, Jesse and Bryce strode in to collect their cash. They suddenly found themselves surrounded by special agents, demanding to know where the animals had come from.

The guilty pair knew the game was up. They confessed to their thefts.

Jesse and Bryce were arrested on crimes that can carry a ten-year prison sentence. Because conspiracy and stealing livestock? In Oklahoma, it's not OK.

DUDE, WHERE'S MY CAMEL?

In June 2010, in Saint-Liboire, Quebec, a twenty-two-year-old car thief, "Richard," spotted a nice truck in a motel parking lot. The truck was hooked up to a long silver trailer—the sort of thing you could use to transport livestock. It was an expensive-looking rig, and Richard probably figured a trailer like that would be easy to sell to local farmers, so he climbed into the driver's seat and drove away with truck and trailer.

After he was a safe distance from the motel, Richard stopped to check the trailer. He realized he'd taken on more than he'd bargained for. The trailer had animals inside it—and these were definitely not the kind local farmers would buy. At one end of the trailer were two camels. At the other end, locked behind several layers of cage, was a three-year-old, four-hundred-pound, male Bengal tiger.

According to a report on Reuters, the animals were in the process of being transported from a circus in Nova Scotia to a zoo in Ontario. The driver had stopped for a rest break at the motel, about forty-five miles east of Montreal, and that's where Richard entered the picture.

Richard suddenly found himself with the responsibility of looking after the three exotic animals. He moved the trailer and its animals to his barn in Drummondville, about twenty-five miles from the motel. He couldn't just abandon the creatures—he wasn't that heartless—but he knew they needed food and water. He did what he could. He went to a local store and picked up a large bag of cat food. It was plenty for a regular cat, but no more than a midday snack for the tiger.

In the meantime, news of the theft had got out. It was all over the media, not just in Quebec, but worldwide. The owners were frantic with worry—they feared that the animals might be mistreated, and they were particularly concerned about the tiger, which would not live long without water—especially in the hot weather they were having. Police were carrying out an intensive search of the area.

The pressure on Richard stepped up another notch when the zoo offered a $20,000 reward for the lost animals. Everyone was on the look-out. A vehicle theft was risky enough, but this trailer was way too hot to handle. Four days after stealing the trailer, Richard got rid of it, leaving it under a group of trees. The abandoned trailer was quickly spotted by a local resident and the animals were recovered.

A veterinarian examined the creatures and said they were in good health—a great relief to the owners. Richard also got rid of the truck, which was found later.

There was speculation that the zoo might have paid Richard a ransom for returning their animals. If they did, he didn't get to enjoy it for long. A few weeks later, police raided his barn and found evidence that the animals had been kept there. Richard was arrested and charged with possessing stolen goods and breach of parole. It was then his turn to be given food and water while waiting behind bars.

BACK-SEAT DROVER

For as long as people have been keeping livestock, other people have been stealing them. But there have been some unusual approaches to cattle rustling.

Back in 1978, three young men in Ogdensburg, New York, had their criminal sights set on the livestock at a local farm. They got onto the farm without raising an alarm and stole two animals—one a Holstein calf, the other a 350-pound Angus bull calf.

They led the animals away to their own vehicle. And this is the "dumb" part. You might think they'd brought an animal transporter truck for the theft, or at least a pickup truck. But no, their vehicle was a regular car—an everyday sedan with plush seats in the front and back.

Still, there was always the trunk. They hoisted the Holstein inside and managed to close and lock the lid. They now had the problem of where to put the big Angus calf. They figured that if a back seat was good enough for a human, it was certainly good enough for a prize calf, and so, working together, they managed to squeeze the surprised animal into the back seat, and one of the team squeezed in next to him to keep him company. As they drove away, the rear of the vehicle strained under a quarter ton of livestock.

As the gang drove along the highway, they saw flashing lights. According to an Associated Press report, they had been spotted by two state troopers. It might have had something to do with the horrible sounds coming from the car's muffler as it scraped against the asphalt.

The guys tried to look innocent as the officers peered in at the car's occupants. The two in the front were nervous but normal—but who was that muscular character propped up in the back seat?

While the thieves were trying to justify the presence of this bull with some bull of their own, the car suddenly gave a jolt. Then another. The vibrations were coming from the trunk. The second calf was tired of being confined and was starting to kick. The officers popped the trunk and released the nervous animal.

Of course, the men were arrested. Their unusual approach to cattle rustling got them charged with third-degree burglary. We're guessing it also ruined their muffler.

IF YOU'RE BUYING, I'M SHELLING

A rare African spurred tortoise named Millennium was a popular attraction at a reptile-focused animal shelter and educational center in New York. The tortoise had been a beloved staple of the center for a decade, and anyone could come and see him in his enclosure for a small optional donation. But one turtle enthusiast, "Lou," didn't want to wait for viewing hours—he wanted a tortoise like that around him twenty-four hours a day, seven days a week. He couldn't afford to buy one—a single tortoise of this breed costs $2,500. Instead, he decided to kidnap Millennium in a cold-blooded heist, reported by the *Queens Chronicle*.

Lou waited until the reptiles had been put to bed, then cut a hole in the tortoise enclosure. Millennium was big, weighing in at ninety-five pounds, and it was a struggle for Lou to haul the enormous creature back to his car. But he kept at it, finally hoisting the animal inside, then drove his new best friend across state lines. The next morning, the educational center staff arrived and were devastated to find Millennium's enclosure an empty shell of its former self. They began a search for the missing tortoise.

African spurred tortoises are the third largest of their kind. They're not the easiest tortoises to keep. They have specific dietary needs, including hay and occasionally kale, and they need the right kind of enclosure, because they spend most of their days digging deep holes in the ground. Perhaps it was Millennium's time-consuming care routine— or all the fresh craters in the lawn—that led Lou to change his mind about keeping the turtle a few days later.

A nice guy would have returned the tortoise to its owners. Lou had different plans. He placed an ad on Craigslist, offering the tortoise for sale. A prospective buyer haggled Lou down to a mere $300. Lou wasn't sure until the buyer offered to throw in a musk turtle. Lou accepted this very uneven trade, and the deal went down at a subway station the next day, which must have been quite the sight for commuters.

But tortoise enthusiasts talk to each other, and Millennium's new buyer learned about the theft of the big tortoise on the news. Could this be the animal he had just purchased? He went to the police. They soon confirmed that his tortoise was indeed the stolen animal. Now they asked for the buyer's help in tracking down the thief. Lou had used his phone to contact the buyer, and police were able to use the number to identify him.

Millennium was returned to his pen, and Lou, for his trouble, received six months in another kind of pen.

THE BEAR FACTS

Animal crimes aren't always about stealing animals. Sometimes the animals themselves do the stealing.

California's Lake Tahoe region is a major tourist destination. It's also a hot spot for black bears. In late 2021, a huge black bear went on a crime spree, breaking into multiple homes. According to the *New York Times*, the bear weighed around five hundred pounds—perhaps because he had decided to forgo his hibernation and instead enjoy a diet of pizza and chips. The bear was easily identified by his size and his very dark coat. People called him "Hank the Tank." He used his enormous strength to break through garage doors or tear down the front door to a home, then ransacked the house in search of food. The "bearglur's" activities were extensive—he broke into nearly forty homes.

Local homeowners were alarmed at the activities of this animal supervillain. His activities generated hundreds of calls to the emergency line. Some of these calls were made in the middle of a break-in, while others were just concerned citizens giving the police advice. There were so many of these calls that police had to post a notice on Facebook: "Please stop calling to give your opinions about Hank."

The bear showed no fear of humans. He had been known to smash his way into occupied houses and push past the occupants to get to the food. But, in a *New York Times* report, one local bear expert pointed out that Hank had good manners. Aside from his violent entry to the house, he displayed no aggression toward the occupants—no attacks, no snarling, no growling. She said, "He just sits there and eats."

But many people believed the bear was a dangerous menace. It was just a matter of time before Hank hurt someone. They demanded his death. Things were not looking good for Hank.

Fortunately, authorities were not going to pass sentence without an investigation. We humans can't always distinguish between individual bears—especially when the bear is currently bursting its way into your living room. Investigators took DNA samples from the crime scenes and discovered that the break-ins had not all been carried out by the same bear. Sure, "Hank the Tank" had been responsible for some break-ins, but others had been carried out by at least two "copycat bears," both females. The three-bear team quickly acquired the nickname "Hanks the Tanks."

After the new information came to light, a spokesperson for the California Department of Fish and Wildlife announced that no bears would be killed. The three culprits would instead be tagged and relocated into a suitable wild habitat.

STUCK IN A LIFE OF CRIME

MAKE 'EM SQUIRM

Being a burglar often involves squeezing your way into a building. In many cases, criminals stop halfway.

In December 2016, a forty-seven-year-old burglar decided to rob a house in Manchester, England, according to the *Sun* newspaper. He waited until the homeowner had gone out to do some shopping, then he deftly scaled the drainpipe to an open bathroom window on the second floor. But as he put his head through the window, he found he was stuck. He couldn't push through the window, and he couldn't pull his head out. His body protruded from the house, suspended high above the street, his knees resting on the windowsill.

He was still there, trapped, when the homeowner, a woman in her sixties, returned with her groceries. She phoned emergency, and police arrived, along with the fire department.

The semi-intruder was removed from the window and arrested. He pleaded guilty to burglary with intent to steal and was jailed for two years and four months.

A would-be burglar in the Mexican city of Morelia ran into a similar problem when he tried to escape the scene of a burglary by squeezing through metal bars on an apartment building. According to *Metro*, he managed to get his head through, but then found he was stuck fast. He remained there for two hours, until people in a neighboring building spotted him struggling and called police.

Onlookers watched and recorded the proceedings on their phones for a couple of hours. One unsympathetic observer commented that he looked "like a rat caught in a trap." Finally, the police arrived—probably one of the few occasions a burglar was happy to see them. The officers cut him free with bolt cutters before taking him in for questioning.

All over the world, burglars are in an arms race against homeowners and shopkeepers. The Nigerian city of Jos has a high crime rate, so shops take extra precautions, installing bars that wouldn't look out of place in a high-security prison.

One thief figured a way into a clothing store that had installed these bars on the doors. He waited until dark, then entered the store by cutting a hole through the roof. Nigeria's *Daily Post* reported that the thief scooped up seven suits, thirteen pairs of shoes, and an array of sheets and blankets.

Since he had successfully entered the store through the ceiling, you might think he would leave the same way, but instead, he chose to go out through the doors.

Unlike the other burglars we've mentioned, he didn't push his head through first. No, he played it safe and squeezed his body through the bars. He got as far as his neck. Of course, he then found himself in exactly the same position as every other person who sticks their head through railings—his body was out in the street, and his head was on the other side of the bars. All his efforts to get free were useless, and he remained there until the following morning, when passersby called police. They had to bring in a welder to cut the bars. The police arrested the thief and returned the stolen items.

In 2020, in Portage la Prairie, Manitoba, the Royal Canadian Mounted Police received several calls about a twenty-five-year-old man who had been causing his own private crime wave in the town. PortageOnline .com reports that the man seemed to have assaulted one person and later entered the home of another, where he threatened the occupants. The police followed his trail, and finally tracked him to a house. The fugitive saw them coming and tried to escape by entering a tunnel under the house. Unfortunately, he got stuck there.

Now, instead of shouting threats, he was shouting for help. The police managed to pull him out of the tunnel and got him free—then they pulled him down to the police station and made him un-free.

The Mounties always get their man, even when the man is down a manhole.

SWEEP HER OFF HER FEET

"Mia" met "Seth" online. Seth lived in Thousand Oaks, California, a suburb of Los Angeles. The couple went out on a few dates, but Seth decided to end the romance. However, as CBS News reported, Mia was determined to make her way back into his life—or at least back into his house.

After the breakup, she was spotted on the roof of his home. Seth called the police to report the incident, but by the time they showed up, she had escaped. It was a little weird, but he hoped that would be the end of it.

A couple of weeks later, in October 2014, Mia made a second attempt to get inside the house. It was around three in the morning. What did she have in mind—a romantic reunion? A vengeful murder? Once again, she climbed onto the roof, and this time she made her way to the chimney. She climbed into the chimney stack and wriggled her way down.

At least, she wriggled partway down. When she was about eight feet into the narrow flue, she got stuck, and it seemed like no amount of squirming or wriggling could get her loose. As she realized her predicament, she became more and more desperate and frightened.

Three hours later, neighbors heard odd noises coming from somewhere on their street, and then screams. They could tell someone was in trouble, but nobody could figure out where the anguished cries were coming from. At last, they narrowed it down to Seth's chimney. Seth was out of the house, but the neighbors called 911, and the fire department were soon on the scene.

The firefighters got onto the roof to see what was going on. Shining a light down into the chimney, they saw Mia's arms and head. She was stuck fast, and try as they might, they couldn't shift her. They used dishwashing soap in an attempt to slide her free. When that didn't work, they knew they would have to do it the hard way—they started dismantling the side of the chimney with a hammer and chisel. After two hours of work, a ladder truck hoisted the sooty Mia from the chimney.

She gave a convincing story to police, and they didn't know about her earlier weird roof high jinks, so they took her to hospital to be checked over.

When Seth arrived home, he found his roof damaged, his chimney destroyed, and the neighbors full of stories about the woman in his chimney. He talked to the police about his relationship with the determined Mia. They charged her with illegal entry and providing them with false information.

Seth said that from now on he'd be more careful who he invited into his house. Hopefully, he'll also tell them to use the big rectangular entrance at the front of the house, not the narrow round one on top.

A FIXER-DOWNER

In Grand Bend, Kansas, in September 2018, a man and woman in their forties pulled their car up to an old farmhouse. According to the *Hutchinson News*, the place was abandoned, and the couple, "Lucas" and "Jenna," figured there might be some things worth taking.

The house didn't have any money or valuables lying around, but it did have copper pipes, and those had some scrap value. The couple set to work hacking at the walls and cutting out the pipes in neat, easily transportable sections.

There was copper wiring, too. A shame to waste that on an abandoned house, so they also pulled the wire from the walls.

The couple loaded the pipes and wire into the car, congratulating themselves on a good day's illegal work. But as they tried to drive the car away, they ran into a problem. The ground was muddy, and the car was heavily loaded. It was stuck in the mud. It was impossible to move it. There was nothing to do but walk down the highway and find help.

As Lucas and Jenna were walking, help arrived—although perhaps not in the form they'd hoped for. A police car pulled up beside them. A pair of friendly deputies explained that a local had spotted the couple walking along the road and phoned in, thinking they might need help. The couple acted grateful and played along. Perhaps these dumb-but-friendly cops would give them a tow out of the mud.

The officers drove the thieves back to the farmhouse, but when they checked the stuck car, it turned out they weren't quite as dumb as Lucas and Jenna had hoped. The officers immediately spotted the load of copper pipes and wiring, and the whole situation started to look suspect. A check of Lucas and Jenna showed that there was a warrant out for Lucas. The police arrested the couple and charged them with burglary. You folks have a nice day.

If you want to keep out of prison, stay away from the coppers.

A DEBASED CRIMINAL

You might have heard of BASE jumping. It's a sport where someone jumps from a high spot and descends to the ground by parachute. The term BASE is an acronym for the objects participants can jump from—buildings, antennas, spans (bridges), and earth (cliffs and mountains). It's a dangerous activity, and it often involves getting to those high places illegally.

In October 2014, a BASE jumper in St. Louis, Missouri, decided this was an A-for-antennas week. Twenty-seven-year-old "Jacob" grabbed his parachute, then he and a companion headed for a local broadcasting tower's mast—a narrow lattice structure supported by guy wires coming out at an angle. The tower he chose belonged to the local PBS television station.

They climbed the tower to a considerable height, then Jacob leaned over the edge and made his jump. His parachute opened—and was immediately blown onto a guy wire.

According to an Associated Press report, Jacob found himself dangling 155 feet from the ground, his parachute and cords wrapped around the guy wire. He was far enough away from the tower that he couldn't reach it. He might have climbed up his parachute cords to the guy wire, but any kind of movement was dangerous—if the tangled cords came loose from the wire, he would fall to his death. While he and his buddy were trying to figure this puzzle out, someone saw him hanging from the tower and called 911.

Luckily for Jacob, the fire department had a team who were trained in rescuing people stuck at great heights. They pulled the team together, along with their specialized equipment, and got them to the scene.

When he prepared his jump, Jacob had anticipated spending just a few seconds hanging from a parachute, but by the time the expert help arrived, he'd been suspended in a tight harness for over two hours, and hanging for that long can really hurt—it's called suspension trauma.

Once the firefighters were on the scene, they climbed up to Jacob and fastened a specialized winch to him. Jacob removed his parachute and was lowered from the PBS mast. A small group of onlookers were watching the process and clapped as the emergency crew brought him safely to the ground. Jacob was in pain but managed to walk to a waiting ambulance.

Once Jacob had been checked over and had recovered from his adventure, he and his companion were arrested and charged with trespassing.

A note to other BASE jumpers: when PBS stations ask for "public support," they don't mean having members of the public supported by their antennas.

CRIMINAL AU FENCES

Criminals often have to deal with fences—and sometimes the fences come out on top.

In 2017, Fox News reported that a Florida man had come upon a stranger outside an apartment complex and, for reasons unknown, hit him on the head with a rock. He then made a run for it. The attacker was immediately chased by police—including an officer with a police dog. (What kind of neighborhood was this?) The criminal found himself cornered in a fenced area. He jumped the fence, which was about five feet high, but his pants were caught on one of the posts. The criminal ended up hanging upside down, suspended by his pant leg, until police tore off his pants to release him. The victim was fine. The attacker was arrested for assault with a deadly weapon.

In the same year, Fox News also reported an even more embarrassing fence–pants experience in Tucson. A would-be burglar had entered the grounds of a local school and was in the process of trying the doors when a locksmith spotted him. The burglar ran and scaled the fence. He got caught on the spikes. The burglar was unharmed, but his baggy pants were impaled. He found himself hanging upside down with his underwear exposed and his pants around his ankles.

The amused locksmith snapped some photos, which went viral, but before he could release the burglar from the fence, the police showed up and did it for him. The humiliated suspect was cuffed and arrested. A police spokesperson said they had no record of an event quite like it.

Not all the inept fence jumpers are burglars. In March 2017, CNN reported on a woman who had tried to get over the White House fence. She was a massive fan of Donald Trump and really wanted to speak with him. She had spent eight years in the US Army, so she had been trained in getting over barriers, and her keen interest in astrology might have given her insight into the right time for the adventure. But either her army training wasn't up to snuff or the stars were misaligned, because after scaling the fence, her shoelaces got caught. Security officers found the Trump fan dangling from the inside of the fence.

Despite court-issued "stay away" orders, the army astrologer made a total of three attempts to get past that fence and into the White House, all unsuccessful. She was charged with unlawful entry and contempt of court.

Perhaps the most ridiculous example of criminals getting stuck on a fence occurred at the US–Mexico border in November 2012, as reported in *USA Today*.

It looks as though drug runners were trying to drive bales of marijuana into the United States in their Jeep Cherokee. Obviously, they didn't want to cross at the border crossing, so they came up with a better idea: they would go to the border fence, place ramps on either side, and drive over.

They set up the ramps—two strips of metal wide enough to accommodate the vehicle's tires, a pair of ramps on each side of the fence—then drove smoothly up to the top of the fence. At that point, they encountered some trouble. Their vehicle was wedged on the top of the fence, unable to drive over the sharp angle at the peak of the ramps.

The criminals saw border agents coming, so they fled, taking their drugs with them. The agents were greeted with the bizarre spectacle of an empty Jeep teetering on the top of the sixteen-foot border fence.

IDOL HANDS

You know that stealing jewels from a religious idol isn't going to work out well for a movie character. It sometimes doesn't work out well for real-life characters, either.

"Subash" was a thirty-year-old with an alcohol problem. A big part of his problem was that he wanted alcohol and didn't have the money to pay for it. According to the *Times of India*, he lived in Andhra Pradesh in India, in a village named Jadupudi. Money wasn't easy to come by, so he turned to crime. He'd tried stealing and selling his mother's propane gas tank, but he'd drunk his way through those funds and now he needed money again.

In April 2022, Subash turned to the gods for help, although not in the way most holy men would approve of. The local Hindu temple contained jewelry—and he made plans to steal it.

He entered the temple by hammering a small hole in the wall. He squeezed through the hole to get inside the building. Once inside, he inspected the religious icons. Many of the sacred figures were adorned with jewelry—the ornaments were small and easily pocketable. He went from one idol to the next, removing the jewelry and stuffing it into his pockets. Then he headed back to the hole he'd made in the wall.

It was at this point that karma caught up with Subash. Although he'd managed to enter the temple without too much difficulty, the affronted gods seemed to frown on him as he tried to leave. He managed to squeeze through the hole as far as his waist, but then found he could move no further, either forward or backward. He was hanging halfway through the hole. His head and upper body were outside the building, hanging just a few feet from the ground, but his lower body was still inside the temple.

He called for help and soon attracted a crowd of amused onlookers, who had a pretty good idea what had happened. Some took photos, while others pulled him out.

Subash had stolen so he could drink, and in a roundabout way, the gods gave him what he wanted. Before handing him over to the police, locals offered the thief a cool drink of water.

A GARDEN OF PLANT THIEVES

AM I THE AZALEA HERE?

In an era where the smallest dispute can lead to a showdown with automatic weapons, it can be nostalgic to read how things were handled in decades past. This story comes from the archives of the *New York Times*.

In 1950, a New Jersey resident, "Percival," was unhappy with the look of his garden. He had noticed another garden in the next county that had some spectacular thirty-year-old azalea plants, and now his own lawn seemed like it needed the same splash of color. But who can wait thirty years for a floral display? So, Percival chose the quick-and-easy approach. In mid-May, late at night, he drove to the house with the azaleas, dug them up, and took them home.

"Douglas" was the owner of the azaleas. When he woke the next day and discovered his prized plants had been stolen, he called the police.

In an impressive act of fairy-tale detection, the cops followed a trail of petals along the road.

The trail ended in Percival's neighborhood, and not far away was Percival's garden, which now featured two lovely azaleas.

Percival was arrested and charged with larceny. It was hard to deny. In court, he pleaded no contest. He was given a one-year suspended sentence and fined $50—a relative bargain, considering that the azaleas were worth twice that.

As for the flowers, Douglas was an expert gardener and didn't think the plants would survive another transplantation, so he told Percival to keep them. He said he would rather see them thrive in someone else's garden than die in his own.

A LYTLE MOTHER'S DAY SURPRISE

Even criminals like to get their mother flowers on Mother's Day—they just don't want to pay for them.

Lytle is a small city in Texas, about twenty-five miles southwest of San Antonio. According to a report in the *Fort Worth Star-Telegram*, "Cody" was pushing his cart around the town's supermarket in May 2022. As he was leaving the store, he spotted a nice $15 flower arrangement that would be perfect for Mom, so he picked it up and tried to walk out.

The store manager spotted the action and moved to stop the thief. Cody made a run for it, leaving behind his shopping cart. He also left the cart's contents, which included his dog, a shih tzu.

The police were called, and they considered what to do with this unusual canine clue. They passed the dog on to animal control, who checked the animal for a microchip—it might tell them the name of the owner. And indeed, it did. The dog was owned by a family in San Antonio and had gone missing two years before. It seems the guy who stole the flowers had also stolen the dog.

The dog's owners were surprised and delighted to get their dog back. The dog, whose name was Leela, had been let outside for a few minutes and never came back. The family searched for months, but finally gave up. They thought she might have been killed by a coyote.

The police didn't manage to catch the thief, but the local police chief was contemptuous of the man's approach to Mother's Day. As he said, "Nothing says 'I love you' like stolen flowers."

HEARTS AND FLOWERS

People have been stealing flowers for almost as long as they've been giving them as gifts. If these 1930s stories from the *New York Times* are any indication, flowers seem to have been a particular target during the Depression era.

In July of 1933, a peasant from the town of Schwechat, near Vienna, was strolling through the park and stopped to steal some roses. The thief's name, ironically, was Joseph Thorn.

The theft was spotted by a policeman, who approached Thorn and tried to apprehend him. Thorn put up a fight, hitting the officer with the stolen roses. The conflict escalated. The officer drew his truncheon to defend himself. Thorn upped the ante further. He pulled out a knife to counter the police officer's stick and tried to stab him.

The police officer dropped the truncheon and pulled his revolver. Thorn couldn't top that, so he gave up. He was arrested for assaulting a police officer.

American justice was sometimes more understanding. In the same year, 1933, a twenty-one-year-old named George Difit was charged with a similar crime in New York. After a chase by police, he was found in possession of two flowers stolen from Battery Park.

In court, things looked bad for Difit. The young man had previously been convicted of burglary. But Difit explained that the flowers were for his mother, as a Mother's Day gift. He went on to say that he hadn't stolen the flowers—they'd been given to him by some other men he'd met in the park. The only reason he'd run was that he saw a patrolman racing toward him in one of those newfangled "radio cars."

His story about the other men wasn't entirely convincing—Difit was found guilty of disorderly conduct—but his Mother's Day excuse seems to have moved the judge. He was given a suspended sentence.

Another New York flower thief operating in 1930 seemed to exude pure class. His name was William C. Minter, and for some time he had been sending lovely bouquets of roses and orchids to young debutantes in New York.

The recipients and their wealthy families were puzzled by the gifts. Nobody could remember meeting this Mr. Minter, but he obviously knew *them* and admired their daughters. Was he someone from Harvard? From the regatta, perhaps? Why, who the devil could this fellow be?

If they had seen him in person, they would not have been disappointed—he looked every inch the suave, fashionable gentleman. But Minter had never met most of the socialites he sent flowers to, and despite his generous gifts, he didn't have the slightest interest in their daughters. He was a con man.

His modus operandi was to enter a flower store and order a nice bouquet, something valued at around $12—roughly $200 in today's money. He had previously selected the name and address of a girl from the society column, and he would ask the florist to send the flowers to her address. The florist, glad to get the upper-crust business, didn't question an order from such a well-dressed man, and going to a prestigious recipient.

Once he'd made the order, Minter would pull out his wallet to pay for the purchase and discover . . . oh dear! How embarrassing! He had left his cash at home. Fortunately, he had a money order for $48. He offered to sign that over to the florist to pay for the flowers—and the florist could give him $36 (around $600 today) in change. The florist usually agreed. The money order was signed over, the change was given, and the flowers were sent—accompanied by Minter's engraved calling card, to add a touch of style. It was only much later that the poor florist would discover the money order was forged, and he was out of pocket for both the change he'd given and the cost of the flowers.

William C. Minter was a pseudonym—one of many. The con man's real name was Herbert A. Gordon, and he had a long criminal record. Although flower shops were one of his favorite targets, he used similar methods to buy tickets to expensive theater shows.

So far, the scam may not sound too dumb. But, like many thieves, Gordon played the same trick once too often. His downfall came when he tried to buy an expensive watch—probably one he genuinely wanted for himself. The watch was worth $29.75, and using his usual "cash at home" ploy, he presented a money order for $38. The canny jeweler said he was willing to accept it—as soon as they'd both taken a quick trip to the post office to check that the money order was legitimate.

Realizing he was about to be exposed, Gordon grabbed back the money order and ran from the store. The jeweler ran after him and shot at him with a pistol. Then a traffic cop caught Gordon and hauled him to the police station, where a queue of florists and ticket sellers confirmed that he was the man who had defrauded them.

He was charged with possessing and passing forged money orders, which, it turned out, had been stolen from a Brooklyn post office.

While his debutantes were "coming out," their flower donor, William C. Minter, was going in . . . for a long time.

TREE STRIKES AND YOU'RE OUT

Although a tree can be worth thousands of dollars, it's difficult to steal one—it's too big and heavy. But what about a bonsai tree? Now you're talking. At least, that was the logic of two crooks back in 1963, as reported in *Newsday*. "Rupert" and "Ashley" planned a forest heist in miniature.

A botanical garden in New York was exhibiting a dwarf Japanese white pine. The rare tree was valued at $3,000 (equivalent to around $30,000 today), and the high value attracted the attention of the two criminals.

The pair paid their admission and found their way into the area with the bonsai tables. Rupert stood lookout while Ashley snuck the petite pine into a bag. The thieves made off with it with no one any the wiser. It wasn't until later that staff noticed the sizable empty space next to the exhibit label.

It didn't seem to have occurred to these dimwits that a $3,000 tree is only worth that much money if you can find someone to sell it to, and there wasn't much of a market for rare bonsai in 1960s New York. The months went by, and Rupert and Ashley were unable to find a buyer for the bonsai—but as they contacted people who might be interested in the tree, some of their contacts became suspicious. One of the potential buyers tipped off the police that Rupert had a rare tree for sale.

The police sent one of their undercover officers to contact the thieves. "Gail" told them she was a bonsai collector interested in making a purchase. She expected the pair to jump at the chance to sell their tree—and they would have, under normal circumstances. Unfortunately, the pair were better at larceny than horticulture, and the stolen tree had been involved in a miniature forest fire. (Perhaps a misplaced cigarette.) But the crooks didn't want to let this opportunity slip through their fingers. They promised Gail that, if she could wait a few days, they would find her a new tree, just as good as the one they'd previously had for sale. Gail said sure.

It didn't take much imagination to guess where the thieves planned to get the new tree. Based on Gail's report, the police staked out the botanical garden, and sure enough, late at night, Rupert and Ashley turned up, preparing to grab another tiny tree. They were arrested and charged with grand larceny.

When someone tries to sell you a bonsai tree at a bargain price, it's probably a "little shady."

THE SCIENCE OF CRIME

PHYSICAL ATTRACTION

There's an old story about a famous physicist, Robert W. Wood, who went to traffic court after running a red light. The physicist claimed that, as he approached the light, the color was changed by the Doppler effect—the waves of red light were squeezed together to a higher frequency and appeared to him as green. The judge was ready to let the charge drop, but one of Wood's students, who had recently been flunked by the physicist, pointed out that, for colors to be changed in this way, the driver would have to be moving at around a quarter of the speed of light. The judge considered this, then dropped the original charge and fined the physicist for speeding.

That story is probably not true, but some prominent physicists have got into unusual legal scrapes.

In his memoir, *Surely You're Joking, Mr. Feynman*, the physicist Richard Feynman describes his time working on the top-secret Manhattan Project near the end of World War II. During his time off, he entertained himself by cracking the combination locks of safes and filing cabinets around the Los Alamos complex, placing warning messages inside that described how easy the safes were to pick. The administrators dealt with the problem promptly—they told everyone not to let Feynman near their safes. They should have paid attention to his warning, because a real spy was also at work in the facility, collecting secrets for Russia.

Feynman probably broke some laws, but he was too important to the project to face any legal repercussions.

But in 2011, another top physicist got into a different kind of trouble.

"Chase" was a sixty-eight-year-old physics professor. He was British by birth, but now worked at the University of North Carolina. He had divorced from his wife three years earlier, but he was starting to feel lonely on his own and wanted to get married again. Come to think of it, he wouldn't mind some children, too.

The *New York Times* describes how it seemed like all his wishes were about to come true when he met a woman online, "Trinity." She was exactly the kind of woman he wanted—she was a successful bikini model, but she was so *tired* of men admiring her for her pretty face, dark hair, and naturally large breasts. What she wanted was to settle down and have children with an extremely intelligent older man. But what chance was there that a man like Chase could ever be interested in a young Czech bikini model?

Chase assured her that, yes, indeed, he would be willing to give it a try. She was delighted, and their online relationship continued. It all seemed too good to be true, but Chase had googled her, and Trinity was definitely a real model. They communicated by text. Sometimes he suggested a phone call, but the supermodel was surprisingly shy and always found an excuse to avoid it.

Eventually, Trinity suggested that they should meet in person. She told Chase that she happened to be doing a photo shoot in Bolivia— why didn't he fly down and join her? She would even send him the tickets.

Chase jumped at the chance and flew down. But he ran into a problem with the tickets he'd been sent. It took him four days to arrive in Bolivia. When he finally arrived, he discovered that Trinity had been called away to another photo shoot, in Brussels. But all was not lost—she promised to send him another ticket so he could join her.

She had one tiny request. She had left a suitcase behind in Bolivia. Could he bring it with him, from South America to Europe? He said sure. The ticket and suitcase were delivered to him.

In the meantime, Chase chatted with one of his friends, a man who was both a physicist and a lawyer—and probably a real authority on the laws of physics.

Chase told his lawyer friend about his rare good luck in snagging the girl of his dreams, even if it did involve some unwanted globetrotting. He described the suitcase delivery. The lawyer had been puzzled by the whole relationship, but when he heard about the luggage, everything became clear. He told Chase not to take the bag—it certainly contained cocaine.

Chase refused to believe that his darling Trinity would be trying to use him as a drug mule, but he looked inside the suitcase just to be sure. The case was empty. He texted Trinity to ask why she needed an empty suitcase. She texted back to explain it had sentimental value. Satisfied, he put some of his own clothes inside it and set off.

He flew from Bolivia to Argentina, then waited for an e-ticket to Brussels. Instead, he was questioned by Argentinian police. They asked him to identify his bags. He explained that he was delivering one of them to his girlfriend. They had already opened it. It had a package hidden in the lining containing two kilograms of cocaine. Chase was arrested.

In jail, he slowly realized that the doubts expressed by his friend were true—there had never been a bikini model interested in him. Trinity was a real model, but she had never communicated with him. Instead, he'd been exchanging text messages with a fake—probably a man pretending to be a woman.

He called his ex-wife from prison—she was still on good terms with Chase. When she heard what had happened, she said she was "flabbergasted but not surprised." She described her husband as "a very good scientist with the emotional age of a three-year-old."

Chase told his story in an Argentinian court—how he had been in love, how he was taking the suitcase as a favor. They'd heard such stories before from other drug mules. He was sentenced to four years and eight months in prison. In 2015, after serving half of his sentence, he was released and deported to his native England.

Chase had learned a valuable lesson. Physics can be a wonderful way of understanding the universe. But if you want to operate in the world, you also need a grasp of psychology.

CATCH OF THE DAY

Working as a scientist studying river fish doesn't seem like a great opportunity to make an illegal income, but it worked out that way for a biologist in Wisconsin whose field of study was the sturgeon.

The sturgeon is a big fish that has been swimming around at the bottoms of lakes and rivers since before the time of the dinosaurs. In fact, with the crocodile-like ridges running down its back, it has a distinctly prehistoric look. It can grow to more than six feet in length and weigh over two hundred pounds. Up to a quarter of that weight comes from its eggs.

Unfortunately for the sturgeon, humans have another name for its eggs: caviar. It is one of the most expensive foods on earth, associated with status and power. People catch the sturgeons mostly for their eggs—and removing the eggs usually means killing the fish. These ancient fish are in trouble, and their numbers are declining all over the world, but the rarer they become, the more their caviar is worth, and that high price drives the demand.

Sturgeons still swim in the rivers of Wisconsin. "Sebastian" was a biologist employed by that state's department of natural resources to protect them. Colleagues called him the "Sturgeon General."

But according to Wisconsin's WLUK-TV, Sebastian was also making money from a profitable sideline. His scientific work occasionally involved catching sturgeon and dissecting them. If he collected the eggs at the same time, he could discreetly sell them to a network of caviar processors.

In 2015, one of these caviar processors received more than 65 pounds of sturgeon eggs from Sebastian and put them in jars for the luxury food market. While the lake sturgeon found in Wisconsin doesn't produce the most expensive caviar you can buy, it is still very costly—a tiny one-ounce jar will set you back at least $55.

One of Sebastian's perks from selling the sturgeon eggs was receiving jars of caviar back from the processors. There are reports that he enjoyed the caviar at meetings and shared it with colleagues.

Eventually, word got out that Sebastian was killing and eating the creatures he was supposed to protect. Sebastian was suspended, and detectives moved in to investigate. They found many sturgeon eggs stored in the department's fridges. He insisted he was just keeping the eggs for research into sturgeon fertility. Detectives asked why the storage containers were all marked with the names of different caviar producers. That was harder to explain.

In court, Sebastian pleaded no contest to the charges against him. Since he had probably not harmed the fish population too much, and his career and scientific reputation were in ruins, he avoided a trip "up the river." Instead, he was given a $50 fine—the price of an ounce of caviar. He resigned from his job.

"Quite often, people make dumb choices," the judge told Sebastian. "You made a doozy here!"

BREAKING BADDER

In the TV series *Breaking Bad*, chemistry teacher Walter White pays his medical bills by manufacturing methamphetamine, or "crystal meth." He goes to considerable lengths to keep his activities secret from his friends and family.

But it seems that what worked for a fictional chemistry teacher in New Mexico didn't work quite as well for a real-life chemistry professor in Arkansas.

In October 2019, KATV television reported that people at Henderson State University in Arkadelphia, Arkansas, had noticed an odd chemical smell coming from university buildings.

The buildings were closed and tested, and scientists discovered the presence of benzyl chloride, an extremely hazardous substance. Its applications are tightly controlled. One of its uses is in making poisons for chemical warfare; another is in the manufacture of amphetamines.

Two university professors were arrested, "James" and "Victor." They were charged with the manufacture of methamphetamine and the use of drug paraphernalia. James claimed to be a big fan of *Breaking Bad* but seemed to have missed one of the show's main plot points: if you're going to run a meth lab, you need to do it far away from where anyone can smell it.

While the university spent a month decontaminating and airing out the buildings, police investigated the two rogue profs. The charges were serious. Manufacturing illegal drugs could send the perpetrator to prison for anywhere between forty years and life.

Even so, James admitted that he had been making drugs. He said he and Victor had both been in on it, making meth for personal use and smoking it in their offices late at night.

Investigators discovered some documents in Victor's office that appeared incriminating—they included papers containing the chemical formulas for methamphetamine.

The case went to the courts and took two years to resolve. In *Breaking Bad*, Walter White sells drugs to pay his medical bills. Victor could probably have used the money to pay his legal bills, but instead he conducted his own defense.

Despite James's claims that they had smoked drugs together, Victor denied everything. He said he knew nothing about the drugs. The police had found vials of meth in the safe in his office, but he said he had no idea they were there—and, in any case, the safe belonged to James and had been left in Victor's office for . . . safekeeping?

As for those papers, the ones with the chemical formulas, Victor could explain that. He said that students sometimes came to him with questions about *Breaking Bad* because it was such a popular show. Since the series was about the manufacture of methamphetamine, he kept papers on hand to explain the chemical steps. It's certainly an unusual approach to chemistry class.

But Victor's story seems to have convinced the jury that there was at least some reasonable doubt. He was found not guilty.

James, meanwhile, made a plea deal. He pleaded guilty to making methamphetamine, using drug paraphernalia, and manufacturing a controlled substance, phenylacetone, which is used as a final step in making meth.

He avoided a forty-year sentence, but he did get 120 days in jail and six years of probation. He also had to pay $150,000 in restitution to the university to cover the costs of cleaning up his chemicals from the buildings.

Victor walked free—although the university refused to give him his old job back. Their professional relationship wasn't working. The chemistry was all wrong.

TICKET TO NOWHERE

Psychologists seem like they should be good at getting away with a crime—in theory, their knowledge of the human brain could give them an edge when it comes to anticipating and manipulating others. But it doesn't always work that way in practice.

Cyril Joad was a psychologist and philosopher. In 1940, he appeared on the panel of a British radio show called *The Brains Trust*. The format was simple—the listeners, many of them soldiers, would send in their questions on difficult subjects: How can a fly land on a ceiling? What is the meaning of life? The panel offered intelligent answers, sometimes disagreeing and debating.

It was wartime, and the BBC hoped the show would give soldiers a taste of the intellectual freedom the Allies were fighting for.

The show was hugely popular and continued for many years. For its first seven years, Professor Joad was the star. His answers were both witty and smart, yet phrased in the sort of commonsense language anyone could understand. He believed that many seemingly difficult questions were just the result of muddled language, and his answers often started with the phrase "It all depends what you mean by . . ." followed by a sensible clarification of the question. He was outspoken, controversial, and fun. Ordinary people loved his style, and he became an intellectual superstar, considered by many to be one of the smartest men in Britain.

But Joad had a secret. He was an amateur criminal. His specialty was evading fares on trains, and he used an elaborate range of techniques to travel for less, or for free. Now that he was a celebrity, you might think he would change his ways, but instead he seemed to feel invulnerable and kept trying new techniques. In one of his books, he had written about his dislike of railway companies, boasting that he cheated them whenever he could. This quote caught the attention of railway officials, and they began to watch him.

In 1948, Joad was caught traveling on a train from London to Devon. He was sitting in an expensive first-class seat. The ticket inspector asked, "Could you explain why you only have a third-class ticket?" Joad might have started, "It all depends what you mean by 'explain' . . ." but no matter what the inspector meant by "explain," Joad couldn't. And on this occasion, the official wasn't going to treat it as a mistake or let him off with a warning. Joad was trying to cheat the system, and the railway officials all knew it.

Joad was charged with fare evasion and pleaded guilty at the Tower Bridge Magistrates' Court. It was revealed that his boast about cheating the railways was not a false one—in fact, he had developed cheating into an art. He routinely lied about where he'd boarded the train and where he was going. He carried cheap tickets in various pockets, so he could produce the wrong one and claim an honest mistake. He would go to great lengths to avoid ticket collectors at station exits, escaping train stations by squeezing through hedges or crossing fields. He was a train fare supervillain.

The punishment was minor: Joad was fined £2 and charged additional costs of just over £26. He could afford that, but the damage to his reputation hit him much harder. His career was destroyed. He was revealed as a dishonest petty thief, and it was suddenly hard for the general public to take his views on philosophy and morality seriously. He was mocked and criticized in the newspapers and fired from his radio show.

He might have been a smart man, but he was a very dumb criminal.

CRIME TRAVELERS

THE MAGNA-TUDE OF THE CRIME

Tourists with an interest in the law can view a copy of the Magna Carta in Salisbury Cathedral, in England. (A purist might say just "Magna Carta" without the "the.") The document was signed by King John in 1215 and lays out legal rights that are still the basis for many of our laws today.

But while the Magna Carta has been invoked in countless legal cases, it's not often that it's the victim of a crime. The *Guardian* reported one such case.

"Robert" was a forty-five-year-old man who didn't like the state of the law in 2018 England. He had a history of convictions for theft and criminal damage, and he thought those convictions were unfair, so he took out his anger on the system. He spray-painted the doors of a police station in Exeter. He cut into municipal benches with an angle grinder. And he heaved a concrete block through the window of a law firm.

Despite all his efforts, the system refused to change.

Robert decided that the root of the problem was the Magna Carta. He got it into his head that the document was a fake. It's not clear where he thought the real one had gone, or what it had to say about vandalizing park benches, but he was sure there had been a switch. He made plans to visit Salisbury Cathedral, where one of the four remaining copies of the document is kept. He would steal it, then give a prepared statement sharing some of his nutbar theories.

The precious document is well protected, lying behind two glass screens connected to an alarm system, and watched over by security cameras. But those safeguards weren't going to deter a thief like Robert.

Around 5 p.m. on an October day in 2018, he entered the display area and put on gloves and safety goggles. He messed with the camera and pulled a fire alarm as an ill-considered "distraction," then produced a claw hammer and started smashing at the glass.

Other visitors were in the room. One of them, an American tourist, was appalled at what he saw. He assisted two cathedral officials as they grabbed Robert and wrestled him to the ground.

The police arrived a few minutes later and took Robert into custody.

He had managed to knock a few holes in the outer case, but the inner glass was mostly intact, and the ancient document was undamaged.

Robert was sentenced to four years in prison. That is, after he was tried and found guilty by a jury of his peers—one of the fundamental rights guaranteed to all citizens by the Magna Carta.

HE TURNS AND STAIRS

The Spanish Steps are a famous landmark in Rome. Known locally as *la Scalinata di Trinità Dei Monti*, it's a stairway of 135 steps built in the 1700s, connecting a church on one street and the site of the Spanish embassy, which is on a lower level. The steps have featured as a location in many films—most famously in *Roman Holiday*, when Audrey Hepburn eats an ice cream cone there and Gregory Peck wishes he could have a lick.

In May 2022, Britain's *Sunday Times* reported on a more unusual visit to this location.

"Asad" was a tourist visiting Rome from Saudi Arabia. He was a thirty-seven-year-old engineer and wanted to drive one of those expensive Italian cars, so he rented a Maserati Levante luxury SUV. He wanted to see the sights of Rome, and what better way to do it than from the driver's seat of a high-performance four-wheel-drive vehicle?

In the early hours of the morning, Asad was trying to navigate the streets of Rome. He had a Romanian woman in the seat beside him—he'd met her at a nightclub and they seemed to be hitting it off. But that would soon change. After taking a wrong turn, he found himself at the top of the famous steps. His GPS said he should continue straight down (or so he claimed), so he did just that. In a scene like something from the heist film *The Italian Job*, he simply turned his car onto the steps and drove down, bumping and grinding against the stone steps as he went.

The Maserati Levante has a top speed of over 187 miles per hour, but its speed on stone steps is much less. Nobody was there to stop Asad, but cameras caught it all on video.

Asad could feel that something was wrong and brought the car to a stop on the stairway. His passenger didn't seem impressed by his driving. She started yelling at him. He is seen leaving the car and holding his head in his hands while she shouts at him.

Asad changed his mind about the route he'd chosen. He tried reversing, but it got him nowhere. He made a call to a tow truck, and while he was waiting, tried to get help from passersby. Eventually, he got the car moving and back on the road again before the tow truck arrived, scratching and scraping his way back the way he'd come.

Asan kept quiet about his adventure driving over the landmarks of Italy, but the license plate of the rental car was clearly visible on the camera footage. When Asad was ready to fly home, he returned the car to the rental company in Milan's Malpensa airport. The police caught up with him there and arrested him. His excursion had cracked several of the steps and done minor damage to many more. He was charged with aggravated damage to cultural heritage and monuments.

In Italy, if you break steps, the police will take steps.

I'M LOOKING FOR THE PRESIDENTIAL SUITE

If you're looking for a place to commit a casual break and enter, it's not usually a good idea to choose the country's best-guarded location.

Romania's capital, Bucharest, is the site of the world's most expensive administrative building, the Palace of the Parliament. The brutal communist dictator Nicolae Ceaușescu had ordered its construction in the 1980s after seeing what his counterpart in North Korea had built. An entire downtown neighborhood was demolished, and the new palace and its grounds replaced it. The imposing edifice was finally finished in 1997 at a cost of more than $4 billion, although Ceaușescu never got to enjoy living there—the corrupt dictator had been deposed, tried, and executed eight years earlier.

The palace is a mammoth structure and dominates the heart of Bucharest. It has more than a thousand rooms. The utility bills alone are more than $6 million a year. The decor is very ornate, with many marble columns and crystal chandeliers. It houses the Romanian parliament and several museums.

As you might expect, the security around the building is tight. The palace is guarded by five thousand soldiers working in shifts.

But all the guards must have been on a coffee break at 4 a.m. on December 27, 2021, because, according to the *Daily Telegraph*, that's when "Sean," an Irish tourist who had had much too much to drink, climbed over the six-foot wall and strolled across the lawns and fountains in the courtyard. He made it all the way to the palace without anyone approaching him. He then smashed a window and climbed inside.

Sean spent a while exploring the big building. He wandered the cavernous corridors, admired the works of art, and tried to open the locked doors.

Eventually, the folks in the security department rubbed the sleep from their eyes, checked their monitors, and thought, "That doesn't look quite right."

Security officials moved in and arrested the intruder.

Sean was interrogated. Officials asked him to explain his presence in the building. Sean said he had been out drinking in the old part of the city and had then returned to his lodgings. Unfortunately, he'd mixed up the buildings, mistaking the palace for his own hotel. Presumably, it was one of those hotels where patrons who want to enter after-hours just smash a window.

The guards grilled him about how he'd hopped the wall, and about that broken window.

Sean said he didn't remember doing those things. It was the alcohol, you see . . .

The break-in made headlines in Romania. His arrival at the police station was on TV. He was charged with trespassing and damaging a public building.

Several hours of court hearings followed. He could have faced thirty days in jail, but the prosecutors decided he could go free after twenty-four hours, because he wasn't a danger to the public—and perhaps also because the ease with which he'd entered the building and carried out his idiotic exploits was an embarrassment to the security chiefs.

MAKING A HUMAN PYRAMID

The Egyptian authorities prohibit people from climbing the Great Pyramid of Giza, but it wasn't entirely against the law, and many people tried to get to the top despite the prohibition.

But in 2018, the UK edition of *Metro* reported on a Danish couple who went too far. They caused such outrage with their "ascent to the peak" that laws were changed.

"Magnus" was a twenty-three-year-old photographer from Denmark. He describes his photographic interests as "urban exploration, nude art, travel stuff."

In November 2018, he visited Egypt. He had set his heart on a photo session on the Great Pyramid, the largest pyramid in Giza. The huge structure is over 450 feet tall. In ancient times, it was considered one of the Seven Wonders of the World, and it is the only one of the seven to have survived to the present day. The pyramid was built as a tomb for the pharaoh Khufu (also known as Cheops). It was then the tallest human-made structure in the world, and it remained the tallest for 3,800 years.

Magnus wanted to celebrate its rich heritage by climbing to the top and taking some nude photos. He'd brought along a Norwegian model who would pose with him.

The two made several attempts to climb to the top of the pyramid, but each time, they had to stop. On one occasion, they were arrested by police. They were interrogated but released with a warning.

Magnus figured it was just a question of greasing the right palms. He contacted an Egyptian woman who said she could put him in touch with someone, a camel driver. He would help Magnus climb to the top without being caught.

The camel driver agreed to help for four thousand Egyptian pounds (around US$212 at the time). With his help and advice—and perhaps a bribe so that certain officers would look the other way?—the two Danes made a successful ascent. Once at the top, they stripped and took photos of themselves lying together. Were they having sex? It looked like it, although Magnus later claimed the girl was just a model, not his girlfriend, and the act was simulated.

When the photos went onto the internet, Egypt was shocked and appalled. Having tourists climb the pyramid was against the rules, but everyone knew it happened now and then, and they could turn a blind eye to the occasional overenthusiastic tourist. But this was another thing entirely! Using Egypt's greatest symbol as a backdrop for pornography? (That's how the images were described by Egypt's prosecutors.) The actions of these scandalous Scandinavians were entirely unacceptable. The outrage was discussed in Egypt's parliament. It was a violation of public morality. Magnus and his woman must be punished.

Unfortunately for Egyptian justice, Magnus couldn't be punished.

He had returned to Denmark and, after learning what they were saying about him in Egypt, he didn't think he'd be paying another visit any time soon.

With the real criminals out of reach, the Egyptian authorities had to content themselves with arresting the people who had assisted the couple—Magnus's Egyptian contact and the camel driver she had put him in touch with.

With the incident still fresh in their minds, the government also passed new laws, making it a criminal act for anyone to climb the country's pyramids, punishable by a minimum of one month in prison and a fine of up to $6,200. And those fines are doubled if the climb involves acts that "violate public decency."

So that may be the end of the "Nile High Club."

BAD HABITS

In May 2009, seventeen members of a British soccer team went off for a boozy team getaway to the Greek island of Crete.

According to the *Guardian*, they stayed in the resort town of Malia, which is infamous for rowdy, alcohol-fueled behavior, especially in the summer months. Locals were getting fed up with it. The behavior of British tourists was considered particularly bad.

The men took full advantage of the party mood at the resort, but they really crossed the line in the eyes of some locals when they dressed up in that year's costume theme: "naughty nuns." Their costumes were homemade—plain black dresses in various lengths, some sporting white collars, some accessorized with crucifixes. The outfits were described as "rudimentary," with the emphasis on "rude." Some of the players had added sexy lingerie to their nun outfits, including thongs. Locals complained that some of the "nuns" displayed their buttocks—"and the rest."

The party had not gone on for long before complaints of the irreligious display reached the police. They reacted quickly, arresting the whole team and putting them in the back of a police van. The players were charged with "scandal and misrepresentation of a costume or uniform."

The footballers were shocked. They hadn't had a problem like this before. On previous trips to Cyprus and Portugal, the men had also dressed up to match various themes. In Cyprus, they all dressed as babies. In Portugal, they dressed as schoolgirls from the *St. Trinian's* films. That raised eyebrows but didn't lead to any arrests.

It is a serious crime in Greece—and many other countries—to pretend to be a nun or a priest, but this law usually applies to people who are fraudulently pretending to be members of the clergy, not people dressing up for an obvious party.

The dress-up theme was also considered to be insulting to the Catholic church, another crime in Greece.

The seventeen men were thrown into a single prison cell. They were still wearing their homemade nun's outfits. The players were appalled at the conditions in the jail. There were only eight "beds"—made from concrete—they had to pay for any food they ate, and the cells were filthy.

The next day, they were paraded out to appear in court—still in their "naughty nun" outfits, now looking a little wrinkled. They escaped any charges, though, because the witnesses who had lodged the complaint didn't show up to testify against them.

The men were allowed to go free. Still in their outfits (which were becoming a habit), they made their way back to the resort, where they tried to continue their holiday in their day clothes and grumbled about how they hadn't meant anything by dressing up as nuns.

No offense meant? Nun taken.

BORDERING ON THE ABSURD

HUNTING THE HUNTER

"Marcus" was a hunter from Fairbanks, Alaska. In August 2017, he was hunting near the Canadian border when he spotted a Dall sheep, a wild animal that likes mountainous areas. The sheep are mostly white, with large, curling horns. The animal was a very desirable target for a hunter, and Marcus was licensed to shoot one in Alaska.

Marcus took aim and killed the sheep.

Yukon News reported that there was one small problem: the sheep wasn't in Alaska. It was across the border, on the Yukon side, in Canada.

A wide band of cut trees marks the boundary between the two countries, but Marcus later claimed he hadn't realized the sheep was more than a hundred yards away, on the other side of the border, when he shot it.

Whether that claim is true or not, he was certainly aware that he'd done some cross-border shooting when he crossed the border himself and posed for photos with the dead sheep. He used the usual hunter trick of holding the camera close to the head, so the dimensions of his victim were exaggerated and it looked as though he'd brought down a beast the size of a moose.

He then dragged the sheep back to the American side, butchered it, and took the parts he wanted back home. He checked in with US authorities, telling them that the sheep had been killed in Alaska, although he knew full well it was shot in Canada.

Marcus posted his pictures on a Facebook sheep-hunting group (there's a group for everything, isn't there?) and bragged about shooting a "Yukon zebra"—referring to the dark markings on his sheep. A Dall sheep with these markings is sometimes called a Fannin sheep.

It seemed like he'd avoided being caught for cross-border poaching, but the act caught up with him the following year, when an anonymous tipster sent copies of Marcus's photos to Canadian officials, suggesting that this American hunter had been killing Canadian animals.

The officials who monitor illegal hunting go to considerable lengths to investigate these reports, and they were soon on the case. They took a helicopter to the area where Marcus had killed the sheep and explored it, trying to find an exact match for the landscape in his photo. This was no small task. The photo showed only nondescript rocky hills and a few tiny trees. But at last, they found the precise spot and took a photo to match the one taken by Marcus. They marked an arrangement of ten small features—little trees, small ridges on rocks. Individually, none of the features would have clinched the case, but when they were viewed together, the new photograph showed conclusively that Marcus's earlier photo had been taken in Canada. It was an impressive sleuthing job.

Marcus was charged with unlawful hunting and unlawful export. The crimes could carry heavy fines, from $5,000 up to $300,000.

In his favor, when Marcus was confronted with the charges, he cooperated and pleaded guilty. He also handed back his trophy, the mounted head and shoulders of the dead sheep. In court, he asked for the minimum fine: $5,000.

The prosecutor agreed he'd been cooperative, but wanted to deter other trigger-happy hunters. He asked for a $12,500 fine and a five-year hunting ban.

The judge compromised—Marcus wasn't a wealthy man, so she gave the hunter a five-year ban and an $8,500 fine. Of that money, $7,500 went to the Yukon's program for tipsters.

Only one person profited from Marcus's crime: the person who turned him in. He received the remaining $1,000.

WELCOME TO SCAM-DINAVIA

Many people from the Indian subcontinent would like to start a new life in Europe, but can't qualify for immigration. A few try the illegal route.

"Oleg" was there to help them. At least, he said he was. He was actually a scam artist, looking to take their money.

We don't know too much about Oleg, but he was from central Asia, part of the former Soviet Union. He promised the migrants he could get them into Europe by routing them through Russia, which borders a number of countries in the European Union.

Oleg claimed he had provided his services to thousands of customers over the years. That was true, but the services involved taking them on a long trip, then telling them they were in Europe when they were actually still in Russia. By the time they realized the truth, Oleg—and their money—had vanished.

In November 2019, Oleg transported four South Asian men in his car. According to the Russian news agency Interfax, each man had paid over $11,000 for Oleg's services as a "conductor." Oleg drove them toward Finland, an EU member. First, they took the main roads, then they turned off onto bumpy country roads. It was then time to leave the car and endure a long trek around the Vyborg region—a forested area of Russia dotted with a few lonely farms.

Oleg led his clients on a march around a lake. To build a sense of tension, he gave his clients an inflatable boat to carry—"Just in case," he said, although he knew perfectly well that they wouldn't be using a boat.

At last, they arrived at their destination in the forest—supposedly, the Russian–Finnish border. This was an easy border to cross, said Oleg. It certainly was, but it didn't lead them to Finland. Oleg had built the "border" himself in the middle of the Russian forest. The real Finnish border was another fifteen miles farther west.

Oleg took the migrants through the border and said goodbye, then left them to fend for themselves.

The four migrants wandered around the swampy forest, believing they were in Finland, until they were spotted by Russian border guards and arrested. They were astonished to learn they were still in Russia. Images on Russian media showed them emerging from behind trees with their hands raised.

The migrants were quickly processed at a court in St. Petersburg and deported back to their own countries.

As for Oleg, the authorities caught him, too. He faced charges of fraud and violating the (real) state border.

LIKE A DOG WITH A DRONE

Canada's gun laws are much stricter than those in the United States. It's particularly difficult for Canadians to get hold of the kinds of small, easily concealed handguns favored by criminals. That means there's money to be made smuggling pistols from America to Canada. But if you get caught at the border, you're in trouble.

Gunrunners have tried many approaches. They have hidden guns inside the gas tanks of cars, and they have attached them secretly to the vehicles of unsuspecting tourists. (The smugglers track down the cars later and remove the illegal packages.)

But, in a modern twist, a group of smugglers in Michigan hit on what they figured was the perfect approach: they would use drones. A big drone could just about carry fifteen pounds, which translates to ten or eleven average-sized pistols. The state of Michigan is separated from neighboring Ontario only by a river in many places. It's a good place to sneak something across.

On April 29, 2022, around 4 a.m., the American gunrunners went to a point on the US side of the St. Clair River and attached a bag holding eleven guns to a $7,000 drone. The drone had been modified for covert use: its lights had been disabled so it couldn't be easily spotted.

The drone's operator, "Tom," was at the controls on the Canadian side. As far as we can tell, he'd driven his pickup truck to the planned landing spot, about fifteen miles east of the Detroit suburbs.

Once the drone was loaded with weapons by his colleagues on the American side of the St. Clair River, his partners signaled him, and he launched the vehicle.

The trip over the river was fairly short—less than half a mile. With the weight of the guns, the battery life of the drone was being pushed to the limit, but Tom had accounted for that. It was all going perfectly.

The area had many trees, but Tom had chosen an open area for the landing spot—the backyard of a house situated beside the river in the little town of Port Lambton, about twenty miles downriver from Sarnia.

Tom congratulated himself on the flying. Weather conditions were good—not too much wind. Now, as he carried out the most difficult part of the operation, landing the drone, he needed all his attention. Not that there would be many interruptions. That's why he'd chosen four in the morning for the transfer—he wasn't likely to be interrupted by anyone.

But he was wrong about that.

According to the *Globe and Mail*, the occupant of the house near the landing spot was woken by his little Yorkshire terrier, who felt a pressing need to "go outside." The bleary-eyed owner dragged himself out of bed and opened the door for the dog.

But as the homeowner looked down toward the river, he noticed movement in his yard. This was weird. Someone was out there, trying to stay hidden. He shone a flashlight toward the figure and called out. The little dog bounded out to investigate.

Tom was trying to get the landing right, and this was the worst time to be distracted by bright lights and a yappy dog. It threw Tom off his game. The drone, instead of landing, swerved to one side and found a nearby tree. And it got stuck there.

Tom panicked. He didn't want to risk a ten-year sentence for gun trafficking. He ran for his truck and sped away, leaving behind his

$7,000 drone, which was carrying a bag of guns he could have sold for $22,000 to criminal buyers in Toronto. The drone and its cargo were picked up soon after by the Ontario Provincial Police.

Police are still working on technology to protect against smuggling by drone. In this case, though, a low-tech approach worked just fine. The criminals were unable to do their business—because the dog wanted to do his.

SO LONG, SUCKERS!

Canada's border control agents often catch criminals trying to smuggle exotic animals into the country. The creatures are usually reptiles, like tortoises and snakes, but in May 2019, they stopped a man smuggling something a little more unusual.

At Toronto's Pearson Airport, *National Geographic* reported, a trained sniffer beagle picked up an interesting smell from one passenger's luggage and drew the attention of officers to it. When they looked inside a grocery bag in the man's carry-on luggage, they found five thousand squirming leeches.

The owner of the bag, "Sergey," had flown in from Russia. He claimed he was going to use the leeches himself, pouring their wastewater on his orchids. It didn't sound plausible.

Government naturalists identified the leeches as *Hirudo medicinalis*—also known as European medical leeches. These are voracious parasitic worms, distant relatives of the earthworm, that love to latch onto humans and suck their blood. They are called medical leeches because the same species has been used since ancient times in medicine. People once believed that removing surplus blood could cure disease, and leeches are enthusiastic about removing surplus blood—which, in the leech's tiny mind, is as much of it as it can eat. In the 1800s, demand for the wriggling horrors reached such a high level that wild leeches became endangered, leading to strict rules on their international trade.

Medical use of leeches today is very limited—their anticoagulant saliva can occasionally be useful in keeping blood vessels open after certain surgical procedures, but that's about all. However, there is a steady demand for them in the "quack medicine" market.

The medical leeches bred for use on humans are raised in clean conditions. An analysis of Sergey's collection showed that they were leeches taken from the wild, and that they had been dining on whatever they could find in their stagnant ponds or dirty streams. A New Ager using one of these to "cleanse bad blood" might end up with a serious infection.

A single medical leech can sell for $10, meaning that Sergey's haul was worth up to $50,000. It didn't seem likely he'd bought them for his flowers. Officials guessed he was intending to sell them to gullible alternative-medicine customers. The leeches were confiscated, and Sergey was charged for trying to import a protected species. After a guilty plea, he was banned from importing any more live animals and given a $15,000 fine.

Case closed. Bag emptied.

Except for the pesky question of what to do with the five thousand leeches.

The creatures posed a real problem for the officials. They didn't want the fuss and expense of looking after such a large number of bloodsuckers. The leeches were lively, and good escape artists. Twenty escaped after a water change and had to be recaptured. The leeches weren't native to Canada, so it would be an ecological problem to release them into the wild.

Furthermore, while most of us might look at a leech and think, "Kill it! Kill it with fire!" the fact is that they are a threatened species. So, in the end, the leeches were spared a fiery death and patiently cared for at taxpayers' expense while officials tried to find a place for them. It took a few months, but eventually the leeches were safely passed on to interested researchers at various museums and academic institutions.

The final tally: five thousand bloodsuckers were relocated and confined for the rest of their lives, and one was released after paying a large fine.

CHARGES THAT STICK

Criminals know that crossing a border can be a good way to escape the law. But it doesn't always work out the way they hope.

"Victor" was a Canadian man in his twenties who had ambitions to be a globetrotting criminal. He had set his sights on Singapore, a small but very wealthy country. But there was a problem: Singapore is famous for the harsh punishments it gives to criminals. Drug dealers are often executed, and other criminals are caned in addition to getting jail time. Victor didn't want the pain and humiliation of a caning, so he intended to carry out his robbery and get out fast.

According to the *Straits Times*, Victor arrived in Singapore in June of 2016. He stayed in various hostels in Chinatown for a week while he planned his big heist. Finally, all the pieces were in place.

In July, he walked into a local bank and put a bag on the counter with his right hand inside it. He passed the teller a slip of paper claiming that he was holding a gun hidden in the bag and that this was a robbery. The part about the robbery was true enough, but the gun was a lie. Still, the terrified cashier didn't want to take any chances and handed over the money—just over 30,000 Singapore dollars (around US$20,000). Victor then fled the bank.

You might be surprised that this rudimentary robbery took a week to plan, but like most of the criminals we've encountered, Victor doesn't seem to have been too smart. Even so, he moved just fast enough to avoid getting caught. While the police were checking bank security footage and DNA from his hotel room, Victor was on a flight to Thailand with a bag full of cash.

Home free!

Well, not quite. A few days later, Victor was under arrest in Thailand, because that's what happens when you come into a country with a bag full of cash, no customs declaration, and no way to explain where the money has come from. He was charged with money laundering.

News of his arrest made its way back to Singapore. Singaporean officials asked for Victor to be extradited to face charges there. Thailand refused. They didn't have an extradition treaty with Singapore, and besides, they'd already confiscated the cash.

So, Victor spent more than a year in a Thai jail—not for robbing a bank, but for carrying the loot into Thailand. In 2018, at the end of his sentence, he was deported and put on a flight back to his home country of Canada. His nightmare was over.

Or so he thought.

His flight to Canada made a stopover in London. Once he was on British soil, Victor was detained by the authorities. The Singapore police had not forgotten about his robbery, and they had contacted the British police, because Singapore and Britain *do* have an extradition treaty.

The fact that Singapore canes bank robbers was a problem for the British, who don't support capital or corporal punishment, and won't extradite criminals to face such punishments. The British told their counterparts in Singapore that they could only return Victor on the condition that he didn't get caned. The Singapore officials agreed, and Victor was flown to Singapore to face trial for his bank robbery.

Despite the no-caning promise, the prosecution demanded a harsh sentence for Victor's crimes: six years in prison and nine strokes of the cane. The judge went easy on him and sentenced him to five years in jail—and six strokes of the cane.

Officials in Britain were angry at the betrayal, and for a while, it wasn't clear whether Victor would get caned or not. Finally, the Singapore government stepped in and said it would stick to its promise and spare Victor the caning part of the sentence. It was a minor win for this dumb criminal to relish as he serves his five-year term in a Singapore cell—his second prison sentence for a crime that netted him nothing.

GONE IN SIXTY SECONDS ...
GIVE OR TAKE

BE CAREFUL WHO YOU TRUST

In May 1960, a twenty-year-old man, "Eric," had a problem with his car. He saw a passing policeman and asked for help. He explained that he'd locked himself out of his car and now he couldn't get in.

According to the *New York Times*, the officer, "Charles," seemed like one of those old-fashioned, friendly types. And he knew just how to help. He went to a nearby store and got a length of wire. He used it to reach inside the car. In a few minutes, the car was unlocked.

Eric was deeply grateful and thanked the officer for his assistance. He got behind the wheel.

"Just one last thing," said the officer. "Could I please see your registration and license?"

Eric handed over the documents and waited nervously while the officer looked them over. One glance was enough. Charles could see they were obviously false. Another quick check showed that the car had been stolen three days earlier. It was owned by the city and had been assigned to the medical examiner.

Eric had displayed a rare level of chutzpah, and an even rarer level of dumb, in asking a police officer to help him break into a stolen car. Friendly Officer Charles arrested Eric and charged him with stealing a vehicle and forgery.

He later said he hadn't been doing anything unusual in asking for the documents. He just made it a practice to always ask for the paperwork for any car he had anything to do with, especially one he had to open with wire.

STUCK IN THE CAR

Car thieves usually want to get from the outside of the vehicle to the inside, but every now and then, they have a pressing need to go in the other direction.

That's what happened to a thief in Abbotsford, British Columbia. The *Abbotsford News* reported that a man had broken into a cargo van late at night in July 2018. It seems the thief got into the van through a rear door. But as he entered, the door closed behind him.

The thief, a thirty-eight-year-old man, suddenly discovered he couldn't open the door from the inside. You might think he could just get out through the front doors. He probably thought so, too, but he soon discovered that the van had a metal barrier between the cargo area and the driving compartment. He had created a prison for himself.

The thief tried to smash his way out of the van. He had no luck getting the doors open, but at two in the morning, his hammering woke the neighbors. They saw the van shaking violently and called the police.

The officers unlocked the van and locked the thief in jail instead.

CTV News reported on another thief in British Columbia who took a more audacious approach. In September 2020, a man came out to his car, only to discover a stranger sitting inside—the car thief was in the midst of stealing it.

The owner told the intruder to get out of his car. The intruder, a forty-year-old man, said it was his own car, then locked all the doors so the car's real owner couldn't get in.

Police were soon on the scene. The owner proved the car was his by using his key fob to unlock the doors. The intruder used the opportunity to run from the car, taking the owner's jacket with him. He was caught, arrested, and charged with theft under $5,000.

Scandinavian thieves seem to be more cooperative, though no less dumb. In December 2018, a seventeen-year-old thief broke into a Volvo parked outside a dealership in the city of Trondheim, in Norway.

According to the *New York Daily News*, the thief was unaware that the car had a centralized locking system. Once he was in, the car locked, and he was completely unable to get out.

The teenager was already known to the police, so he figured there would be no problem asking for their help. He phoned them, and they were indeed happy to get him out of the car—and into their custody.

In June 2022, a female car thief in Australia was trapped in an even more unusual way.

According to BBC News, the twenty-four-year-old woman had wandered up the driveway of a rural house on the outskirts of Brisbane. There was nobody around, so she made herself at home, taking a shower and changing clothes before going outside to steal the family car, a red Volkswagen Polo.

She was just getting ready to drive away with the vehicle when the homeowners returned. The family had been on an outing and were shocked to see their car being stolen.

The owner approached the car and told the thief to give up. But despite repeated requests, she refused to get out of the car and was still determined to take it.

The man said, "Well, OK. You want to play it that way. I've got an alternative option."

The man happened to own a forklift, parked nearby on the dirt driveway. He climbed on, wheeled the vehicle around, and scooped up the family car.

Before the thief knew what was happening, she found herself trapped inside the car, six feet in the air. She couldn't drive, and the position of the forklift made it impossible for her to get out. She could only wait until police arrived.

She was charged with burglary and unlawful use of a motor vehicle.

STUCK WITH A STICK

Car technology is constantly changing. In the past, thieves could just hot-wire a car. Today, they may need to get past layers of digital protection to make the car move. But sometimes it's the simplest technologies that are most effective in deterring crime.

"Luke" and "Adrian" were a pair of aspiring teenage car thieves in Nashville, Tennessee. According to Fox News, one evening in May 2022, they went out to steal a car. They had decided to take a bare-bones approach to their crimes. They didn't know how to get past computerized anti-theft systems, and they didn't intend to learn. Instead, they would go with the carjacking option—find a person who has stopped their car, then take it while the keys are still in the ignition. They'd likely seen it done a hundred times in *Grand Theft Auto* video games—pull the driver out, climb in, and drive off in their car. Easy.

After wandering around a multistory parking garage, they spotted a suitable victim, a woman sitting in her car. They ran up to her, catching her by surprise, then grabbed her and pulled her from the car. At least, they tried to pull her from the car. It wasn't quite as easy in real life as it looked in the video games. While they pulled, she screamed, and she held tight to the steering wheel as she sounded the car's horn.

It wasn't supposed to work like this. Luke and Adrian panicked and ran away.

After they'd calmed down, they decided to try again. Maybe the trick was to wait until the person had just left the car—eliminate the problematic "pull them from the vehicle" stage.

They walked to a new parking garage and soon found a new victim—also a woman. They watched her as she parked her car, shut it off, then opened the door, still holding the keys.

Now was the time to make their move. They ran into the woman, snatched the keys from her hand, and jumped into her car. Luke got into the driver's seat. Adrian rode shotgun.

"Say goodbye to your car, lady!"

The criminal pair were just getting ready to peel away, leaving only the smell of burning rubber.

Then they hit a snag.

The car had three pedals instead of two! And what was this gear shift that went in different directions?

The car had a manual transmission. The thieves were utterly bewildered by the stick shift. While their victim watched their efforts in disbelief, they tried and failed to make the car go. They finally gave up, and once again, they ran away.

We can only imagine what they intended next. Perhaps they could look inside the car first and double-check that it was automatic before stealing it. Or ask the owner a few questions about the car before carrying out the theft. Whatever their plan, they didn't get a third chance. Their previous victims had reported them.

The police were on the lookout now, and they soon caught up with the inept car thieves as they wandered the streets. They appeared in juvenile court later, charged with carjacking, theft of property, and attempted vehicle theft.

Statistics say that less than one-fifth of drivers today know how to drive a car with a manual transmission. Although stick-shift cars are still common in Europe, they have become unusual in North America, and younger drivers are particularly disinclined to learn to use them. Many American car dealers don't even bother stocking the humble "standard."

Some drivers deliberately choose the manual transmission precisely because it gives them good protection against having their vehicle stolen. It seems *Grand Theft Auto* is a more appealing game than *Grand Theft Manual*.

OOPS, I STOLE YOUR CAR

Not every car thief has criminal intentions.

A report on CBC News tells the story of a man who stole a vehicle entirely by accident.

In 1998, seventeen-year-old "Julian" was working as a lifeguard and swim instructor in Winnipeg, Manitoba. He was on his break, and he needed to pay a ticket at the police station, but it was hard for him to get there. Julian didn't have his own car—it was out of commission after he hit a cow on the highway a month earlier. (That's life in the Prairies!)

"Don't worry," said "Emma," his colleague. She threw him her car keys. It was a hot day, and she suggested that he could run his errand, then come back with a couple of icy Slurpees for them both. Emma's car was the white Ford Taurus in the parking lot.

Julian went out to the parking lot and found the car. He didn't even need the keys to get in—the windows were down and the door was unlocked. He slid into the driver's seat and tried to start the car. He had some difficulty turning the key, but after a few attempts, he figured it was because he hadn't yet put his seat belt on. He finally started the car and drove off on his errands.

What Julian didn't realize was that this wasn't his colleague's Ford Taurus. The Taurus was a common car back then, and he had unwittingly stolen a car owned by one of the people swimming in the pool. It was a sheer fluke that the keys were just similar enough that, with a little effort, Julian had been able to start the stranger's vehicle with Emma's key.

Julian drove to the police station, locked the car, and tried to pay his parking ticket. The police told him he couldn't pay the fine there—he'd have to pay at the Public Safety Building. Julian went back out to the vehicle, but he couldn't get the car door to open again. Some officers came over to see what he was up to. He explained that he was driving his friend's car, but the keys weren't working. The parking attendant came to help. He gave the key more of a jiggle and managed to open the car door.

Once Julian was inside the car, he had just as much trouble starting it. It took him ten minutes to get the key to turn, and this time the seat belt didn't make any difference. He worried that he'd damaged the locks of his friend's car, and it seemed like it might be an expensive thing to fix.

Feeling guilty about the damage to the locks, he finished his ticket-paying errand, then bought the Slurpees.

In the meantime, back at the pool, his friend Emma was in the midst of a drama. A woman had finished her swim at the pool and discovered that her Ford Taurus had apparently been stolen. The distraught woman wanted to report the crime, but couldn't remember her car's license plate number. She had gone home to find the information and call the police.

When Julian returned, that drama was over. He gave Emma her Slurpee and handed over the keys with an apology, saying he was afraid he might have damaged her car.

Later, when he returned for a second shift, he was *sure* he had done some damage, because Emma was gone, but the Taurus—the one he thought was hers—was still sitting in the parking lot.

When he saw her the next day, he apologized profusely for rendering her car undrivable. She didn't know what he was talking about— she had driven her car home after work. It was then that Emma told Julian about the stolen car drama, and they realized he'd driven off in the wrong car.

Later that day, the car-theft victim showed up at the parking lot with the police to tell them exactly where her white Ford Taurus had been when it was stolen. To her amazement—and embarrassment—the car was right where she had left it. The police left, probably thinking the woman was a little crazy. She drove off, unable to figure out what had happened.

Julian lived with the guilty secret for many years, but is now searching for that other car owner, so he can say he's sorry and fill her in on the missing parts of her car theft story.

THIS CAR COULD BE YOURS

In September 2021, "David" was in the market for a new car. He knew he could save a significant chunk of the purchase price if he traded in his old one. It was too bad he didn't have an old car to trade in—but problems like that don't trouble the criminal mind for long.

According to *Motor Illustrated*, the fifty-year-old man went to a local Chrysler Dodge Jeep dealership in Lake City, Florida, and stole one of the cars off their lot. Problem solved. Now he had a car to trade.

Three days later, he went shopping for a new car. He found one he liked. When asked if had a car to trade in, he said yes, indeed—and it was a beauty.

The salesperson at the dealership was pleased—he was making a sale and picking up a trade-in that looked perfect. He did the paperwork, which included running a routine check on the vehicle identification number of the trade-in. The dealership staff were taken aback to discover that the trade-in had been reported as stolen. But what was more surprising, it had been stolen from their own dealership!

David was taken in and interrogated by the police. He confessed that, yes, he had stolen the trade-in car. The details he gave of the theft matched the security camera footage police had been working with.

He was charged with grand theft of a motor vehicle, dealing in stolen property, criminal mischief, and "petit theft" (it's *petit*, not *petty*, in Florida).

Police said David hadn't put up any resistance when he was arrested. Perhaps, in the back of his mind, even he knew how dumb this scheme looked.

THE GOOD-FAITH THIEF

Some of the excuses that criminals give for their crimes are amazing—a bizarre combination of the lofty and the ludicrous.

Newsweek described the strange case of a Florida man accused of stealing a car.

"Ernest" had come out of a Florida bar late on a February night in 2022 and driven away in someone else's car. But, as he later explained to police, he hadn't really stolen a car. What happened, he said, was that he was unable to find his own car, so he just took someone else's, in what he called "a good-faith effort" to find his own car—because it's well known that, if your own car is missing, you can take your pick of other people's vehicles without needing to ask.

Ernest's good-faith effort was impressive. It took him speeding off into the night, traveling down the highway for many miles—to figure out where he'd parked his own vehicle before walking to the bar. A cynical observer might think Ernest had stolen the car solely to take it on a joyride. But Ernest denied this.

Ernest brought the "borrowed" car to a halt on some train tracks. A train was approaching. Ernest got out. Was he destroying the stolen car for kicks? No, indeed, said Ernest. He explained that the car had suddenly stopped dead on the tracks, just like that. Why, he'd escaped just in the nick of time.

Moments later, the train smashed into the car, sending it hurtling through the air and smashing into a nearby house.

On witnessing this spectacle, Ernest did what any reasonable person would do—he walked away. A little farther on, he found a fruit stand. He vandalized it, and then tried to steal a forklift—apparently in a good-faith attempt to cause as much chaos as possible.

While Ernest was trying to figure out the forklift controls, the cops came by to investigate. Ernest tried to play the honest citizen. Since the police were approaching anyway, he acted like he was hoping to see them. He walked into their spotlight and flagged them down, explaining that he was looking for his missing car—you know, the one he hadn't reported earlier.

Nobody recorded his explanation for trashing the fruit stand. Perhaps: "I checked under the cantaloupes, officer. My car isn't there."

He also didn't seem to have mentioned that the other car he stole had just been catapulted into somebody's home. Fortunately, the homeowners were uninjured by the four-wheeled projectile.

Ernest was arrested, of course, and faced various charges, including grand theft and criminal mischief. If that was his "good faith," we'd hate to see the trail of destruction he leaves when he's feeling insincere.

WOULD ANYONE WHO ISN'T A CAR THIEF PLEASE STEP FORWARD

In July 2020, police officers were on patrol in Newberg, Oregon, a town about twenty miles southwest of Portland. They had received a report that a Toyota Land Cruiser had just been stolen. Minutes later, the officers spotted it as it passed by and turned on their lights and siren.

According to CBS News, the driver of the Land Cruiser hit the gas and tried to make an escape. The police kept on his tail as he led them on a high-speed chase through the town.

Every police officer knows that these chases pose a risk to innocent members of the public, so you can imagine their horror when the thief's truck went out of control and smashed into another car, a Buick Regal.

The officers rushed from their cars to check on the condition of the two drivers. The car thief was a twenty-seven-year-old man. He was OK. They grabbed him and arrested him.

The driver of the Buick was a twenty-year-old woman. They checked her over and, thankfully, she didn't seem to be hurt. In fact, on closer examination, she seemed far from hurt. She seemed intoxicated.

Police checked the plates of the Buick and made another odd discovery. This car had been reported stolen three days earlier. They realized that, quite by chance, one car thief had collided with another.

In the movies, this kind of "meet cute" would be the start of a wonderful romance between the two young rebels. In real life, they were both arrested and charged with a range of crimes, including unauthorized use of a motor vehicle.

UNHOLIER THAN THOU

NUN LEFT

An eighty-year-old nun—we'll call her "Agnes"—had recently retired from her position at an elementary school in Torrance, California.

The *Guardian* reported that she had spent sixty years as a nun, and for twenty-eight of those years, she had been the school's principal. She would be the first to tell you that running the school wasn't always easy—there never seemed to be enough money to buy all the books they needed, or to pay for all the supplies, or the school field trips.

But Agnes also knew the main reason why money was so short—it was because she'd been taking it. For at least the past ten years, she'd embezzled school funds by the bucketload, taking a hearty bite from donations, tuition, and school fees, and keeping it for herself. By the time she retired, she'd stolen at least $835,000.

She used the cash for "personal expenses"—including her hefty credit card bills and trips to Lake Tahoe and Las Vegas. She was also an enthusiastic gambler and had thrown a lot of cash in that direction.

Agnes oversaw the school savings account, and the school's accounts at the credit union. She looked after charitable donations and managed a fund to pay the living expenses of the nuns employed at the school. These were all useful sources of income. She kept her theft hidden by submitting falsified monthly and annual reports to the school administration.

After Agnes retired in 2018, the school carried out a routine audit and was horrified to see how much money was missing.

Officials from the church confronted the elderly nun to ask what was going on. Agnes seemed to view it as a feminist issue. She told them that priests got paid more than nuns, and she deserved a raise.

For someone who had taken a vow of poverty, she had certainly given herself a generous income boost—roughly $83,000 a year.

The church handed the issue to the courts, where Agnes tearfully pleaded guilty to wire fraud and money laundering.

She acknowledged her sins but asked the judge not to send her to jail. The prosecutor disagreed—Agnes was a terrible example to the kids she had taught. He wanted her locked up for two years.

Parents and students from the school were divided. Some wrote to the judge, begging her to give the nun a light sentence. Others were less indulgent and said he should throw the book at her.

Agnes was sentenced to a year and a day in prison and required to pay back over $825,000 to the school.

WHAT'S UNDER THE HABIT?

In 1926, a group of four nuns was entering the United States from Canada. Customs officials noticed something strange about the nuns: their garments seemed large and somehow padded.

Were these real nuns? Or were they women in nuns' clothing, smuggling contraband?

The answer to both questions was yes.

The nuns came from various convents in the United States, according to reports in the *New York Times*. They had been on a retreat at a Canadian convent. And under their clothes (just how did they carry out that search?), they were wearing more than $5,000 of rare Breton lace—the equivalent of more than $80,000 today. Travelers were supposed to pay duty on such valuable goods.

The nuns were locked up while the customs officials tried to sort the situation out.

The church sent a representative and a lawyer, and the matter was settled without any criminal charges. It was decided that the nuns hadn't been trying to defraud the government; they were just "naive." They were allowed to go after paying $4,000 in duty on the lace. The church representatives paid the money, and the overdressed nuns were allowed to continue their journey.

NUN ON THE RUN FOR FUN

Nuns are supposed to live quiet lives of religious service. But there have always been a few rule breakers in the crowd, even in the Middle Ages. News about one of these naughty nuns came to light around 2020.

In the eyes of church officials in the 1300s, a nun called Joan of Leeds was a very foolish, wicked woman, and her actions were worse than criminal—they were scandalous, breaking the laws of God.

Today, people might view her adventures differently.

According to *History.com*, Joan had entered a Benedictine nunnery in York, England, and she hated it. It's likely she was young, but we don't know how young. Girls as young as thirteen could enter a nunnery. Some had been put there by exasperated parents, or by fathers who didn't want to pay a dowry so their daughters could marry. Many of the girls were hard to control.

Joan wanted to get out, but it was hard to escape. Once women were in a nunnery, they tended to stay there. Death was the only sure way out, so that was the exit Joan planned to take. Not a real death, but a fake one.

She probably worked with some convent conspirators. First, she pretended to be ill. Over time, her illness apparently became worse and worse, until finally the terrible news went out that poor Joan had died. Nobody doubted it—that was just how things were in the Middle Ages; people were dropping dead all the time.

This "black-and-white sheep" had constructed a dummy to serve as her own dead body. After the announcement of her unfortunate demise, the "body" was taken out and buried in a solemn ceremony.

Meanwhile, Joan made her escape. She left the nunnery, confident that nobody would come looking for her.

But later, someone who knew Joan and believed her to be dead was surprised to spot her in a town about thirty miles away. Not only was she very much alive, she was also living with a man. The church community was shocked. Joan had taken a vow of chastity! And what about that funeral? A fake body buried on sanctified ground. It was a huge scandal, an unholy mess.

Everything was now clear to the church authorities. Joan of Leeds had left the nunnery to pursue a life of "carnal lust." Or, as we might say today, because of a boy.

One of the most important clerics in England, the Archbishop of York, heard of the case and ordered Joan to return to the nunnery, but there is no evidence to suggest that she did—and, after the trouble she'd taken to escape, plenty of reasons to believe that she didn't.

KEEPING THE POOR IN THEIR PLACE

With its fast cars and casinos, Monaco is a playground for the super-rich. A third of the population are millionaires. A Monaco thief wouldn't have to look to find rich victims. What doesn't make so much sense is working as a thief in Monaco and robbing the poor.

According to the French news site *The Local*, that's what one church official did in 2017. "Jules" was a sexton at the Saint Nicholas Cathedral, taking care of the church property. The pay wasn't high—at least, it wasn't high enough for Jules. In addition to his regular home expenses, he had a son's wedding he needed to pay for. He decided to top up his income from another source.

One of Jules's jobs was to empty and sort the money from a collection box—money for the poor. He sorted it into two piles: one for the church and one for himself.

He probably thought the crime would be hard to detect, but a smart young priest at the cathedral tracked the amounts coming in from the collection box and noticed the sudden drop in income. He suspected Jules and relieved him of his money-counting duties. He also asked Jules to return the key to the collection box.

But Jules wasn't going to give up so easily. Before returning the key, he went to a locksmith and had a second copy made. Now he could extract the money at the source before it was counted. It might even help his case if the collection stayed low. He kept on pilfering from the poor.

Jules didn't realize that the priest was still suspicious and had been in discussions with the police. He had added some extra security to the cashbox.

When the sexton next opened the collection box, he was snared by a booby trap. A mechanism inside the box sprayed red paint onto his hands. He was literally caught red-handed.

Jules was arrested and charged with the crime. He admitted he had stolen a total of around 3,000 euros ($3,500) from the box. The court fined him 1,000 euros and gave him a five-month suspended prison sentence.

A MULE'S PARADISE

In 1999, a forty-seven-year-old man dressed as a priest walked through the international airport in São Paulo, Brazil. He had tickets for Portugal.

Police were suspicious of him and searched under his cassock. According to the *Irish Times*, they found many small bags of white powder fastened to the inside of his garments. He was carrying nearly twenty-five pounds of cocaine.

But what surprised them more was that the priest's robes were not a disguise. The man really was a priest.

Father "Miguel" was originally from Lebanon, but had moved to Brazil nineteen years before and worked at a church in São Paulo, a huge "melting pot" city.

He admitted that he had been regularly running drugs between Brazil and Europe. He'd made four trips just in the past year, earning more than $120,000 for his illegal efforts. He claimed he used the money to help the poor.

Police searched his house, which he shared with his mother. They found photos of him kissing a woman. They identified her as a twenty-nine-year-old sales clerk, "Lucia." They suspected she was an accessory and rushed to her home to bring her in. They were just in time: she was hurriedly packing her car. Her suitcases included two priest's cassocks and an assortment of plane tickets to destinations like Amsterdam, Berlin, and Milan. The tickets bore two names—hers and Father Miguel's.

Lucia was seven months pregnant, but claimed that she and Father Miguel were "just good friends."

Further investigations showed that this wasn't the first time Father Miguel had been in trouble. He had previous arrests for drugs. Nine years earlier, he had been caught in Australia. On that occasion, the powder was hidden in his suitcase, and he only had around five pounds of it. On the downside, it was heroin.

A church spokesman for Father Miguel's São Paulo church was shocked that nobody had ever notified them about the priest's criminal history. He added, "I would like to distance the Catholic church from this man. His behavior horrifies us all."

Some church regulars had never been impressed by the priest, who seemed to be the clerical equivalent of a nine-to-five worker. Said one, "He arrived, prayed, and left. He didn't make friends with anyone, and he didn't get involved in any of our church projects."

Perhaps that was just as well. The church doesn't need opiates for its masses.

PREPOSTEROUS IMPOSTERS

ROBERT DE ZERO

In July 2008, Romanian police in the city of Iași (pronounced YASH-ee) stopped a car in a routine roadside check. According to the *Guardian*, the driver wore a designer suit and sunglasses. He told them his name was Robert De Niro, and he seemed to resemble the actor.

The police asked for some identification. The man presented a Romanian driver's license showing the name Robert De Niro. He also had a credit card with the name Robert De Niro. But the police suspected they were being given a pile of raging bull. After all, why would a big Hollywood star be driving around a remote part of eastern Romania, all alone?

(Note to the real Robert De Niro: if you're planning to take a trip to Romania, you need to travel with your entourage.)

Looking more closely at the famous actor's ID, the officers found more reason to be suspicious. It said his parents' names were Madonna and Antony, but a quick search on the internet turned up their real names: Robert and Virginia. The address was odd, too. Robert De Niro has had homes in New York and California, but according to the driver's license, his house was right there in the town of Iași, and when police checked out the address, it was a local cemetery.

They arrested the celebrity imposter while they tried to figure out what was going on. They soon discovered that this De Niro was actually a local forger, part of a criminal gang providing counterfeit documents to Moldavian workers who wanted to enter the EU.

But why would this man present such a ridiculous alias to the police? After all, if he had shown a license with an ordinary local name, nobody would have questioned it.

It turned out that the fake Robert De Niro identity wasn't for the benefit of the police. The imposter had been going to various banks around town, using the fraudulent persona to borrow money. The banks had proved more gullible than the police, and he'd been approved for loans of around 60,000 euros.

"Robert De Niro" was charged with fraud and embezzlement and sentenced to nine years in prison.

Did he learn his lesson? In part. When the imposter was finally released on probation, he made no further attempts to play Robert De Niro, the actor. Unfortunately, he was still determined to act like one of De Niro's gangster characters. Shortly after getting out of prison, he was arrested again—for drug trafficking.

STUMBLIN' JACK FLASH

On a February night in 2022, in Naples, Florida, "Seth" had already been kicked out of a seafood restaurant for being drunk and abusive. While a band was performing, he staggered in again and got onto the stage.

According to NBC News, he claimed he was Mick Jagger, front man for the Rolling Stones, and he tried to start fights with the other patrons.

At fifty-nine, Seth was nineteen years younger than the real Jagger, with none of the moves or vocal ability.

Eventually, the middle-aged non–rock superstar was kicked out of the restaurant for the last time.

The police had been called, and officers later found Seth walking along the street. When they tried to talk to him, he ignored them and kept walking. An officer stood in his way, and faux Jagger walked aggressively right into him, then, losing his balance, fell slowly onto the sidewalk and started crawling—a "beast of burden" pose, perhaps.

The crawling rocker wannabe challenged the cop, threatening to "mess him up" and "take him down." He started tugging on the cop's pant leg.

The officers grabbed him, put him in the back of their cruiser, and took him to the jail. On the way, he barfed on the car seat.

Seth faced charges of battery of a police officer and disorderly intox-ication. He wasn't put in jail because of "medical reasons"—perhaps they didn't want to clean up after him.

But from the moment he'd got on that stage, he was completely intoxicated, completely wild, completely out of control . . .

Hmm—maybe it was Mick Jagger after all.

THE SOUND OF SIRENS

In February 2010, Paul Simon walked into a New York branch of Citi-bank prepared to carry out the scam of a lifetime.

The *New York Post* reported that, when he was greeted by the teller, the man said he was Paul Simon—yes, *the* Paul Simon, the singer-songwriter from Simon and Garfunkel, creator of such hits as "The Sound of Silence," "Fifty Ways to Leave Your Lover," "Mrs. Robinson," "You Can Call Me Al," and many, many more.

And now, the musical legend wanted to withdraw some money from his account.

"I'll take $4,300. In cash, please."

The teller asked the music legend for some identification.

Paul Simon confidently pulled out some convincing cards. He had everything they needed—a credit card, a social security number, and a driver's license.

The teller checked the ID and checked the man again. He looked like Paul Simon, more or less. The musician had an account at the bank, and the address on the ID matched the one in their files. And while the man in front of her looked closer to fifty-four than Simon's sixty-eight years—well, perhaps that was just the result of plastic surgery.

Only one thing seemed odd. The teller had thought Paul Simon was quite a small man, yet the person standing in front of her was definitely on the tall side.

The teller took another look at the driver's license Mr. Simon had presented. It looked legit, and yes, his height was printed right there: five foot three. Yet, the man now standing in front of the wicket was much taller—around six foot one. He would have towered over Simon. For that matter, he would have towered over Art Garfunkel, who, at a paltry five foot nine, was no match for this Tall-Paul Super-Simon.

The teller asked the giant of the music industry to wait a moment while she made some calls.

Sensing trouble, the phony singer bolted for the door, and before anyone could stop him, he was running down the street.

But the police have their ways of finding people. After the incident was reported, they managed to track the fraudster down. The deluded imposter was arrested and went slip slidin' away to the police station, where he was charged with attempted larceny.

BRIGHT LIGHT, DIM BULB

Some drivers are envious of the freedoms that the police seem to enjoy: speeding down the highway as fast as you like, running red lights, and pulling over anyone who tailgates you.

"Mark" wanted some of those freedoms for himself. The eighteen-year-old from Dallas, Texas, was proud of his cream-colored pickup truck, with its spiked lug nuts and lowered suspension, but he wanted to race it down the highway, and other drivers were always getting in his way.

His genius idea was to install red-and-blue emergency lights in his pickup, so it would look like a cop car. Now he would rule the road.

In January 2022, Mark invited a couple of friends over, and they took his truck out for a nighttime drive, enjoying the new sense of power. He sped along the expressway. He spotted a car up ahead—some idiot driver doing the speed limit. He would show them. He turned on the flashing lights.

The driver of the other car reacted and moved into the right lane.

Mark's friends were impressed.

Mark decided to have some fun. Lights still flashing, he pulled up behind the slowpoke. The other driver responded the way most people would when they see flashing lights behind them—he pulled over onto the shoulder. Mark loved it; his friends loved it. Then he turned off the flashing lights and hit the gas, speeding off down the road.

According to the *Dallas Morning News*, he had picked the wrong person to harass. The driver of the other car was a police officer in an unmarked car. When he saw those flashing lights, he really thought he was being pulled over, but when he got a look at the truck, with its chrome and stickers, it didn't seem like the usual undercover vehicle. He got on the radio to report it.

Dallas police were immediately on the lookout for Mark's truck, and before long, they spotted it, tearing down the road at over a hundred miles per hour—this time without the benefit of the flashing lights. The police moved in to bring it to a stop.

When they inspected the truck, they found the red-and-blue lights that had been illegally added. There were a few other custom modifications—the truck also had a siren, loudspeakers, and, for really inattentive drivers, an air horn.

It seems as though Mark might have noticed the police attention earlier and made an emergency pit stop, because the wires to the flashing lights had been cut.

The passengers were released, but Mark was charged with impersonating a public servant.

UNINFORMED AND UNIFORMED

At thirty-two, "Denis" worked as a carpenter in Cantley, Quebec, about ten miles north of Ottawa. His day job was building staircases for a construction company. But in his spare time, he liked to talk about his military background.

He said he had been a sergeant with the Royal Canadian Regiment, and he was proud of it. He had even dressed in his military uniform when he got married.

His friends and coworkers might have been bored hearing about his army exploits, but they never suspected it was all a pack of lies.

In November 2014, a CBC-TV reporter covering the Remembrance Day ceremony talked to some of the soldiers and veterans attending the somber event. Denis stepped forward to be interviewed as a sergeant in the Canadian Armed Forces. This turned out to be a big mistake.

Even members of the public might have noticed a few oddities about Denis's appearance. His beret was on the small side, and his beard and sunglasses looked a little more "hip" than you might expect of a soldier.

Sharp-eyed military types spotted a host of other irregularities about his appearance. The insignia on his collar were at the wrong angle, and his brass buttons weren't the correct ones for his jacket. He was also missing a regimental sash that noncommissioned officers would be expected to wear with their dress uniform.

Immediately, TV viewers phoned in, asking questions about the supposed sergeant. Was he for real? The media did some digging. It turned out that nobody with his name had ever received the rare medals and awards he claimed to have received. In fact, nobody with his name had ever served in the army, period. Except for a couple of years in cadets, Denis had never been in the military. He'd purchased his uniform and medals online.

Soldiers and veterans were furious. Pretending to be a member of the military is a crime in Canada, as it is in many countries, and it seems particularly inappropriate at a ceremony remembering real soldiers who died in real wars.

Thousands of military members criticized Denis. Some said his actions were an insult to the services. One commented that it was disgraceful to impersonate a soldier on Remembrance Day. Denis even received death threats. His employers were appalled and suspended him, with pay, while they figured out what to do with him.

According to the *Ottawa Citizen*, Denis was arrested on four charges: falsely representing himself to be a public officer, misleading use of a badge or uniform, unlawful use of a military uniform, and unlawful use of military decorations. These were potentially serious charges. Impersonating a public officer can carry a five-year prison sentence. But as the investigation progressed, it started to look like Denis's behavior was more deluded than fraudulent. The most serious charges were dropped.

The courts took a "restorative justice" approach. Denis was taken on a tour of Ottawa's National Military Cemetery and also made to hear statements from real veterans. Denis seemed to take it all in and to regret his choices.

He avoided jail, pleaded guilty to illegally wearing the uniform and decorations, and was sentenced to community service and a year's probation.

HELL, NO . . . CAN I PLEASE GO?

In 1966, America had its hands full with the Vietnam War. It was an unpopular war, especially with the young people being drafted, and many were burning their draft cards or trying to escape to Canada. Those who got caught faced criminal charges.

But twenty-one-year-old "Don" had just the opposite problem, according to a 1966 *New York Times* story. Don wanted to join the army, but couldn't. He worked as a night-shift computer operator at the

University of California in San Francisco. He had tried to enlist but was classified as 4-F because of a physical disability.

Despite being rejected, Don was determined to join the army somehow, and in June 1966, he found an opportunity. He was at a party, talking to a soldier, an army engineer who was back home on emergency leave. The soldier was dealing with family problems and wanted a hardship discharge but couldn't get it. He had to go back to Vietnam in a few hours.

The men realized that, if they switched identities, they might both be able to get what they wanted. Don exchanged clothes with the soldier and was soon on a plane to Vietnam.

He arrived in Saigon and went to the army engineer battalion. He was close enough to enemy action to hear the gunfire, but alert administrators spotted that something was wrong here. After a quick check, Don was identified as an imposter. He was turned over to the United States Consulate for repatriation to the United States.

Meanwhile, the other soldier faced a court martial for going AWOL. He probably improved his chances by voluntarily turning himself in.

It wasn't all bad for Don. When the commander of the battalion learned what had happened, he was impressed at the young man's determination. He proposed making Don an honorary member of the group.

ON THE SCROUNGE

In the 1940s hit musical *On the Town*, three lovable American sailors have twenty-four hours' liberty in New York. They see the sights, fall in love, and with time running out, must hurry back to their ships. But stories like this had played out even earlier on Broadway.

In the summer of 1928, a patrolman watched three sailors on Broadway who seemed to be in the same kind of predicament, according to the *New York Times*. They wore their navy uniforms, which showed that one was from the USS *Colfax*, one was from the USS *Seattle*, and one was from the battleship USS *Texas*. They were desperate to get back to the navy yard. They stopped pedestrians, asking for nickels to cover their fare, so they could get back in time and return to their duties.

The officer watched the three with growing disapproval. Finally, he decided that, however badly they might want to return to their ships, they were obstructing traffic. He arrested all three.

The sailors appeared before the court in their uniforms. An officer from the USS *Texas* was also present. He said that none of the three men were real sailors. They were imposters, using the uniforms to beg for nickels. They were held without bail.

Three sailors on Broadway. Imposters who don't want romance or adventure—they just want change. As a stage show, it has "flop" written all over it.

FLEE(C)ING THE NAZIS

For sheer audacity, it's hard to beat an imposter named Heinz Schilling, who impersonated Nazi officials and Gestapo officers in World War II Germany, often for trivial purposes.

Historian Robert Gellately uncovered Schilling's records in the German archives. Schilling, who had some background in the theater, had been in trouble with the law since he was twenty years old, creating fake documents and pretending to be a German official. By the time the war began, he was thirty-two and serving a six-year prison sentence for forgery.

In January 1941, Schilling managed to escape the prison. No sooner had he escaped than he got back into his old line of work—impersonating officials. He had an idea for a moneymaking scam. We don't know the details, but it seemed he wanted to arrive at his intended victim's location in a police car, posing as an official. Of course, for that, he needed a police car.

He arrived in the city of Düsseldorf and phoned the deputy chief of police in the nearby city of Essen. He said he was a public prosecutor from Berlin, "Dr. Schmidt," and he needed a police car, because his own car had broken down. His story was that he wanted to arrest a couple of thieves. His accompanying officer had gone ahead by streetcar.

This Dr. Schmidt certainly sounded convincing, and the deputy chief was anxious to help, but he told Herr Doktor that it was against the rules to arrange these things over the phone. The deputy was sorry, but the request had to be made in writing, and it had to be presented in person.

That might seem like the cue to give up on the scam, but Schilling was bolder and more determined than that. He wanted that car, so he went looking for the paperwork. He also needed to look the part—finding a coat and briefcase would improve his chances.

Schilling dropped into the courthouse to see what he could find there. First, the briefcase. He approached a lawyer and claimed he was a Gestapo official from Berlin. The lawyer wanted to stay on the right side of the Gestapo and was happy to lend this official a briefcase.

When Schilling saw that the lawyer was a soft touch, he also asked him for a letter on official stationery, asking for a car. The lawyer had his secretary type it up on official stationery, and Schilling signed it himself.

Next, he needed a coat. He went to the courthouse's prison area and told the guard he was a justice official from Berlin. He asked if a man named "Schmitz" was being held in the prison. He had deliberately chosen a common name. The guard said there were several men called Schmitz, and he started listing them.

Schilling jumped on one of the names at random. "That's the one! When he was admitted, did he have a *coat* with him?"

The guard said yes, he did.

"I thought so. That coat was stolen!"

The prisoner was brought out and, despite Schmitz's protests that the coat was his own, it was immediately confiscated. The coat was a little light for the time of year, but Schilling took it anyway and handed over an illegible receipt.

He had no badge and no paperwork. His manner was so confident that everyone believed him without question.

Wearing the coat and carrying the briefcase, Schilling went to the Essen police station. He presented the freshly typed letter and asked again for the car. But there were other bureaucratic problems. The police said they were still unable to give him the vehicle, because judicial authorities were not allowed to use police cars.

Again, a sensible person might give up at this point—but a sensible person wouldn't have attempted the crazy scam to begin with. Since he was getting nowhere with Essen's regular police chief, "Dr. Schmidt" doubled down. The police were wasting his time! The criminals he wanted would soon escape! This was intolerable. He demanded to see the head of Essen's "Kripo."

The Kripo was the Nazi-controlled criminal police agency. Like the Gestapo, it was then part of the SS. The organization was widely feared by Germans.

The imposter got his meeting. Nazi Germany was a country that ran on cards, badges, and identification papers, but even in Kripo headquarters, Schilling had such confidence and authority that, when he strode into the room, nobody dared question him.

Essen's head of Kripo was completely taken in by his visitor and wanted to help. "Yes, of course, Dr. Schmidt, I can provide you with a car."

But Schilling's cover story about arresting thieves seems to have made the Kripo nervous. Providing a car was no problem, but here was an important German official who wanted to drive off, all alone, to arrest two criminals? He seemed sure of himself, but what if something went wrong for Dr. Schmidt? It must have crossed their minds that if he was hurt—or worse, killed—they might get the blame for not providing him with better help. The chief could not allow Dr. Schmidt to go alone to arrest the thieves. He insisted that one of his own detectives accompany him and carry out the potentially dangerous job of making the arrests.

Schilling agreed to this—he might even have seen some opportunities in being able to drive around with a genuine detective under his command. While they waited for the detective, he chatted casually about the current trends in German crime. The police chief could tell his guest knew a lot about the subject.

The detective arrived, and it looked as though everything was settled. But then the head of Essen's Kripo said he just needed to dot a few *i*'s and cross a few *t*'s. He asked to see Dr. Schmidt's papers.

It might be just a formality, but it wasn't one that the imposter Schilling could fake his way past. Despite having experience as a forger, he only had one piece of paperwork with him, and that was the letter he'd tricked officials into typing at the courthouse. It wasn't enough.

It was time to abandon the plan. But Schilling remained completely cool. "My papers. Of course."

He reached for his papers, then reacted with surprise and alarm. He didn't have them! Where had they gone?

Dr. fake-Schmidt then fake-remembered. Why, of course—he must have forgotten his papers when he presented them at the courthouse. The rules must be followed. He would fetch them immediately.

The head of Kripo still suspected nothing, but because he believed his visitor was real, he tried hard to be courteous. He didn't want to put the important gentleman to any trouble—he would phone the courthouse to see if the papers were there.

"No, I would prefer to get them myself," Dr. Schmidt insisted.

He rose and left the office, assuring the officials he would return soon with the documents. As soon as he was out of the building, he made a quiet getaway.

It had been a crazy scheme, and Schilling didn't get away with it. When he failed to return to Kripo headquarters, police finally became suspicious. They checked with officials at the courthouse, who were also asking questions about their mysterious visitor. Police searched for the fraudster, who they now suspected was the escaped convict Schilling.

Meanwhile, Schilling had appeared on a ship in another German city, posing as a police officer, and placed the captain "under arrest" for currency offenses. Of course, it was necessary for him to confiscate the currency. He was so confident that he even told people where he was heading next. The police phoned ahead and caught Schilling when he arrived at his destination.

Schilling was arrested and packed off to prison. But even as he was being taken away, he passed the officer an official-looking notice that instructed him to send Schilling instead to a police station in a different city, where he hoped he would find a new way of escaping. It fooled the guard, but Schilling didn't manage to escape that time.

When a senior police officer wrote up the reports for this case, he had to admit a grudging respect for Schilling's cool-headed audacity, as well as his cunning and ability to think on his feet.

We don't know what happened to Schilling after that. In Hitler's Germany, impersonating high-ranking officials doesn't seem a recipe for a long life. Then again, perhaps he managed to find other ways to work the system.

LAUGHING ALL THE WAY
TO PRISON

WHAT A DING-DONG

Sometimes the criminal aspect of a prank comes from the ding-dongs who take it too seriously.

One January evening in 2003, a group of teenage boys were out roaming the streets of Calgary. They were bored, so they decided to play "ding-dong-ditch"—ringing doorbells and running away before the resident comes to the door.

They picked a house, and one boy was dared to ring the bell. He hit the bell, then ran away with his friends. For a few seconds, the group was disappointed that no one had come out to yell at them.

Unfortunately for the group, they had chosen the wrong house. "Devin" and his wife, "Hannah," had been pranked many times before by kids, and they were no longer going to stand for it. They had talked with police about the issue, and the two were under the impression that they could make a "citizen's arrest" of the troublemakers. They could see the kids huddled outside. "This time, we've got them!"

After the boys ran away, Devin grabbed a broken hockey stick and ran after them. Hannah joined the hunt, getting into her car and searching the streets. About twenty minutes later, Hannah found the kids. She chased them and almost ran them down. She jumped out of her car and grabbed the boys, screaming, "Stop, you hooligans! I'm calling the police!"

"This woman is crazy," one boy thought to himself, and he ran for it. Unfortunately, he wasn't looking in front of him. Devin was approaching from that direction, and the kid ran straight into him. Devin saw the kid coming and applied his hockey skills, body checking him. The boy's face was cut and bruised by the broken hockey stick, then he was knocked backward into the street.

When the police arrived, Devin asserted that he had done nothing wrong in capturing the criminals. But it turned out that the kids they had been chasing were not the ones who had bothered them on previous occasions—these boys had only rung one doorbell. Worse, the boy they'd injured had been against the doorbell-ringing game from the start—he was entirely innocent.

Devin's body-checking "citizen's arrest" led to his own police arrest. He was charged with, and ultimately convicted of, assault.

HAVING A GAS AT THE GAS STATION

A group of four teenage girls in Dothan, Alabama, loved tricks and games and jokes of all kinds. One night in December 2021, the fun-loving gang had an idea for the best prank ever: they would pretend to rob a gas station.

According to Alabama's WDHN-TV, they went to a local gas station and walked into the convenience store. One girl was wearing a mask and carried a joke knife. More accurately, it was an actual knife with a sharp blade, but because it was being used as part of a joke robbery, that made it a "joke knife."

The girl with the knife walked up to the counter, pointed the weapon at the store clerk, and demanded all the money in the cash register. The clerk didn't hand it over.

The girls then grabbed some alcoholic drinks from the cooler and ran from the store. When they were far enough away, they sat down to unwind at a local park. Good times.

That's where they were caught by police officers. All four were arrested and taken to the police station.

The girls were questioned. They told the police the robbery was a joke. Can't people even take a joke? Sheesh!

But the way the police saw it, their "joke" was convincing enough to pass as the real thing. They had pulled a knife on the store employee, demanded money, stolen from the store, and fled from the scene. It checked all the boxes for a serious crime.

Three of the girls were minors. The fourth was charged as an adult. Her bail was set at $60,000.

It didn't matter that they hadn't been successful in getting the money they demanded from the register—the big problem was that they had used a knife to try to get it, and as far as the law is concerned, a knife is a deadly weapon.

The girls were charged with first-degree robbery, which, in Alabama, is a class A felony, with punishments that can range from twenty years to life.

And that's no joke.

ALL FIRED UP

They say that repetition is one of the key ingredients in comedy. It was certainly the comedic technique that forty-three-year-old "William" excelled in.

He lived in an apartment building in Guelph, Ontario. *Guelph Today* reports that, in April 2021, while COVID was raging, William kept himself entertained with a practical joke he found amusing. He went to a certain area of the building, covered the security camera, and pulled the fire alarm. Bells sounded, tenants went outside, and firefighters sped to the scene.

People wondered, "What's going on? Is there really a fire?" William could join in the worried speculation while privately enjoying the entertainment.

Finally, the firefighters declared a false alarm. Everyone went in. Will returned to his apartment with the sense of a prank well executed. Hilarious.

After a few days, he did it again—covered the camera, pulled the alarm, then shared in the frustration and confusion.

William kept going, and as far as he was concerned, the joke just kept getting better. His neighbors were going crazy. "Not again!"

The fire crews weren't too happy, either. With each alarm, as many as twenty-two firefighters had to speed to the scene.

People speculated about the identity of the phantom alarm puller. The cameras showed nothing.

Over the next few weeks, he repeated the same priceless gag—cover the camera, pull the alarm. In total, he did it nine times.

And again, cover the camera, pull the alarm.

And again, pull the alarm.

Oops. Did he remember to cover the camera?

No, the clown prince of fire alarm crime had forgotten this vital step. Now it was William's turn to be alarmed. His identity was revealed. He was arrested and charged with nine counts of mischief and setting off a false fire alarm.

FOUR APRIL FOOLS

April Fool's Day pranks occasionally go too far. A few ill-conceived gags have led to criminal charges.

On April 1, 2021, fifty-eight-year-old "Makayla" was sitting at her workplace in the suburbs of Wichita, Kansas, and wanted to play an April Fool's Day gag on her adult daughter "Amber." Deciding that the simplest pranks are the best—and apparently not understanding what "prank" means—she called Amber and told her she'd been shot, then hung up. Man, what a great joke that was! The kid totally fell for it!

Of course, as a responsible, rational young woman, Amber was horrified. She sped down the highway toward her mother's place, while calling 911 for help.

According to KWCH-TV in Kansas, the emergency services mobilized fast and headed for Makayla's house—fire trucks, paramedics, and many police cars, including a sizable SWAT team.

Police surrounded the home, blocked streets, and attempted to contact whoever was inside. When there was no answer at Makayla's door, the police broke it down. They entered the house with shields up and guns drawn. There was no sign of violence and nobody home.

Police caught up with Makayla at her workplace. When they learned that her report of a shooting was meant to be a joke, they played a great joke back: Makayla was arrested for unlawful request for emergency service assistance and was held without bail.

The key to any good April Fool's joke is in the details. But we're not sure that applies to idiotic 911 pranks like this one reported by WHIO-TV.

A fifty-seven-year-old Ohio woman, "Lauren," had been well pranked by her sister "Stephanie" in 2020 and wanted to get her back. She worked out a detailed backstory for her April Fool's stunt.

Lauren worked at a manufacturing plant. She texted Stephanie that an employee of the company who had been fired the previous day had got into the building. He was angry, he had a gun, and he was shooting up the place. She added that all the employees were hiding in an office with the door locked and the lights off.

When Stephanie got this message, she wasn't just "fooled," she was terrified. Showing some presence of mind, she decided to not even text back, in case the notification sound on Lauren's phone attracted the attention of the shooter.

Instead, Stephanie called 911.

Police descended on the factory. Because they didn't know which person was on the shooting spree, they called to employees one by one, and workers walked out with their hands on their heads, at gunpoint.

The employees were fooled, too—many of them thought there was an active shooter! This led to further 911 calls. The employees' family members believed that their loved ones were in danger.

We don't know Lauren's reaction, but she probably wasn't chuckling anymore. She might have had some suspicion that her prank had gone horribly wrong.

Roughly twenty minutes passed before emergency responders figured out that the call had been a hoax.

When it was revealed that Lauren had caused all this trouble, she was fired from her job, arrested, and charged with inducing panic, a felony that can lead to up to a year in jail. Some people just can't take a joke!

Sometimes, April Fool's Pranks can be a blast in the wrong way.

In June 2000, "Stephen" was a civilian and former pilot who wanted to prank some of his air force friends, according to CBC News. During a party in the officers' mess at an air base in Moose Jaw, Saskatchewan, he set off a "bear banger" noisemaking device designed to scare away bears. That would surprise them!

It did surprise them. The explosive isn't meant to be used indoors. Two people were injured by the blast.

Stephen was charged with four criminal offenses, including possession of an explosive substance and criminal negligence causing bodily harm.

The colonel in charge of the air base was a friend of Stephen's. He had allegedly tried to cover the prank up by attempting to convince his subordinates not to mention anything to the military police. He also tried to save Stephen's hide by stopping an investigation.

The colonel was court-martialed and ultimately found guilty of "conduct prejudicial to good order and discipline." He was fined $5,000, reprimanded, and demoted.

Sometimes, the problem with an April Fool's prank isn't the prank itself, or the reaction—it's the reaction to the reaction. The *Wagoner County American-Tribune* reported such a tale.

In 2013, in Oklahoma, eighteen-year-old "Cassandra" was just trying to play a fun prank on her boyfriend, "Evan." It wasn't too bad. She told him she was pregnant as a joke.

Unfortunately, Evan didn't find it amusing. Instead, he got angry. In response, Cassandra continued her joke by bringing out a silly little knife.

Her boyfriend reacted to that. He threatened to call the cops. The situation escalated, and it kept escalating until Cassandra slashed Evan across the throat with her knife, then bit him twice. This left him in stitches—it took seven to close his wounds.

When questioned by the authorities, Cassandra said that everything was a joke right up to the point where her boyfriend threatened to call the police. She was charged with assault.

THE JOKE DIDN'T FLY

Here's a quiz: What's something you shouldn't talk about out loud when you're on a plane? Bombs, right? You might think this is common knowledge, but it seems not everyone got the memo—like "Therese," a fifty-three-year-old woman from Montreal.

Therese had taken a break from the cold Quebec winter by flying to Florida along with her boyfriend. In February 2019, they were getting ready to return home again on an Air Canada flight. According to the *South Florida Sun-Sentinel*, the plane was on the tarmac in Fort Lauderdale, preparing for takeoff. Inside the cabin, flight attendants were doing their final checks.

One attendant noticed a bag in an overhead compartment. It was too big to fit there and needed to be moved. The flight attendant asked, "Whose bag is this?"

It was then that Therese offered a priceless zinger. Laughing, she turned to her boyfriend and said, "There's a bomb in it!"

Her boyfriend warned her to be careful. "Don't make jokes like that! They'll kick you off the plane."

But it was already too late. The flight attendant had heard Therese's remark, and she reported it to the captain. It was probably nothing, but the captain couldn't afford to take any chances, so he ordered everyone off the plane.

The passengers were deplaned, and the plane was de-luggaged.

Officials organized the clearing of Terminal 2. When the terminal was cleared of passengers, the bomb squad moved in to examine all the bags and cases.

Of course, they didn't find a bomb.

The plane finally left two hours late—without Therese, who had some legal work to get through.

When she was questioned by the police, Therese denied that she had laughed and said, "There's a bomb in it." No, she claimed she had said something like, "I hope there's not a bomb in there," in a very serious tone of voice. Because what's funny about a bomb on a plane?

Her lawyer described the incident as "a horrible joke gone wrong." We'd beg to differ. Here's a horrible joke:

> **Flight Attendant:** Whose bag is this?
> (*Therese points at an old man sitting next to an old woman.*)
> **Therese:** I think she belongs with that guy.

People will be insulted and offended, but you won't get arrested.

But the reply "There's a bomb in it" doesn't seem like a joke at all. It doesn't even answer the question the flight attendant asked. It's a non-joke, a random word burp. Still, Therese couldn't be punished for being unfunny, so instead the officials charged her with "making a false report of a bomb, explosive, or weapon of mass destruction."

She was released on bail. The judge set a $5,000 bond.

And Therese resisted the urge to quip, "Did you say a $5,000 *bomb*?"

THE BAD PENNIES

CHUMP CHANGE

"Jake" was a forty-year-old resident of Palm Beach, Florida, and he was going through some personal problems. At least, that's what he told "Andrew," another local man. Andrew felt bad for Jake and tried to help. He even offered Jake a place to stay in exchange for assistance with some work. But "no good deed goes unpunished," as this story from the *Palm Beach Post* shows.

The two men talked, and Andrew told Jake about his passion: rare coins. Andrew had inherited a nice coin collection from his father, and he had added to it over the years. Now he had a large collection—a hundred thousand coins in eighty boxes. Some were rare and valuable. The entire set was worth more than $350,000. Andrew saw the coins as his retirement policy. If he needed money, he could take a few coins and sell them.

In December 2018, Jake decided he wanted a retirement policy of his own. He had discovered where the coins were stored and knew they were protected by security cameras. He broke in and carefully placed blue tape over the camera lenses. We know this because he was clearly visible on camera as he entered the room and applied the tape.

But it gets dumber.

After breaking into Andrew's storage cabinets and stealing pretty much the entire collection, Jake needed to turn the coins into the kind of cash he could spend. He put the weirder-looking coins together and took them to a local store specializing in coins and jewelry. The store owner gave him $2,300 for the lot.

The rest of the coins looked like regular American change, so Jake went around to the local supermarkets and looked for those machines that turn loose change into store credit, minus a service charge. That's right. All those unusual, collectible coins were sold for their face value. Andrew's rare presidential dollar coins were worth a thousand dollars apiece. Once they'd gone through the machine, each one netted Jake around eighty-eight cents.

Andrew reported the theft of the coins, and the police soon had an idea who might have done it—they had received a tip about Jake, who had had earlier run-ins with the law. In February, they booked him. A search of his backpack revealed a few remaining coins, along with various illegal drugs—which probably explains why he needed the money. It was too late to recover the most valuable coins.

Jake was charged with grand theft and ten drug-related charges. He was sentenced to five years in prison, to be followed by ten years' probation.

CHANGE OF VEHICLES

In November 2015, twenty-six-year-old "Evan" broke into a post office in his hometown of Port Talbot, Wales. According to *WalesOnline*, he entered the building through the roof and smashed open the cash registers. He got away with thousands of pounds in cigarettes, and thousands more in cash. But the cash was in the form of one-pound coins—it was a heavy bag.

The robbery was caught on camera and publicized in the local news. Although the video showed glimpses of Evan's face, nobody came forward to identify him. A month later, he still hadn't been caught. He seemed to have got away with it.

Evan was flush with cash and feeling confident—or was it just the nicotine coursing through his veins? He decided he needed a car. He could afford a used one now. Nothing fancy. Just something to get him from A to B . . . where B stood for break-ins.

He checked the used car ads to see what was available. He found a little Renault he liked the look of. He visited the seller, checked out the car, and made an offer—a thousand pounds, cash.

To show he was a man of means, Evan swung a bag of coins weighing twenty pounds.

While running your thumb along a fan of bills might be a tempting inducement to accept a buyer's price, bouncing a huge bag of loose change is not. The seller declined the offer, and Evan left, looking for other automotive deals. But it was a strange encounter. After checking the news, the seller learned about the robbery of one-pound coins the previous month. The seller called the police, who showed him the security camera photos.

"Yes, that's the man."

Evan's stolen hoard could have kept him in small purchases for years. Trying to use the coins all at once bought him a quick trip to the police station. He was arrested and charged with the post office robbery. He was sentenced to two years in prison—where maybe the stolen cigarettes came in handy.

COINS? I AIN'T SEEN NO COINS

"Kenneth" was not your typical criminal type. In the 1980s, he was living in Columbus, Ohio, but he had a dream to hunt for underwater treasure. He had worked as an oceanic engineer and he figured there was big money to be made if you could build a submarine that went deep enough. He planned to build a robot sub. It would cost more than $12 million.

The *Guardian* reports that hundreds of people and companies chipped into the project, and Kenneth raised the money. You might think he disappeared with the cash, but no. He built that robot submarine, and his mission was a huge success—off the coast of South

Carolina, Kenneth's robot found the wreck of the SS *Central America*. The ship had been sunk in a hurricane in 1857, and it was loaded with literally tons of gold, which had been intended to create a gold reserve for banks on the east coast of America. At the time, the loss of the gold was considered such a disaster that it contributed to an economic panic.

Today, the cargo of gold from the ship would be worth around three-quarters of a billion dollars.

Kenneth and his team used their robot to retrieve some of the treasure. They hauled up ingots and coins worth as much as $150 million—and there was still plenty more at the bottom of the sea.

In 2001, a single ingot from the wreck was sold at auction for $8 million.

But there was a snag. The sunken ship had been insured, and thirty-nine companies that had paid out on the insurance claim more than a century earlier now figured the gold was theirs. They sued. The legal situation quickly became messy.

The investors demanded their share. They'd put up the money to build the submarine but hadn't seen any return. They also sued and demanded that Kenneth give a full accounting of what had been spent. Lawsuits were flying in all directions. The company filed for bankruptcy.

Some people said that Kenneth had taken a large portion of the bullion and stashed gold coins away for himself. Kenneth denied hiding any treasure and said that any missing funds had gone to pay legal fees.

Kenneth didn't show up for a court date, and he hid from the law for years. He was finally arrested in 2015.

The investors were livid with Kenneth. So was the judge. In 2015, Kenneth was held in contempt of court. He offered to hand over five hundred gold coins, worth about $2.5 million, but later claimed he no longer had access to them. He has been fined $1,000 for every day he refuses to reveal the location of the coins. Usually, a person can only remain imprisoned on contempt charges for a maximum of eighteen months, but Kenneth has remained in prison for six years.

It doesn't seem like a smart choice. Then again, we don't know how much gold he has hidden away.

HER MAJESTY AND THE WALRUS

In January 2022, the Ontario Provincial Police started getting reports of some unusual counterfeit coins circulating in the province.

According to CBC News, the coins were two-dollar coins, commonly known as "toonies." At a casual glance, the fakes looked like the real thing—a large silver-colored coin, with a gold-colored disk in the center. But the counterfeiters had made certain errors that made it possible to distinguish the phony coins from the real ones.

For example, the real coin is printed with the inscription "Elizabeth II." On the fake coin, the Roman numerals were printed incorrectly: "Elizabeth I-I."

There was another error in the text. The real coin has the words *D. G. Regina*—short for *Dei Gratia Regina*, meaning "Queen by the grace of God." On the fake coin, it says "PG Regina," meaning . . . what? Parental guidance? Paying guest?

The counterfeiters also made a slipup on the coin's date. The coin was stamped "1990," but the first Canadian two-dollar coin wasn't introduced until 1996.

The text on the other side of the coin also displays an error. Where it should say "2 Dollars," the fake coin says "Z Dollard."

But it's the errors in the coin's images that are most striking. The image in the center of the coin should be a majestic polar bear, but instead features a fat walrus. And the head of Queen Elizabeth has been replaced by the head of what appears to be a wrinkled old man.

All in all, it doesn't feel like the counterfeiter's heart was really in it. The terrible counterfeits were mocked by the press and called "ridiculously fake." Then again, that might have been part of the plan. If a fake is bad enough, the counterfeiter could claim that the coins were just playthings.

When first contacted, the Royal Canadian Mint said it was debatable whether the coins were counterfeit currency. Later, they decided that the coins definitely were counterfeit. After all, most people don't closely examine the coins they receive, and the public was reporting that the coin was turning up in their change. And no matter what the coin looks like, if someone knowingly passes off fake currency as the real thing, they're committing a serious crime.

There have been no arrests yet, and police are still working the case. But for all the effort the counterfeiters put into creating these bizarre fake coins, it doesn't seem like they made much money.

WANT A MINT

If you want to stay in business as a criminal, don't make an enemy of someone who is much smarter than you are. That's what one counterfeit coiner did, and the results were gruesome.

In England in the 1600s, coins were real money. Silver coins were made of silver, and the high-value coins were gold. When coins are made of precious metals, there are many profitable ways to mess with them. One common method back then was "coin clipping"—trimming the gold off the edge of the coin to make it a little smaller. The government fought back by giving the coin a milled edge so that tampering would be obvious, and many coins still have that feature today.

A more subtle method was "sweating"—putting gold coins in a leather bag and shaking them for a while. The coins naturally wear down, and gold dust appears in the bottom of the bag.

If you were caught doing either of these things, you could be put to death, so most "coiners" figured: in for a penny, in for a (forged) pound— they might as well just produce their own fake coins. It was a big risk with big payoffs.

William Chaloner was an expert in coin counterfeiting. He had started as a con man, fake doctor, and fortune teller, and had also practiced a wide range of other nasty scams, but faking coins was where the real money was. His coins looked convincing, including realistic milled edges, but instead of being gold or silver, they were made of a cheap alloy or had a very thin layer of gold applied to a cheaper metal.

He made so much money in the phony coining business that he was able to live like a gentleman. He owned a big house and drove around in a carriage. He also started to make important friends. As he got used to his new station in life, Chaloner raised his ambitions. Why take chances producing coins secretly, like a criminal? He could make a lot more money if he were running the country's official supplier of coins—the Royal Mint.

Chaloner wrote pamphlets describing the problems with the way the mint was being run. He said coins were too easy to counterfeit. (He knew this all too well, because he was still busy counterfeiting them himself.) He also claimed that the mint was corrupt and that it handed over coin-making tools to counterfeiters. He offered his ideas for doing it right, and his services in overseeing the process.

His pamphlets were a big mistake. He had insulted the man in charge of the Royal Mint, who at that time none was other than Sir Isaac Newton—widely considered the most brilliant scientist in history. Newton was getting on in years and had been given the position because of his scientific fame. Running the mint was considered an easy job that would give him a good income. But that wasn't how Newton looked at it. From the moment he took over at the mint, he was deadly serious about his responsibilities. He looked for ways to streamline and improve operations and improve security.

As far as Newton was concerned, counterfeiters were the enemies in a war. When a counterfeiter was arrested, Newton would often show up to the interrogation. He recruited spies and picked up clues in bars.

Newton was incorruptible and could also be vindictive. William Chaloner was already on Newton's radar, and when the scientist read the pamphlets falsely accusing him of running a crooked operation, Newton's desire to punish Chaloner became personal.

Newton had Chaloner arrested and put on trial for counterfeiting. Chaloner used his influence with his powerful friends to get acquitted.

But Newton was just getting started. He now brought all his powers to bear—his network of spies and informers, and statements from Chaloner's old contacts. In the second trial, one informant testified that Chaloner had boasted that he had forged more than 30,000 golden guineas. Another described how Chaloner had produced counterfeit French coins. The judge selected for the trial had a reputation for being ruthless.

Chaloner realized he had no hope. He tried accusing the witnesses of accepting bribes. He tried pretending to be mad. Nothing was working. He was trapped.

Meanwhile, Newton's case was calculated with scientific precision. It was methodical, detailed, and airtight.

Chaloner was found guilty and sentenced to death.

And that was even worse than it sounded. Newton might have been a leading figure in modern science, but his approach to justice was positively medieval. He wanted to deter counterfeiters, and he made sure that the traditional punishments were enforced.

The day after the trial, William Chaloner was hanged, then publicly disemboweled. He had dared to match wits with Isaac Newton. How do you like them apples?

HOUSE THIEVES

WHY, NO, OFFICER, I'M JUST MOVING HOUSE

It's common for a thief to slip into someone's garden shed and walk away with items from it. It's not so common for the thief to walk away with the shed itself, but that's what CTV News reported happened in 2022.

Apparently, a thief in one small Ontario town was checking out properties when he spotted a golden opportunity. It was a yellow pallet jack—one of those sturdy, hand-operated forklift devices used for moving heavy loads. You slide its forks under a pallet, pump it to raise the forks hydraulically, and then you can pull a heavy load along on wheels.

The pallet jack was ripe for stealing. But the thief also noticed another tempting target: a stylish garden shed in dark blue with white trim. It had a door and a tiny window. But how do you steal a shed? Obviously, you use the pallet jack.

The thief slid the pallet jack under the shed to lift it a few inches off the ground, then trundled off. He escaped on foot, awkwardly pulling the shed behind him.

The owner soon noticed that the shed and pallet jack had both been stolen and reported it to police. They likely assumed someone had loaded it onto a truck and driven away.

But the thief was still walking, and he kept walking for hours. After night fell, he was across town, struggling his way along the sidewalks of the town's main street.

When the police spotted the crazy guy pulling his house behind him, it wasn't hard to guess that he might just be their shed thief.

Images taken by the astonished officers show a stocky man in a dark jacket, sweatpants, and sneakers trying to manipulate the shed past closed shops and banks, along a deserted, rain-soaked street.

The police took the shed thief and returned the jack and the shed to its owner.

The police chief commented, "This might be a first."

It might be possible for one man to steal a small shed, but for a larger one, it takes two men and a van. In July 2020, in the English city of Hull, the *Guardian* reported that two thieves had gone to a sports center and stolen one of the buildings. The wooden hut was large—about nine feet wide and thirty feet long. The men worked in broad daylight, making numerous trips to load the pieces of the hut into a white van.

It took the men about six hours to complete the work. The staff of the center asked them what they were doing, but they seem to have managed to continue. By the time the police appeared on the scene, the men were gone, and so was the hut.

In this case, the crime was dumb enough, and audacious enough, that the thieves got away with it.

A DIFFERENT KIND OF HOUSE ROBBER

Three burglars broke into a New York home on April 29, 2015. While ransacking the house, they found the property ownership documents. It might have been while looking these over that they got the big, dumb idea to supersize their robbery. Why steal the contents of the house when you can steal the house itself? Imagine—a little place of their own in Queens.

According to the *New York Daily News*, the burglars changed the locks and made the place their own for the day. That evening, the occupant, a woman in her sixties, returned home from work. When she tried to open the door, her key didn't work. The criminals had figured out a way to deal with the homeowner. They came to the door and told her they represented the bank that held the mortgage for the house, which was now taking possession of it.

They insisted that the woman would have to sign over the ownership to them if she wanted to come in. The woman was understandably shocked, and the crooks seem to have been confident enough that she believed their story. She told them she didn't own the house—it was all in her husband's name. And right now, he was away in China.

The thieves told the distraught woman to phone her husband and to email him documents to sign, including a deed transfer. She did what she was told, but her husband wasn't so easily fooled. He refused to sign over the ownership. The gang stayed put and refused to let his wife enter.

She came back the next day. The poor woman pleaded with them. She needed things from her house. The gang grudgingly allowed her to come in and take her property out of the house. But their time was valuable—she had to be done in ten minutes. When she entered the house, she was shocked at the state of it. These bank employees sure were messy.

It was more than two weeks before the husband returned from China. He hired a locksmith to open the door. They found that the house had been emptied of valuables. The fake bankers also had an unusual fondness for knives—those were all missing, too.

The police were finally brought in and had no trouble tracking down the criminals through their mobile phones. They were arrested and charged with burglary, criminal mischief, criminal trespassing, and unlawful eviction. The locks on their next residence may not be so easy to change.

HIDDEN AWAY IN THE COUNTRY

In June 2022, in Saskatchewan, CTV News reported that a house had gone missing. It was being moved from Tisdale, a little town about sixty miles northeast of Saskatoon. The house was a small wooden bungalow, and it had been lifted onto a trailer for transport by truck. Around midnight on June 14, someone took it. The house was gone.

The Royal Canadian Mounted Police investigated and learned of a disagreement between the owner of the home and a thirty-two-year-old man, "Sam." The previous day, the men had had an "altercation." It seemed obvious who had spirited the house away. Police charged Sam with theft. They also charged him with uttering threats and assault with a weapon. A court date was set.

The only thing the Mounties couldn't figure out was what he'd done with the house.

A house isn't the smartest thing to steal. Obviously, you can't live in a stolen house—the theft will be discovered as soon as anyone visits. It seemed that Sam was not much good as a criminal, although he might have a bright future as a magician.

As of this writing, the house mystery remains unsolved, but perhaps the RCMP can draw some clues from a similar case in Oregon, in 2015. There, too, a residence went missing from a very isolated area about forty miles from Klamath Falls. And if you've never heard of Klamath Falls, it's a small town about 230 miles south of Portland. We're talking "out of the way." In this case, the missing structure was a 1,500-square-foot log cabin, complete with deck. The owner turned up one day to find an empty lot—the foundation was there, but the cabin was gone.

The local police had never come across a case like it. They scoured the area and found signs that the house had been jacked up and moved on a truck. They talked with neighbors and informants, but it was finally the department's "forest unit" (we're imagining cartoon animals) who solved the case—the cabin's new location was less than a mile from its original site. In fact, if someone had thought to stand on the old lot and gaze across the large meadow behind it, they might have spied the cabin through the distant trees.

It seemed like the cabin snatcher was the most audacious thief in Oregon—either that, or he had logs for brains. But when police talked to the occupant, it turned out that he wasn't a thief at all, and the situation was complicated.

The man who had arranged for the cabin to be moved had bought it in good faith from another man who claimed to own it. That's because three different people had their names on the title to the cabin—the man who had reported its absence, his ex-girlfriend, and her ex-husband. The ex-girlfriend had reconciled with the ex-husband, and her ex-boyfriend moved away. Later, without informing the other owners, the now "ex-ex-husband" sold the cabin to an unsuspecting buyer, who hired a company to remove the cabin he'd purchased and shift it to his own property.

The case of the vanishing cabin went from baffling to messy as police tried to figure out whether a crime had even been committed by the seller, whether the cabin's former owners needed to sort out their disagreements in a civil court, and who was still an "ex" of who.

UNORTHODOX ACTIONS

Russian churches often contain valuable religious icons, and these are sometimes targets for thieves. But in 2008, BBC News reported that villagers in Russia had gone further and stolen the entire church. The priest showed up one day and the building was gone—all that remained were the foundations and a few pieces of wall.

The church was located near the village of Komarovo, in a rural area about 180 miles from Moscow. The building, which belonged to the

Russian Orthodox church, was a two-level structure that had been built in 1809. It had originally been a schoolhouse before being sold to the church. It wasn't being actively used at the time, although church officials claim they were thinking about reviving services in the building.

The priest last saw the church in July 2008. In the months that followed, the villagers struck a deal with a local businessman who was looking for building materials. They offered him as much of the Church of the Resurrection as he wanted. They disassembled the building and sold it to him for one ruble (about four cents) per brick.

When the priest returned in November, the church had disappeared—disassembled and converted from rubble to ruble. It remains to be seen whether the Church of the Resurrection will be resurrected.

The priest was appalled by the theft. He accused the villagers of blasphemy and said their actions were a sin.

Which certainly makes it sound like those villagers need a new church.

LEASE UP, HOUSE DOWN

There are also cases in America where locals have torn down buildings in order to use or sell the building materials. It was more common long ago, when most buildings were more substantial than they are today and were constructed brick by brick.

The *New York Times* describes a case in June 1938 in which a crew showed up to demolish a group of ten buildings in Chicago. But the buildings had already vanished—they had been completely disassembled by local residents.

The police commissioner was on the case, though. He advised his officers to be "suspicious of anyone carrying a crowbar"—especially someone who "was eyeing a building." Yep, that should fix it. Good job, Commissioner.

Chicago seems to have been a popular place for spontaneous home removals, going back a long way.

In another incident, way back in June 1885, a hardware dealer was renting a large, two-story house in a busy part of town. His lease expired, and he moved out, but a rumor spread that the building was being given away to the poor. The hardware dealer had barely left the site when a group of men appeared and started removing pieces of the house. It was broad daylight and the gang seemed so focused on their activity that none of the passersby thought much of it at first, assuming they were just hired workmen. But when the work continued into the night, people started to become suspicious—or perhaps just annoyed at the nonstop racket. Neighbors called the police. The police didn't make any arrests and just told the impromptu demolition team to move along.

The workers left for a while, but as soon as it was light again, they were back, and hard at work once again, taking the building apart and carting away the bricks, tiles, pipes, and timbers.

The owner of the building had arranged for a new tenant to move in, paying a rent of $25 a month. The landlord traveled to the site after breakfast, intending to check on the place and see if there were any little repairs that needed doing. He arrived to find a vacant lot. All that remained of his two-story moneymaker was the foundation.

Despite the neighbors' complaints, the theft had been carried out openly. The Chicago police were ridiculed for their failure to stop the destruction.

EMPIRE STATE BILKING

Con artists often steal buildings by fraudulently transferring the ownership to themselves. It would be difficult to sell the stolen property, but they don't have to. They can use the ownership documents to get a quick mortgage from a bank, then walk off with the money, leaving a confusing situation for the bank, the city, and the homeowner to sort out.

New York is a hotbed of mortgage crime, partly because of the high value of the land. In one typical case, a New York woman stole her grandmother's home this way, taking $445,000 in cash for herself. She was arrested and got a year's sentence for fraud.

In 2008, the *New York Daily News* wanted to show how easy this kind of fraud was, and how lax bureaucrats were in checking the information provided. Journalists put together a deliberately dumb crime, with a set of fake documents giving themselves ownership of the Empire State Building.

The paperwork was filled with odd names, to see if anyone was paying attention. The company claiming the ownership of the two-billion-dollar building was named Nelots Properties LLC. (Read *Nelots* backward to see what they did there.) The name of the notary was Willie Sutton, a notorious bank robber. One of the witnesses was Fay Wray, who starred in *King Kong*. In the movie, she was carried up the Empire State Building by the giant gorilla.

Despite the oddities, the transfer of ownership was processed in ninety minutes, with no checks. The newspaper later returned the building, without getting a loan on its value, but they boasted that they had pulled off one of the biggest heists in American history.

INSURANCE SCAMS

HOOPS, I MADE A MISTAKE

Professional basketball players get health insurance, and that coverage continues after they have retired. "Jerry" was a former player who felt he was owed a bigger retirement package, and he saw a way to turn the players' health insurance plan into profits for himself. His idea was not too original—it involved submitting false insurance claims to the NBA's health plan—but rather than using his own claims, he decided to do it on an industrial scale.

According to NBC News, Jerry talked to at least eighteen others, mostly NBA players, and convinced them to submit their own claims. He would arrange everything, he assured them. It was easy—he would provide the fake invoices for them to submit. They would just send off the forms and collect the checks. When they received their money, they'd send Jerry a substantial cut for his part of the work. If the insurance company had any questions, Jerry would field them all, pretending to be a health-care provider. A dentist and a doctor worked with Jerry on the scheme, providing some of the forms and information.

Jerry gave one of his associates an invoice for a series of root canals. According to the invoice, six teeth had been drilled on April 30, 2016. On May 11, crowns had been put on the same six teeth. The bill totaled tens of thousands. The associate submitted it, and when the money came in, Jerry got his share.

But inventing the medical details seems to have been too much work for Jerry, so he got lazy. He reused the same root canal information. He gave a nearly identical invoice to another player—the same dates, the same root canals, the same crowns, and all in the same teeth.

Apparently, he was proud of this invoice, because he used it yet again on another one of his players. Six root canals followed by six crowns on exactly the same teeth, also on April 30 and May 11.

The players' imaginary dental woes didn't end there. Jerry sent two of the men back for more work two years later. This time, they each got thirteen root canals in the same thirteen teeth on exactly the same date, followed by crowns on twelve of those teeth—the same twelve, naturally.

Jerry was a busy man. Between 2017 and 2020, he submitted medical and dental claims totaling nearly $4 million, and took in hundreds of thousands in kickbacks. On at least one occasion, one of his NBA associates didn't want to pay Jerry his share, so Jerry tried to intimidate him by posing as an official from the insurance company. He claimed he had flagged a problem with the invoice—a problem the player would need Jerry's help to fix.

Jerry thought he was getting away with his fraud, but his sloppy methods were raising red flags. Most of his documents weren't on regular letterhead, and his letters often contained grammatical errors you wouldn't expect from a health-care professional. Batches of documents related to a case often had the same dates, even though they were supposed to have come from different offices. As he got greedier, his scheme set off alarm bells at the insurance companies, eventually triggering a huge police operation.

Investigators soon discovered impossible and incriminating discrepancies in the claims. Some players claimed to be receiving health care in the US when they were elsewhere. One was playing basketball in Taiwan at the same time he claimed to be getting $48,000 in dental work in Beverly Hills.

The police made coordinated arrests across the US. Players were all charged with conspiracy to commit health-care fraud and wire fraud, while "Jerry" was also charged with aggravated identity theft. His career had started in a basketball court. It ended in a law court.

THE SMALL PRINT

"Pazir" was an immigrant from Afghanistan working at a low-paying factory job in Gloucester, England. His ex-wife, "Minnie," had triplets to care for. She came up with a daring scheme to supplement the family's income—they could use the money from Pazir's life insurance policy. The one problem with that was that Pazir was still alive, but they could deal with that together.

In 2006, Minnie persuaded thirty-four-year-old Pazir to get a fake death certificate for himself from Afghanistan. Getting the documents there would be easier than doing it in England, and harder to check. Using that document, his ex-wife could go to the insurance company and collect a fat payout.

According to the *Daily Mail*, Minnie submitted the claim to the insurance company, along with the death certificate. She claimed £300,000. The first death certificate they sent to the insurers was lost in the mail, so Pazir got another one, and they sent that.

The death certificate said that Pazir had died from "brain trauma" in March 2006. The brain trauma might have explained what came next, because instead of lying low until the money arrived, Pazir carried on with his normal life. He kept up his work at the factory, showing up every day, as usual. He also went to his doctor's appointment in September 2006—a fact that made its way back to the insurance company. For a man who had been dead six months, Pazir looked pretty healthy.

The insurance company confronted Minnie and told her she had lied and committed fraud. She crumbled. She admitted she had lied about her husband's death to collect on the policy.

They then turned to Pazir—they were sure he was in on it. But Pazir denied it. He claimed he knew nothing of this scam. It had all been done by his greedy ex-wife.

Investigators didn't believe him—and they had strong evidence on their side. They showed Pazir the "small print" on his death certificate—that is, a small fingerprint that matched his own. How exactly did his fingerprint end up on a death certificate he claimed to know nothing about?

The couple both confessed their guilt. In court, the prosecutor was struck by the simpleminded nature of the scam, calling it "an unsophisticated offense."

The judge said the couple deserved prison, but perhaps not immediately. They were given a suspended sentence of nine months.

I'M NOT A THIEF, I'M A FRAUD

In 1949, "Max" was living in Wood River, part of greater St. Louis, on the border between Illinois and Missouri.

According to the *New York Herald-Tribune*, Max had a straightforward scheme to make some easy cash: his car was insured against theft, and the beat-up old vehicle would earn him much more money if it were stolen than he could hope to get by selling it. He recruited his friend "Tim" to steal his ride.

Max's plan was simple. Tim would take the car and drive it several states away. Then he only had to hide it somewhere in the woods, set fire to it, and find his way back home.

In the meantime, Max would report the car stolen, collect the insurance payout, and they would split the money between them.

That sounded like a fine plan to Tim.

Tim filled up the car (and the trunk) with gasoline and set out on his road trip. But as he was driving through Missouri, daydreaming about the money that would be coming his way, he was pulled over by the police. It was just for a minor offense, but when the police checked the license plates, they saw that the car belonged to a man back in Wood River.

The police phoned Max. They asked if he was the owner of the car with the license plates they'd just found.

Max told them he was the owner, and, thinking that the police were now examining a burned-out wreck, told them that the car had been recently stolen.

Suddenly, Tim's minor traffic offense had become a more serious crime: car theft. Tim was dragged before a judge in Missouri and charged with driving a stolen car across a state line.

Tim didn't want to get into more trouble by explaining about the big insurance swindle, so he kept his mouth shut. Max stayed out of it, too. Tim was sentenced to three years in Leavenworth prison, the maximum-security federal penitentiary in Kansas.

After a month behind bars, Tim had had enough of prison life. He wanted to tell the whole story in the hope that he might get out. He explained to the authorities that he hadn't stolen the car, and that it was all part of a scam gone wrong.

The officials weren't sure what to make of all this, but the FBI investigated his claim. They reviewed the files, paperwork went back and forth, and finally, a year later, they decided that Tim's version of events checked out.

The FBI investigators said Tim and Max wouldn't face any further charges. The charges of driving a stolen car wouldn't stick because the car hadn't been stolen. They also couldn't be charged with insurance fraud because Max hadn't submitted a claim. And, while they had planned to destroy the car, there was no federal law against burning an automobile, never mind intending to burn one.

Tim was released from Leavenworth, having served a year for a crime he didn't commit and having been paid nothing for it.

POISON ON THE HOUSE

In 1933, a group of five men in New York City came up with the idea for what was then an unusual crime.

According to *Smithsonian Magazine*, they had a mutual acquaintance named Michael Malloy. Born in Ireland, Malloy had once worked as a firefighter, but now, at sixty, he was a pitiful character—homeless and usually out of work. The one thing he could do well was drink. He had run up a big bar tab at Tony Marino's speakeasy (it was the final year of Prohibition), and there didn't seem to be much chance of Tony getting the money that Malloy owed him.

Tony and a group of his regulars discussed Malloy. The way the guy was going, it didn't seem like he would live long. One of them proposed the idea of taking out life insurance on old Michael. He had no close friends or family. It would be easy to collect.

Tony knew how to do it. In fact, he had done this sort of thing before, letting a homeless woman drink herself to death and collecting $2,000 from an insurance policy he'd bought on her life. They could do the same with Malloy, with an even bigger policy. Then, all Tony had to do was give Malloy free drinks. It was hardly even murder—the guy would certainly drink himself to death. He'd die happy.

One of the gang members, Frank Pasqua, ran a funeral parlor. He offered his services in burying Malloy, and in the meantime, he was also willing to help set up the insurance. He contacted a crooked insurance agent he knew, and over the next few months, the gang bought three policies on Malloy's life. These included a double-indemnity clause, so that if Malloy's death was accidental, the policy paid double. All told, the gang would earn $3,500—equivalent to about $80,000 today.

Once the insurance was in place, they started plying their victim with drinks. Malloy didn't understand why his credit was suddenly good again. Marino explained to Malloy that there was so much competition between bars these days that he had to loosen his rules. It meant Malloy could drink as much as he wanted.

Malloy wasn't going to question the new policy. He took Tony at his word. He knocked back one drink after another. He'd been a heavy drinker all his life, and he drank prodigious quantities in front of Tony, then walked out, saying he'd be back the next day.

Malloy kept this up for several days, drinking volumes of alcohol that would have killed most men, yet apparently taking it in his stride.

The drinks were getting expensive, so Tony tried to speed up the process. He added wood alcohol to the drinks. Wood alcohol is very toxic, and many people have died from drinking it accidentally. But it didn't slow down Michael Malloy. Even when Tony served him shots of pure wood alcohol, he just kept drinking.

Things weren't going according to plan, and the group was getting concerned. Frank Pasqua had a new idea. He said he had once seen a man eat oysters with whiskey, and then the man died. Frank assured the gang that the combination of oysters and whiskey was deadly. Everyone knew Malloy loved seafood—they could try it on him. Tony agreed. They served Malloy the combination. Just to make extra sure, they soaked the oysters in poisonous wood alcohol. Malloy ate it. Of course, he didn't die.

They tried spoiled sardines, laced with poison. And how about some carpet tacks to go with it? Malloy ate the meal and seemed to relish it. Again, he survived. He was soon back, asking for more drinks.

The group was starting to get desperate. This venture was expensive, and on top of that, they were paying insurance premiums each month. Years of drinking bad alcohol seemed to have turned Malloy's guts to iron. There was no way they were going to kill him with booze or poison. They needed something more certain.

It was winter, and on one bitterly cold night, they decided to freeze their victim to death. This was the method Tony had used to finish off his previous life insurance victim. They gave Malloy enough drinks to make him unconscious, then dragged him outside and dumped him in the snow with his shirt open. For good measure, they also poured water on his chest.

The next day, Tony found Malloy in the basement of his building. Somehow, he had made his way back.

One of the gang suggested a car accident. He knew a taxi driver, Hershey Green, who would help, for a price.

Once again, the gang got Malloy falling-down drunk, then took him out in the cab. They stood him in the middle of the road, while the taxi raced at him. The driver took two passes, trying to hit Malloy, but each time, by some miracle, the drunken man managed to jump out of the way. But the third attempt was more successful: Green hit Malloy at high speed, then backed over him, just to be sure. The men saw another car coming then, so they fled from the scene.

They were sure Malloy was dead, but when one of the gang, posing as the victim's brother, phoned around, he could find no record of a fatal accident. They checked the local papers for reports of accidents—again, nothing. Weeks went by. It seemed Malloy had simply vanished.

Frank Pasqua, the undertaker, suggested they could kill a different drunk and pass him off as Malloy. But before they could act on this suggestion, Malloy walked into the speakeasy and ordered more drinks.

They asked where he'd been. He told them he'd been in the hospital, with some broken bones. But he was all fixed up now and ready to drink with his buddies.

It was February 23, 1933, and the gang was at their wits' end. This time there would be no half-measures. They got Malloy drunk and unconscious, then put him in his room. They ran a hose from the gas tap to his mouth. The coal gas from the tap had a high percentage of carbon monoxide. They were sure he would not survive that. And this time, they were right. It took an hour of exposure to the deadly gas to kill him, but Michael Malloy was finally dead.

The gang had a friend, Dr. Manzella. He was brought in on the scheme. He signed a death certificate saying that Michael Malloy had died of pneumonia. Undertaker Frank Pasqua made sure Malloy was buried the same night. Carbon monoxide gives its victims' skin a distinctive red flush. One look at that telltale sign, and any coroner worth his salt would know in an instant that this man hadn't died from pneumonia.

Once Malloy was in the ground, the gang celebrated. It had been harder than they imagined, but they had finally killed him. They joked about it over drinks.

The gang's loose lips were their undoing. The police had contacts in the speakeasies. They started hearing strange stories about "Iron Mike Malloy," "Mike the Durable," and the "Irish Rasputin," and they got suspicious.

The insurance companies were suspicious, too. Although one company agreed quickly to a payout of $800, another wanted to see the body first. When they were told it had been buried on the day the man died—well, that was strange. They started a more detailed investigation.

The police eventually had the body exhumed and examined. It didn't take long to determine that Mike had been killed by carbon monoxide poisoning, and his death was soon connected to the insurance records. Police arrested the five participants and charged them with murder. The case was a sensation. Newspapers called the men "the Murder Trust."

The taxi driver, Green, hadn't been paid what he was promised, so he talked to authorities and told them all he knew. He got off relatively lightly, with some prison time.

The doctor was charged with being an accessory after the fact. He claimed he'd made an honest mistake. Not many people believed him, but it was hard for prosecutors to prove otherwise, and his charges were reduced to "failing to report a suspicious death." He was sent to prison for an "indefinite term" of up to three years.

But the evidence was strong against Tony Marino, Frank Pasqua, and the other main participants in the scheme. They were convicted of first-degree murder and sentenced to death in the electric chair at Sing Sing. And, unlike Michael Malloy, they didn't come back for more.

BUMPS ON THE ROAD

THE TINY ARM OF THE LAW

"Jack" was a six-year-old boy in the Boston area. According to CNN, he had been impressed by the story of a little boy who had saved his sister's life by calling 911. He wanted to know more. Jack's mother explained to her son that 911 was the emergency number. She showed him how it worked, and even wrote the number down for him, in case he ever needed to call police, an ambulance, or the fire department.

Soon afterward, Jack had the opportunity to use his knowledge. His father took him along for a trip to the car wash. On the way, Dad made a right turn on a red light.

Jack objected to the move. The light was red, and red means stop. His father should have stopped and stayed stopped until the light was green.

Jack's father explained that, in many places, drivers are allowed to make a right turn on a red light. It was legal in Massachusetts.

Jack wasn't buying his father's excuses. Red means stop. The law must not be violated. He was calling 911. Dad didn't take it too seriously, but when they were back home, Jack went off, found the phone, and made the call.

"My daddy went past a red light," he explained to the emergency operator. "It was in the brand new car—my mommy's car. We had to go to the car wash and then we went past the red light."

His call received a quick response. While Dad was cooking food on the grill, the police phoned the house. Jack picked up and handed the phone to his father. It was the police department dispatcher, who wanted a word.

When Dad realized his son had followed through on his promise, he was embarrassed and apologized. But the dispatcher was OK with it—it made a nice break from the usual calls they received.

Jack's mother was proud of her son. "He thought he was doing the right thing," she said.

Jack himself wants to be a police officer when he grows up. We're guessing his father had better keep to the straight and narrow.

A DIFFERENT KIND OF AMBULANCE CHASER

On a June night in 1990, an ambulance crew was dispatched to a house in the suburbs of Birmingham, Alabama. The paramedics arrived to find a woman, "Betty," nursing a cut on her hand—the result of a domestic dispute.

The paramedics tried to treat her, but Betty didn't want their help. They couldn't force the issue, and her injuries weren't that serious, so they just shrugged and left. A new call had just come in—a medical emergency at the Fairfield City Jail.

As they sped away, Betty decided to go after them. Did she change her mind about wanting treatment? Did she have a grudge against the ambulance crew who had tried to help her? We don't know, but she was determined to chase that ambulance, and she did it on foot!

The paramedics had no idea they were being followed. The *Gadsden Times* reported that, when the ambulance arrived outside the jail, the paramedics left the engine running (which was standard procedure) and hurried inside. Moments later, Betty sprinted up to the ambulance. The vehicle was unattended and, in a blinding flash of dumb, Betty decided this was a rare opportunity to make this vehicle her own. She leapt into the driver's seat and backed out of the space—smashing into a gas pump in front of City Hall. Unfazed by the minor fender bender, she sped off across town.

The theft was immediately spotted, and since an ambulance is a conspicuous vehicle, police were soon on Betty's tail, chasing her through the city streets.

There was no way Betty was going to stop for some cop. She grabbed the microphone of the ambulance radio and swore a blue streak at her pursuers. She also demanded money from them. Oh, and she wanted guns, too—yes, she could definitely use some guns!

Betty smashed the ambulance into a random car. Nobody was injured, and it looked like her joyride was over. But Betty was a woman with a mission. She drove away from the crash site and continued her race through town. The wild ride finally came to an end when she had a second crash. This time, the ambulance was no longer drivable, and Betty could go no farther. She was arrested and charged with first-degree theft, then somebody finally took a look at that cut on her hand.

ANOTHER AMBULANCE CHASER

Ambulances seem to have a strong appeal for a certain kind of thief. In Philadelphia, around 9 o'clock one night in February 2020, an ambulance responded to a domestic disturbance at a local hotel.

According to CNN, the medics were greeted by "Bill," a bearded man in his forties, spoiling for a fight and wearing nothing but boxer shorts. We don't know what he was angry about, but perhaps he had a guilty secret, because as soon as the police arrived on the scene, Bill ran for it. He broke his way into the ambulance, then steered the vehicle directly at one of the police officers.

The officer fired four shots at Bill, hitting him three times in the leg and side, but Bill drove on, injuring the officer, then drove away.

Police cars and a couple of helicopters followed the ambulance across the city for more than an hour in what is described as "a low-speed chase." As he drove, Bill called the police over the radio. He demanded to be taken back to his wife at the hotel. Then he asked the officers if they believed in Jesus Christ.

Bill stopped on a couple of occasions and talked with police, but before they could persuade him to get out of the ambulance, he was off again, cutting across gas stations and going the wrong way down one-way streets. He smashed into at least two police cars.

A tow truck driver tried to block the ambulance, but Bill barreled through it, sending the tow truck into a spin, so Bill was able to make his escape once more.

All this rough treatment had taken its toll on the ambulance. One front tire started to shred, and the other fell apart, so Bill was driving on a rim. Finally, Bill was blocked in by police cars. Officers took him into custody and then transferred him to the place where most ambulance rides end—the hospital.

PLEASE GIVE ME A TICKET

Sit in any traffic court for an afternoon and you will witness a parade of drivers telling lies and giving excuses about why they didn't do the thing they obviously did do. But one Florida driver came up with a unique excuse for his terrible driving—and it happened to be true.

In June 2022, a highway patrol officer in Florida spotted a car moving erratically down the highway. After the driver broke a few traffic laws, the officer pulled the car over.

According to a report in the *Guardian*, the driver, "Paul," sat in a car with three passengers. He seemed ill at ease and had a hard time explaining himself. It seemed to the officer he had a look of despair. The officer took pity on him and let him off with a warning, although Paul didn't seem to appreciate it.

As the officer walked away, he saw Paul make a rude hand gesture. Not acceptable. The highway patrol officer turned on his heel and ordered Paul to step out of the car. Paul did as he was told—with some relief, it seemed. He then begged the officer for help. He was being kidnapped by the men in the car.

Paul was a dog breeder. The three men had shown up at his home pretending to be interested in buying a dog, but instead they robbed him. Then, in a move that turned out to be their dumbest decision, they kidnapped Paul and ordered him to drive them to their next location. While he drove, Paul had tried to attract police attention by breaking traffic laws. He thought he had succeeded when the highway patrol pulled him over, but his heart sank when the officer let him go. His hand gesture saved the day.

The men in the car were found to be carrying knives, guns, and a large sum in cash. They were taken away and charged with assault, unlicensed carrying of a firearm, carjacking, and kidnapping.

The driver avoided the ticket.

TOO HOT TO HANDLE

Some things are not only too dangerous to steal, they're too dangerous to get close to. But nothing stops a determined criminal fool.

Cobalt-60 is one substance you don't want to play with. The metal is used inside hospital sterilization units that resemble stainless-steel ovens. Anything placed inside is exposed to radioactive cobalt-60, which blasts out gamma radiation that rapidly kills germs—and any other living thing—but leaves medical equipment uncontaminated and safe to use.

Cobalt-60 doesn't last forever. After twenty years or so, the material starts to lose some of its radioactive punch as many of its atoms decay from cobalt to nickel. But even as it reaches the end of its useful life, it remains extremely dangerous. The cobalt must be removed and transported—very carefully—to a radioactive waste storage center.

In December 2013, according to NPR, one of these dangerous loads of cobalt left a hospital in Tijuana, Mexico. The material was placed in a shielded container and loaded onto the back of a Volkswagen Worker truck, a specialized flatbed truck with a built-in crane.

The truck should have had GPS tracking and a security guard, but the company seems to have taken a relaxed approach to transporting dangerous materials. The driver made a stop at a service station, where he had a nap—another bad idea.

Two robbers admired the unusual white truck. It seemed like something worth having, so they pulled out their guns and dragged the driver from the cab. After tying him up, they drove off with his truck—and its cargo.

When the driver had managed to wriggle himself free of his bonds, he called the police. The thieves didn't know what they had driven away with, but their actions set alarm bells ringing around the world. The Mexican authorities reported the theft to the International Atomic Energy Agency, the nuclear watchdog for the UN. Some people worried that the material might have been targeted for use in making a "dirty bomb."

The truck with the crane was later recovered about twenty-five miles away. But the container with the radioactive cobalt was no longer on it.

Experts warned how dangerous this container was. If anyone was foolish enough to open the container and remove the contents, the radiation could be deadly.

That's precisely what the thieves had done. The container was found not far away. Ignoring the warning signs and radiation stickers, the thieves seemed to have opened it and examined the cobalt-60 inside.

It's not known who the thieves were, or what happened to them. If they were lucky and didn't stand too close to the material, or stay there too long, the dose of gamma rays they received might only give them radiation sickness—they would feel very sick, then eventually recover. But if they got a little closer or stood a little longer, the radiation could easily be enough to kill them.

RETIREMENT PLAN

"**W**ilt" was a resident of Santa Barbara who, in 2010, figured out a great scheme to get a set of free tires. According to the *Santa Barbara News-Press*, he took his car to Sears and ordered new tires to be installed. The cashier told him it would cost $633 for the tires to be replaced. "No problem," said Wilt—except that he didn't have his checkbook with him that day. But Wilt assured them that, if they started the work, he'd pay when he came to pick up the car. The cashier said that would be fine.

The Sears mechanic did the work and kept the car in the shop overnight, moving it outside the following morning. Later, the shop manager glanced at the outside lot and saw the car being driven away. The manager checked the receipts—the work had not been paid for, and the car keys were still hanging on the hook inside the shop.

Wilt was pleased with himself for outsmarting the shop. He had used his second set of keys to drive the car away, and he didn't care if Sears kept his first set. After all, he could get a new set of keys made for a few bucks—a lot less than the cost of a new set of tires.

You might be thinking, "But couldn't he be tracked down by his license plate?" That's because you are a lot smarter than Wilt. The good folks at Sears had the same thought. They contacted police, who looked up Wilt's license plate and had no difficulty finding him at his home address.

MY OTHER CAR IS A HEARSE

People will go to considerable lengths to get out of paying a traffic ticket, trying to prove that they weren't there, or that the police officer was mistaken, or that the radar gun was malfunctioning. But not many people will avoid a ticket by pretending to be dead.

According to the *Coventry Telegraph*, "Autumn" was a young woman in London, England, who had racked up a series of driving offenses, including drunk driving and driving while disqualified. But despite being banned from driving, she kept at it until, in November 2020, she was out in her BMW and was caught driving carelessly once again.

She gave a false name to the officers, but when she was taken to the police station and they checked the car registration, her real identity became obvious. Nice try. The police requested that Autumn come back to the station later for an interview.

Autumn decided to avoid the problems—and the interview—by pretending to be dead. She phoned the police station under another name, claiming to be Autumn's sister. Putting on her "sad voice," she told the investigating officer that Autumn was sick. Later, she phoned again to say that Autumn had got sicker. Finally, she gave the police the bad news that Autumn had died. She applied for a death certificate so she could prove it.

Did it work? Of course not. She wasn't given the death certificate, because there was no record of any death, and the police weren't fooled for a moment by the claims of Autumn's mysterious "sister."

In fact, it was such a dumb, inept attempt to appear dead that, when the case went to court, Autumn's lawyer used it as evidence that Autumn was not rational.

The judge disagreed—it seemed that some planning had gone into the fake death. Irrational isn't the same as stupid.

Autumn's lawyers tried a range of other excuses. It was suggested that she hadn't been driving the car—it had actually been a male passenger at the wheel. As for the death certificate, how about the idea that Autumn had been feeling suicidal, and planning for her own death, so she wanted to get the paperwork taken care of ahead of time?

The judge said, "I don't accept that for a minute. It's complete nonsense."

Autumn was convicted of the driving offenses, and her attempts to avoid the charges by pretending to be dead got her an eight-month sentence for perverting the course of justice.

BIRTHDAY BRASH

HAPPY BUST-DAY

Birthdays are a time for celebration—and crime, apparently.

Like any twenty-seven-year-old woman, "Courtney" just wanted to have fun celebrating her birthday. And what better way to do it than by having a few drinks? She then got in her car for a birthday drive along the highways and byways of her native Florida, according to Ocala-News.com.

Because Courtney was drunk, her car began to drift off the road and into the grass. Whoops! To fix the situation, she pulled the car back onto the road. Then she fixed it some more by pulling the car into the lane on the other side of the road. Sure, it had cars speeding by in the opposite direction, but they all did a good job of swerving around her as she passed.

Suddenly, she heard sirens. She pulled over—all the way over. She drove the car into a ditch and rolled it.

She was fine. She was fine. No problem, officer.

The police officer said he smelled alcohol on her breath. He asked Courtney if she had been drinking.

She responded, "I had a couple drinks—it's my birthday!" But she assured the police that her driving wasn't impaired. She just didn't get much sleep, and her tiredness caught up with her while she was driving.

The officer peered into the jumbled interior of her car. He discovered an opened bottle of alcohol. After a bit, Courtney discovered it, too, and tried to hide it in her bag.

The officer also found several blue pills—alprazolam, a tranquilizer. Not a great thing to mix with alcohol. He also found a syringe containing a brown oil. He did a field test. The substance was positive for THC.

Perhaps sensing that this situation didn't look good, Nicole tried to stuff another bag of drugs into her pocket. Unfortunately for her, the officer spotted the movement. "Are you hiding something? What have you got there?"

Nicole handed it over. It was more alprazolam. It probably explained her claim to be feeling sleepy.

She was ultimately arrested and charged with driving under the influence and possession of prescription drugs without a prescription. Happy birthday, Courtney!

STEEDING TICKET

People can get in big trouble for drinking and driving—and that applies even when their vehicle is a horse.

In November 2017, in Florida, "Abigail" was heading out to do some shopping, according to WFLA-TV. She enjoyed riding and wanted to buy herself some new spur straps and spurs for her fifty-third birthday. She had already been celebrating the big day with a couple of drinks. And maybe a couple more.

It was midafternoon, and the stores were still open. Time to go birthday shopping. She stuffed $40 in her pocket and staggered outside. She climbed onto her trusty horse, Bo Duke, and then, wobbling in the saddle, headed for the tack shop.

Which route should she take? She decided on the most direct one and rode her horse onto the busy highway, while cars and trucks sped by.

A concerned citizen noticed her meandering progress along the highway and was worried enough to call the police. Deputies caught up with Abigail. She was slumped over in the saddle. She reeked of alcohol. They stopped her four-legged vehicle and asked her to step out of the car . . . that is, step down from the horse, ma'am. She managed to get down, albeit swaying from side to side. Her eyes were red.

Abigail denied being drunk. As for slumping over in the saddle—nahhh. She claimed she just wanted to scratch her leg . . . and she would, as soon as she had found it.

Breath samples showed she was way over the legal limit for a driver in Florida. She was charged with DUI for driving—or riding—drunk. Because she had put the horse in danger, she was also charged with animal neglect.

This wasn't Abigail's first brush with the law. She'd had fifteen previous charges, including cruelty to animals, drug possession, and probation violation. Still, many lawyers in Florida were doubtful that the DUI charges would stick: as dangerous as her actions were, Florida law says that a person riding a horse by the highway is considered a pedestrian, and pedestrians can't be charged with impaired driving. Besides, the horse wasn't drunk.

The horse was taken to the Polk County Sheriff's animal control livestock facility.

When the case went to court, the judge was less focused on the question of drunk driving and more interested in the welfare of the horse. He said the horse should stay in the custody of the sheriff's office—Abigail was not fit to look after the animal.

Abigail didn't go to prison for drunk driving, but the judge ordered her to complete treatment for alcohol addiction.

CRIMINAL BIRTHDAY BOYS

In July 2022, a man in Wales celebrated his thirtieth birthday by taking his girlfriend for a drive in her car. True, his license had been revoked, but hey, anything goes on your birthday. And anyway, her car wasn't insured, so it all canceled out.

He was not a guy to do things by half measures, so before heading out, he got high on drugs.

According to Welsh news site Deeside.com, when police pulled them over, the man realized it might look bad if he was driving, so he and his girlfriend hurriedly changed seats. She slid into the driver's seat, and he moved to the passenger seat. It's hard to do this discreetly, and the exchange was obvious to the officers as they approached the car.

The man was arrested after testing positive for drugs, and he was charged with disqualified driving and driving without insurance. The woman was reported for having no insurance and allowing him to drive the vehicle.

But what if you don't have anyone to spend a birthday with? Here's a bad solution: find a stranger and force them to celebrate with you.

In May 2022, in Singapore, the *Straits Times* described how a local forty-three-year-old man, "Anand," had gone out looking for someone to share his birthday cake with. He went wandering the streets at 11 p.m. He found a cleaner who had just got off work and fallen asleep on a couch in a waste collection center.

He woke the cleaner to offer him a slice of birthday cake.

Either the cleaner didn't want the cake, or he preferred sleep. Anand was offended, and they argued. By the end of the discussion, Anand was so angry that he punched the cleaner in the face, breaking the man's jaw.

Police arrested Anand. He had given them trouble before and had a pattern of being drunk and violent. He was sent to jail, where he will spend his next two birthdays.

Other criminals have tried to use birthdays as an excuse for a crime. It isn't always convincing, as this case from Stuff.co.nz shows.

In New Zealand, in March 2022, police spotted "Tanner" hanging around outside a mall. They had heard he was dealing drugs, so they arrested and searched him. Sure enough, he was carrying five bags of methamphetamine, a large number of smaller, empty Ziploc bags, an electronic weighing scale, and $625 in cash.

Obviously, he was dealing drugs.

But Tanner denied it. He was not a dealer, he claimed. He was one of the dealers' pitiful victims, a meth addict.

"In that case," said the police, "how do you explain the presence of the drugs, the bags, the scales, and the money?"

"Yesterday was my birthday," said Tanner. He described the celebration—one where all his friends had all given him gifts, including drugs and gifts of cash.

"What about the scale?" asked the police. Tanner explained that, when he bought drugs—poor addict that he was—he didn't want to be cheated, so he brought along his own scale to verify the amount.

"And the collection of tiny plastic bags?"

Tanner claimed he was trying to control his habit, and by using the bags, he could portion out his birthday drugs, so he wouldn't smoke them all at once—which would be dangerous.

The police let him tell his story to the judge—who didn't believe the birthday story, either. Tanner was sentenced to twenty months in prison.

SUPERNATURAL CRIMES

CROSS MY PALM WITH DIAMONDS

A New York woman, "Madame Madeline," worked as a psychic. She was not a real psychic—because, news flash, none of them are—but she was one of the more malevolent ones.

Like the worst charlatans, Madeline preyed on people who were distressed or grieving. She offered her services cheap at first. Her clients could justify the visit as a form of entertainment. "Why not? It doesn't cost much." But if she saw an opportunity to draw money from a person, she'd take it.

According to the *Guardian*, one woman, "Julia," went to Madeline and told her she was having relationship problems. Sensing that the woman was desperate and a little naive, Madeline looked into the future. Oh, dear! The future looked bleak. Madeline foresaw that Julia would go on having relationship problems, and remain unloved her whole life, unless . . . yes, she could see a solution . . .

The solution involved Julia buying Madame Madeline a nine-carat diamond ring. Julia believed her stories and did it. Problem solved. Or nearly solved. Because Madame Madeline saw other problems in Julia's life. Demons were circling. Madeline needed to perform expensive spells to protect Julia from them. She collected more money to pay for the construction of a protective gold pyramid that would shield Julia and her family from death.

By the time Madeline was done, Julia was fully protected from magical attacks, and her bank account was sucked dry—she lost more than $740,000 to the psychic.

Another victim, a businessman, was cheated out of more than $72,000. Madeline told him the same things she told most of her clients:

he was suffering from psychic illnesses, and only her expensive magic would remove the problem.

Both victims lost their life savings to the scam. Only in retrospect did they realize that Madeline had made fools of them.

Some psychics can be very convincing. Those who have studied the business say the fortune tellers have many ways of discovering information about their clients, ranging from ID fraud to exchanging notes and recordings with other psychics. Once the victims realize they've been cheated—if they ever do—they may be too embarrassed to go to the police, and when they do report crimes, they are not always taken seriously.

But unlike most of Madeline's victims, the two we've described were angry enough—and courageous enough—to act. They approached a New York private investigator who has made psychic scams his specialty. He listened to their stories with interest and sympathy. In 2018, he contacted a police detective with the information the victims had provided. Madame Madeline was arrested on suspicion of fraud.

Unfortunately, although the police took the matter seriously in this case, the court went easy on Madame Madeline. She avoided prison. She received five years' probation and was ordered to repay a portion of the money her former clients had paid.

The clients were furious at the outcome. After the trial, one commented, "Crime pays."

However, they were successful in publicly exposing Madeline's scam. Gazing into the future, we foresee a downturn in her fortunes.

UNSEEN CONSEQUENCES

Here's a proposal for the perfect crime. You enter a bank, during the day, while security guards are present and cameras are watching the area. You walk up to people holding cash, and you take it from them, just like that. Your victims know they're being robbed, but nobody can stop you, and when you leave with your pockets full of money, nobody knows who did it.

How does it work? Invisibility, that's how. And it can be done. At least, that's what "Babak" explained to "Farid" in 2006—and Babak was one who knew, because he was a professional sorcerer, a wizard, in the Iranian capital, Tehran.

Babak explained that, once the spells were prepared, Farid would be entirely invisible. He could go where he wanted, unseen by others.

But what about the cost?

Babak admitted that, yes, the spells were expensive—if Farid wanted this kind of power, it would cost him five million Iranian rials (about US$540). But, of course, if you were invisible, you might find some easy ways to get your money back.

Farid considered the matter. Yes, he could think of quite a few ways to turn the five million rials into a larger sum. As Babak said, it was expensive, but it was worth it—an investment, really.

Farid was sold. He paid the five million reals to Babak, and the wizard set to work preparing the spells. When the mystic spells were ready and written out, Babak tied the spells to Farid's arm. It was done. Farid was invisible.

Feeling powerful and invulnerable, Farid went to the bank and prepared to put his powers to profitable use. Tellers and customers stood around, clutching their banknotes. They would be astonished when their money disappeared.

Farid stepped forward and started snatching money from the hands of bank customers. But, as *Metro UK* reported, his crime spree didn't continue for long, and the customers didn't react as he'd expected. Instead of looking around in astonishment as their money was whisked away, or running in fear from the spirit in their midst, they looked right at Farid, grabbed him, and overpowered him.

Farid was handed over to police and put on trial.

In court, he admitted that he had made a mistake, and that the man he took to be a true wizard was merely a wizard imposter. "I understand now what a big trick was played upon me," the thief told the court.

You can't trust anyone these days. He could see that.

WAND-ERING THE LOBBY

Twenty-nine-year-old "Spencer" was obsessed with magic. He kept a homemade wand under his clothes.

He was a regular, but unwanted visitor to a hotel in Bloomington, Minnesota. The hotel was sick of him wandering onto the premises and bothering their guests. They had obtained a trespass notice barring him from entering, but it had since expired, and now, in April 2022, Spencer was back.

According to KSTP-TV News, Spencer tried to take a key from a bowl of used room keys, perhaps seeking one that would give him access to the Boss Level. But the keys were guarded by a staff member, who stopped him and asked him to please leave the premises.

Spencer, angered, shouted some insults at the employee and left the hotel. The employee followed him to make sure he didn't come back. Angry at this indignity, Spencer decided to play hardball. He reached under his clothes and pulled out his magic wand.

The employee saw a long object with a metal tip and thought it was a knife. He was licensed to carry a gun, and he pulled it out in response. The two men found themselves in a standoff—the employee's firearm versus Spencer's sixteen-inch magic wand. The wand's powers were unknown, but probably great, considering that Spencer was confidently facing down a man with a loaded gun.

Fortunately for the guy with the pistol, Spencer did not unleash magic missiles or fireballs. Nor did he freeze the employee's firearm in place with an ice blast. Instead, Spencer decided to waste no more time on the puny human. He kicked a garbage can and walked away. Today, the staff member had won. Staff beats wand.

Perhaps realizing his narrow escape, the employee used his 911-summoning spell and let the Bloomington police handle the matter. They were familiar with Spencer and his magic wand, but used their own powers of arrest to bring him in. He was charged with fifth-degree assault and trespassing. Hopefully, he will behave himself and won't do a spell in prison.

COP AND SORCERY

The Maldives is a country made up of hundreds of islands. In 2013, the country was heading into a presidential election. This fight was bitter. One candidate was a former president who claimed he'd been ousted in a coup. The other was a big businessman who was half-brother to a former dictator.

But the *Guardian* reported that, with only days to go before the vote, locals on one of the islands, Guraidhoo, were alarmed to discover a young green coconut that had been left near a polling station. The coconut was covered with Arabic writing. It had been left on the ground where everyone could see it.

The police were called to inspect the fruit. Was it just a joke?

Most of the Maldivian population are Sunni Muslim, but many people also believe in traditional magic, and a common way to perform magical rituals is to carve spells on a coconut.

The polling station was normally a school. There had been problems before with people using the threat of magic to influence elections, and this time around, the school authorities had been so worried about the dangers of magic that they had nearly refused to allow their buildings to be used for the vote. They finally agreed only when election officials promised to take full responsibility if anyone fell under a spell or became ill.

But what was this coconut? Had it been placed as a curse to keep people from voting or to influence the vote with magic?

The police removed the coconut and took it into custody. To put the public at ease, they called a magician into the station and had him examine the writing on the coconut. The magician confirmed that it was just a hoax—the coconut was harmless, and its spells were fake. The election could proceed without risk to the public.

CRIMES OF FASHION

SOCK IT TO ME

There are a surprising number of dumb sock-related crimes.

"Brian" was a big guy—six foot four in height, and weighing around 300 pounds. He needed some socks, but had no money on him, so, in 2012, he went to his local Walmart in Pennsylvania, marched up to the customer service counter, and stole a pair. Nobody was looking, so he put the socks on right there, then walked around the store.

As NBC News reported, what made this unusual was that, although Brian was now wearing a fresh pair of stolen socks, he wasn't wearing anything else. His dress code seemed to involve working from the ground up, then quickly stopping.

Other shoppers were surprised to see this man wandering up and down the aisles, naked above the ankles. As you might expect, they steered a wide path around him.

When the staff realized what was going on, they were alarmed and called the police.

When the police arrived, Brian wanted nothing to do with them. He wouldn't listen to their instructions, so they used a Taser on him. He was taken into custody, struggling and spitting, and faced a number of charges, including retail theft and aggravated assault.

Although Brian had no history of mental illness, police speculated he might have been on drugs.

In March 2021, a homeless man also found himself in need of socks—although this man was fully clothed. As Fox News reported, he went into a dollar store and stole some socks, but the staff saw what he was up to and called the police, who were on the scene fast enough to catch him.

One of the officers spoke to the thief, who admitted he had been trying to steal socks.

The officer appreciated the thief's honesty and, instead of arresting him, paid for some socks, in exchange for the man's promise to stop stealing. He explained that if the man needed other services, he could ask for help at the police station.

The store owner added that if he was in need again, he could let her know and she would help.

In July 2017, in Toronto, thieves pulled off a larger-scale sock heist, stealing 450 pairs of socks from a van.

According to CTV News, the van's owner, "Benjamin," worked at a car dealership. He was sad to discover the crime—the socks had been intended for a homeless shelter. He appealed in the local media, asking the thief to return the stolen socks.

The socks weren't returned, but the homeless shelter didn't lose out. Benjamin's colleagues at the car dealership felt sorry about the theft and held charity events. They raised enough money to buy more than eight hundred pairs of new socks.

HAIR TODAY, GONE TOMORROW

If you steal a fashion item for money, be careful where you sell it.

In 1944, a ballerina named Alicia Markova played the role of Juliet in the ballet *Romeo and Juliet* at New York's Metropolitan Opera House. According to the *New York Times*, she wore a sensational Juliet wig. The color was a gorgeous chestnut, the braids were long and flowing, and the parting was such sweet sorrow.

The wig was worth $100 (around $1,600 today), so, after the show, it was carefully stored in a closet at the theatre.

That's when twenty-five-year-old Francisco Xavier Ortiz took it. He was a male member of the company. But he wasn't interested in playing Juliet—he just needed cash.

A couple of days later, he went looking for a buyer. He dropped in on a famous New York wigmaker, Alfred Barris.

"I have this Juliet wig to sell. What will you give me for it?"

The wigmaker thought the wig looked familiar, and when he flipped it over, he was sure. It had his own label—he had made this wig personally for the ballerina. He knew it had been stolen. He confronted Ortiz with the crime.

Ortiz ran away, leaving the wig behind, but the police soon caught up with him. He was charged with "petit larceny."

He received a thirty-day sentence for the theft, but he'd been well behaved in jail, so the sentence was suspended.

TROUBLE AFOOT

"Sanjay" was a tourist on a bus trip from Dharamshala to Delhi in India, in late November 2017. It was a long trip, taking many hours, and as night fell, the twenty-seven-year-old decided to make himself comfortable. He removed his shoes, then his socks.

The other passengers slowly became aware of something wafting through the air. They exchanged glances, then complaints.

"What is that smell?"

"Was it you?"

"Is it cheese?"

"It's horrible!"

They tracked down the source of the smell. It was Sanjay's socks. Their stench was assaulting the nostrils of everyone nearby.

The passengers complained to Sanjay: "Your socks stink! Throw them out!"

"I'm not throwing them out," said Sanjay.

"Well, put them in your bag!"

Sanjay sniffed the socks. They didn't seem that bad to him. He thought the passengers were being rude and insulting. He refused to put the socks in the bag.

According to the *Hindustan Times*, the argument between Sanjay and the passengers escalated. The driver stopped the bus, and he and the conductor went back to see what was going on.

The passengers explained the problem. Again, Sanjay denied that there was a problem. The driver and the conductor, now within close range of the offending socks, asked Sanjay to discard them. Again, Sanjay refused. Why should he throw away perfectly good socks? The socks might smell a little—all socks smell a *little*—but they didn't *stink*. That was ridiculous.

The bus drove on, and the argument between Sanjay and the other passengers continued. The driver made a couple more stops and made further attempts to negotiate, but Sanjay wasn't budging.

The passengers were getting sock-sick. These socks were a crime! There had to be a law against them. The bus was approaching a small police station, and one of the passengers demanded that the driver make a stop there.

At the police station, the passengers complained to the officers about Sanjay and his socks. Sanjay was outraged and shouted at the lying passengers. The police, who soon caught a whiff of the footwear, sided with the passengers. Sanjay was booked under sections 107 and 151 of the Code of Criminal Procedure—Sanjay and his socks were causing a breach of the peace and were a public nuisance.

The superintendent of police added that Sanjay also created a "ruckus" at the police station.

Sanjay later filed his own complaint against his fellow passengers. He alleged that his socks did not stink and that the passengers had quarreled with him for no reason. As he saw it, he was innocent—and he felt it down to his sole.

THAT'S PRIVATE

You lose a lot of privacy when you get caught as a criminal.

In a small Irish coastal town, a seventy-six-year-old woman, "Edna," felt an urge to lift clothes from a local store. She hid the merchandise and walked out without paying, but didn't realize a security guard had been watching her.

From then on, according to the *Sunday World*, all sorts of details about Edna became public knowledge through the local newspaper. Her neighbors learned that she had stolen three nightdresses, a top, and a cheap pair of shoes. They learned that she had been in poor health for several months, that she had a cataract in one eye, that she was on medication for her arteries, and that she claimed the medication had made her confused.

They learned that she was a grandmother, had previously been caught shoplifting, and had been put on probation.

What was the worst part of having her life put on display before the public?

Edna was in no doubt: "Everybody knows my age now!"

ALL THE NEWS THAT'S FIT TO SNEEZE

In Britain in the 1800s, some people were arrested over a "handkerchief."

Back then, the government taxed newspapers. Every paper was slapped with a fourpenny tax—a hefty addition to the cover price.

Henry Berthold was a German-born journalist living in London. He was opposed to the tax. Like some other liberal thinkers in England, he viewed it as a tax on knowledge and a way to stop working-class people from learning what was happening in government.

Berthold came up with an interesting way to avoid paying the newspaper tax: instead of printing a newspaper, he would print a news-*cloth*. Or, as he called it, a handkerchief.

In 1831, he printed the first edition of his new publication, *Berthold's Political Handkerchief*. It looked like a newspaper, but it was printed on a large sheet of cotton. Some critics complained that the newspaper was messy and left ink on the hands of anyone handling it. Berthold replied that, once the readers had finished reading it and the ink had come off, they could bring the "handkerchief" back and have a new edition printed on it. It was entirely recyclable. And, of course, you could use it as a huge handkerchief—if you didn't mind getting ink on your nose.

The articles in the newspaper were radical in tone. Berthold was a member of the National Union of Working Classes and wanted to give all men the right to vote. (Back then, it wasn't just women who were deprived of the vote—most men weren't allowed to vote, either.) He encouraged people to rebel against the government and fight government debt. He expressed solidarity with the textile workers of England—it was partly for them, he said, that he was printing the publication on cotton.

He published ten issues of the newspaper between September and November 1831. Selling a newspaper without a duty stamp was a clear violation of the law, which, despite Berthold's beliefs, said that a stamp duty must be paid on the sale of all newspapers, whatever material they were printed on. At least one person was arrested for selling *Berthold's Political Handkerchief*, but Berthold himself broke the law and got away with it.

Ironically, he was arrested not for his handkerchief, but for a different article of clothing.

At the age of thirty-three, two years after he'd given up on his news-handkerchief project, Berthold visited the warehouse of a London clothes merchant. While he was there, he stole an expensive feather boa. Nobody knows why an agitator for the working poor stole clothing designed for the idle rich, but he was seen winding the boa around his hand, then stuffing it in his top hat.

He was caught, arrested, and tried.

People who might have grudgingly admired his newspaper were not impressed by his shoplifting, or by his scattered defense in court. Berthold denied that he'd stolen the boa—although there were reliable eyewitnesses. He looked for sympathy, claiming he had lost money in some bad business ventures. He reminded the court that he was a literary man. Then, in a strange departure from his role as a working-class hero, he produced letters he had received in the past from various dukes and lords, which he believed showed his good character. He asked the court why he would commit such a crime (a good question!). Then he pointed out that this was his first offense, and that he'd already spent six weeks in jail since he was arrested. He closed by saying it was better for ninety-nine guilty people to escape than for one innocent person to be punished.

As to his last point, the court were willing to play the odds. Berthold was found guilty and given a seven-year sentence in Australia.

Sadly, life on the far side of the world didn't agree with him, and he died in hospital three years into his sentence. It didn't even make the newspapers.

THEY'RE A BAD INFLUENCER

FOLLOW ME ... IF YOU CAN CATCH ME

"Angela" was twenty-eight years old and living in Florida. She had previously worked as a police officer, but lost that job after hacking into another female officer's phone and posting the woman's nude pictures online.

After being forced out of the police, Angela became a cruise-line worker. But this wasn't her dream, either. She wanted to be a social media star and influencer. She started a website and posted the usual social media selfies, but her posts weren't attracting as many followers as she hoped.

Many of the top influencers attract a young audience, and Angela figured she'd give that a try. And if the kids weren't coming to her, that was no problem—she'd go to them and engage with them one on one.

In May 2021, she saw a good opportunity: a local high school was holding a prom. Angela dressed as an eighteen-year-old, with a skateboard tucked under her arm and a backpack full of promotional flyers, and she snuck into the school.

According to CBS News, she wandered the halls, handing out flyers and trying to persuade kids to follow her, while recording her progress on video.

Security stopped her, asking who she was. She claimed to be a new student. The guard told her she needed to check in at the main office. She moved on and started pestering another group of students, and she also kept handing out her literature. When she ignored the security officers a second time, people got nervous—after all, there had been many instances of attacks on schools—so they announced a "potential threat on campus."

Angela soon found herself surrounded by school officials. Seeing she would get no further, she headed for the exit. Police were on the scene at this point, and they told her to stop. Angela realized she'd pushed things too far and escaped.

Of course, she had left an impressive trail of promotional material behind, so it wasn't difficult for police to track her down through her social media accounts. They surrounded her house.

Angela tried to turn her impending arrest into a social media sensation, with hashtags like #WeMadeIt and #MissionAccomplished. It's not clear what the mission was, beyond handing out flyers.

Angela was arrested and charged with burglary, trespassing, and resisting arrest. There's no word on whether she was also charged for wandering the school without a hall pass.

She appeared in court, posing in an attractive orange jumpsuit and COVID face mask.

EXCESS-MONEY DETOX

One influencer, model, and wellness guru, "Shelby," had more than a million followers on social media. She posted many aspirational lifestyle photos, gazing seductively into the camera while holding a glass of wine, a partner, a dog, or a baby.

Investors poured more than a million dollars into her business, a website where she gave advice on which crystals to place under your pillow and the best ketogenic chocolate recipes.

According to the *New York Post*, the investors later discovered that the business wasn't nearly as profitable as she'd claimed—she was taking investment money and pretending it was income. Her apparent success was just one more manufactured image.

Shelby was arrested in 2019, accused of defrauding her investors by exaggerating the money she made as an influencer. An Australian court ordered her to pay back the money. She sent a letter to the judge pleading poverty—she claimed she couldn't repay the money because of expenses related to her pregnancy. The judge didn't accept this excuse and said the letter represented serious contempt of court.

Shelby certainly had enough in the bank for airline tickets. She and her husband hurriedly relocated to the United States, "permanently." If her pictures are any guide, someone with no money can enjoy a luxurious life in Los Angeles.

Two years later, she returned to Australia and was immediately arrested at the airport. The money she'd taken from investors still had not been repaid, and she had declared bankruptcy.

When her followers asked why she wasn't posting on Instagram so much, she replied that she was taking a step back to focus on her family and her darling son.

She said, "I am choosing to find joy in my motherhood journey."

She is probably finding less joy in her being-sued-for-fraud journey.

IN HIS TRUNKS ON THE TRUNK

"Cody" was an Australian tourist visiting the island paradise of Bali, Indonesia, in June 2022, according to the *Bali Sun*. As he sauntered, topless, through the grounds of a temple, he spotted a giant banyan tree near a cemetery. Cody loved climbing trees.

He told his friends to get this on video—he planned to use the footage on TikTok. Then he grabbed the branches of the giant banyan and pulled himself up, whooping with triumph as he reached the heights.

Locals watched this performance in outrage. The banyan is a sacred tree, representing the earth's divine creator, and this particular tree also stood on a sacred site—for a hundred years, it had grown on the grounds of a Hindu temple. The tourist's behavior was intolerable. Villagers contacted the police, and the police arrested Cody.

He was taken to the police station, where he met with a group of residents, temple officials, and traditional leaders. They patiently explained to him how he had offended their religious beliefs. Cody said he hadn't realized this when he started climbing. (If he had, perhaps he would have recorded a different intro to his TikTok video.) He admitted his mistake and apologized for any distress his actions had caused.

But it couldn't end there. The elders told him that, whenever an act pollutes nature, whether deliberately or accidentally, it is necessary to perform a special ceremony, the *guru piduka*.

Cody fully understood. He cherished and appreciated their spiritual traditions. And it might make a great follow-up video.

They told him that he would have to pay the cost of this ceremony.

"Uh, how much exactly?"

The ceremony would cost half a million Indonesian rupiahs.

Cody wasn't sure he had that kind of money.

It actually wasn't as much as it sounded—the fine was equivalent to $33 in US funds.

But, as it turned out, Cody didn't have *that* kind of money, either. Fumbling in his pockets, he pulled out the equivalent of $10 and suggested maybe he could pay the rest later.

The traditional leaders agreed to the deferred payment plan, but the police nixed it. They'd had enough of this egotistical deadbeat. They took him to the immigration department so that he could be quickly deported.

The sacred sites of Bali seem to be a magnet for irreverent tourists, especially those who flout Indonesia's strict laws against public nudity.

In the months before Cody's adventures, a Russian woman posed naked against the roots of a seven-hundred-year-old tree so she could get pictures for her Instagram account. She was also arrested and deported.

A Canadian actor also offended local sensibilities when he went to a sacred mountain and performed a naked dance for the camera, to demonstrate his connection with God and the universe. According to News.com.au, he, too, was arrested and set to be deported—although in his case, officials ran into a snag: his connection with God and the universe was also his only protection from COVID. He was unvaccinated, and without a vaccination, the airline wouldn't let him fly.

SPEAKING OF MINDLESS DRONES...

A tourist was visiting New York City from Dallas, Texas, in August 2021. "Justin," aged twenty-two, had a great idea to liven up his social media account: he'd fly his drone over the World Trade Center.

According to the *New York Post*, the building was 7 World Trade Center—a fifty-two-story building constructed on the site of a tower destroyed by the September 11 terrorist attacks in 2001, when airliners full of fuel crashed into the Twin Towers.

In the middle of a weekday afternoon, Justin flew his drone near the building, but his navigation wasn't too good. He crashed the drone into the side of the building, and it became jammed in the building's framework.

The crash generated a rapid and massive response from the authorities in New York: the New York Police Department came out, as well as the counterterrorism unit and the FBI.

As Justin describes it (possibly missing the point), it was "quite the New York greeting."

The New York greeting was followed by a New York grilling in an interrogation room. Hadn't it occurred to Justin that New Yorkers might have some sensitivity about flying objects crashing into the World Trade Center? He said no, it hadn't occurred to him, and he didn't even know that the area he was flying his drone over was part of the World Trade Center.

We wonder what his narration of the video would have sounded like. "This is a building. This is another building. I don't know what this is . . ."

Justin described himself as a videographer, crypto investor, and CEO. (Sure you are, kid.) He said he was making a personal travel video to show his followers on social media. "I need to make my YouTube pop off."

Justin appeared to have no grasp of the threats posed by terrorism, or of recent history. He complained that he was interrogated for six hours by the New York Police Department's counterterrorism officers.

He was also interrogated by the FBI. "I've been asked the same questions more than I can count on two hands," he said.

Justin added he "didn't give the cops a hard time," which must have been a great relief to them. He seemed to enjoy being the center of media attention.

He didn't think to look at local regulations before he launched the drone in the middle of the bustling metropolis. If he had bothered to check, he would have learned that flying drones is strictly prohibited in New York—a misdemeanor. That's not just because of the potential for terrorists to use drones, but because the area is densely populated and has a huge amount of air traffic flying in and out of its airports.

Justin says he went to the building to see if he could get his $1,200 drone back, but the building's manager and chief engineer informed him that it was unlikely to be returned. Bummer.

Justin lost his flying toy and narrowly avoided a jail sentence. But he still felt the experience had been important to him. Does this mean he had grown as a human being, gaining humility and sensitivity? Had he learned a valuable lesson?

Not quite.

In newspaper interviews, he crowed, "Now I've got a great New York story!"

LOWERING AWARENESS

Some influencers aren't just about fashion and makeup. They're about making our world a better and safer place. At least, they say they are.

"Caitlin" was an "influencer mom" from Northern California. *Elle* magazine reports that, in December 2020, she was out shopping at a craft store with her two children. As she shopped, she was approached by a couple—a Latino man and woman. They started talking to her and commented on the attractive appearance of her kids.

The couple followed her to the parking lot, then suddenly the man tried to grab her stroller. Fortunately, a passerby intervened, and the couple fled. After the shocking abduction attempt, Caitlin felt the need to post her experiences online, raising awareness, so that other parents could spot the warning signs and stay safe.

Caitlin's videos attracted a flood of support and followers.

The police investigated the "stranger abduction"—a rare crime. But they were disturbed by Caitlin's account, because they had already talked to her shortly after she left the craft store, and her first story was quite different. She had come to the police station to report a Latino couple who she considered to be acting in a suspicious manner. She said she didn't want anyone charged, but she wanted people to be warned about suspicious strangers. The police didn't think there was much in her story, and didn't issue a warning, which annoyed Caitlin. There was no mention of an abduction attempt—just a Latino couple she didn't like the look of.

Now, on social media, her description of the same encounter included a man grabbing her stroller. For someone who claimed she wanted to keep the public safe, this was a strange detail to have withheld from the police.

The reason it was withheld the first time was that Caitlin had invented the whole story. When police took no interest in her suspicions about the couple, she validated those suspicions by inventing a crime for the couple to commit.

Caitlin knew nothing about the couple—and, as it happened, her intuition was lousy. Her "criminals" were an ordinary, honest Latino couple living and working in the area. There was nothing "suspicious" about them. They had no interest in Caitlin or her children. They had only gone to the craft store to buy supplies for a Christmas display.

The police had to investigate Caitlin's new claims. They found video images of the couple from the store. "That's them!" said Caitlin. So, the police put the images online, asking the public for their help in identifying them.

The couple in question saw the photos, recognized themselves, and were horrified. They contacted a lawyer, then talked to the police.

The police believed the couple's version of events. Moreover, there were no witnesses and no evidence to suggest an abduction.

If the couple's story was true, then there was only one way the police could view Caitlin's tale of attempted kidnapping and crime-fighting adventure: it was a racially motivated hate crime.

While the police investigated, Caitlin threw herself into her new career as an influencer-crimefighter. She posted about sex trafficking and promoted herself as a crusader who dared to speak for the cowed victims. She urged her followers to "stay vigilant." Her wild claims became material for a range of conspiracy theories. But her success faltered when the other side of the story became better known.

In April 2021, Caitlin was arrested and charged with lying to a police dispatcher and lying to a police officer.

MEN WITH GUNS

WITH MY MASK OFF,
NOBODY WILL RECOGNIZE ME

In September 2014, thirty-three-year-old "Trevor" sat down at a bar in St. John's, Newfoundland. According to CBC News, he was going to rob it, but first he would scope the place out.

He liked the look of "Laura," the bartender. He asked if he could buy her a drink. She said no, thanks. Keeping things on a professional basis, Laura asked if she could get him a drink. Trevor said no, thanks and suavely pointed to the coffee he'd brought along.

Laura left this big spender alone, but as he ambled over to the slot machines, he could tell she was watching him. Who could blame her?

After he'd seen all that he needed to see, Trevor left the bar. He transformed his appearance by putting on a mask and a helmet, then, an hour after he'd left, he returned holding a gun.

"This is a holdup! Nobody move!"

He knocked over the monitor with the video surveillance, then jumped over the bar. He grabbed the money from the cash register and stuffed it into his sack—which was actually more of a pillowcase. He demanded to know where the safe was.

Laura said there wasn't a safe.

Trevor didn't believe that. He knew there must be a safe. He checked in the kitchen and under the counter, all the while talking to Laura. It was hard to see with his disguise on, so he removed the mask to search more easily. No, she was telling the truth—no safe. Well, that was a surprise. He put the mask back on as he continued his robbery.

Seeing himself as a thief with style and panache, he offered a patron a beer. He asked if anyone else was thirsty.

His tone changed. He suddenly became suspicious of the women by the slot machines. He warned them not to call police. He ordered them to lie on the floor. The women refused—they weren't going to lie on the floor. Trevor was a reasonable man. He changed his mind. They didn't have to lie on the floor after all. But he warned everyone against any sudden movements. "If nobody moves, nobody gets hurt."

One of the women said that, since he'd got what he wanted, maybe he should just leave now.

She had a point. Trevor looked for his car keys. He couldn't find them—no, it was OK, he'd been looking in the wrong pocket. He had found them after all.

Before leaving, he grabbed the hard drive from the bar's computer and smashed it, saying that no one would get any photos of him. He took the drive with him, just to be sure.

Trevor left with his loot—over $4,000—and drove away. Overall, the robbery had taken twenty minutes. In his mind, the crime was slick and professional. Now he was home free.

The police arrived on the scene shortly afterward. The women told them that the disorganized man in the mask seemed to be the same man who had been in earlier—everyone was sure they recognized his voice. But Laura's evidence was the clincher—she had talked to Trevor at the bar, and she had seen the robber later with his mask off while he searched for a safe. It was, unquestionably, the same man.

Based on the excellent eyewitness reports, the police knew that the customer in the bar earlier in the evening was also the robber.

The police then checked the video recordings of the robbery. These recordings were intact because Trevor knew even less about computers than he did about disguises. The video showed what happened in the bar and in the parking lot. Trevor's car and license plate were clearly visible.

The police soon located Trevor's car in the parking lot of a Tim Hortons. He tried to get away, driving on sidewalks, speeding through residential neighborhoods, and swerving through traffic, but they finally brought him to a stop.

Trevor was arrested, and based on rock-solid eyewitness evidence, he was convicted on six counts relating to robbery and four counts related to driving. He was sentenced to four years in prison.

If you want to commit a masked robbery, it's probably a good idea not to show your face to your victims first.

DIAL BANG-BANG-BANG FOR AN AMBULANCE

We associate guns with murder and self-defense, but some people have used them for medical purposes.

Back in 1909, in New York City, a retired pharmacist named Herman Powers had taken the wrong tablets at three in the morning. He realized he had accidentally taken a lethal dose of strychnine.

Telephones were not common in those days, and he needed medical help fast. His solution was to pull out a gun, fire three shots in the air, and shout, "Police!"

According to the *New York Times*, the gunshots woke the neighborhood. People came outside to see what was going on. Powers, frantic with worry, looked down from the top of a three-story apartment building. When he saw that no police had arrived yet, he begged for someone in the crowd to fetch them.

At this point, you might think he would have done better to explain what had happened, so people could call for medical help, but Herman doesn't seem to have been entirely rational. According to his landlord, he had been "sick recently through overstudy," and a nurse had been looking after him until the previous weekend. It's not clear if the strychnine had been a mistake or a suicide attempt.

Fortunately, one of the people in the crowd was a chauffeur—a fellow who drove one of those fancy new automobiles. He drove to the police station and brought back a couple of officers in record time. Together, they went up to Herman's room and escorted the elderly pharmacist outside and then away to the hospital, where he was successfully treated.

Later, he started raving again, and was moved to a private sanatorium, but his doctor seemed confident that he would make a full recovery. It's probably too late to suggest taking his gun away.

THE BULLETPROOF BOUNCER

It was late on a spring night in New York in 1999, and "Chuck," a tough guy in his thirties, was hanging out with two relatives in their twenties, "Joe" and "Ron." The three men headed to a local nightclub, where one got into a loud argument on the dance floor. According to the *New York Times*, a bouncer moved in and told one of the three amigos to leave. This was too much for Chuck—nobody was going to disrespect a member of his family that way. He would teach the bouncer a lesson he wouldn't live long enough to forget. Chuck pulled out his .38 and fired three shots.

Chuck's aim wasn't too good. Two bullets missed the bouncer. The third grazed the bouncer's head. And now the bouncer was angry—very angry—and he charged at his armed attacker. Chuck hadn't expected this kind of spirited response. Suddenly frightened, he turned and ran from the nightclub, with the furious bouncer in hot pursuit.

Joe and Ron didn't like the look of the situation—they wanted to help Chuck, but—understandably—they were wary about fighting the bulletproof bouncer themselves. With an opponent like that, three against one didn't seem like good odds.

They dashed outside and spotted a valet parking attendant in charge of a customer's Toyota. Joe and Ron pushed the valet aside, then Joe got behind the wheel of the car and floored it, heading for Chuck. They figured they could screech to a halt next to him, and he could jump in the car before the ferocious Franken-bouncer had time to catch up.

It seems as if poor judgment and poor coordination went hand in hand in this family, because Joe's driving was just as bad as Chuck's shooting. Instead of pulling up next to Chuck, Joe smashed the car right into him. The car careened on, hitting a row of parked cars before coming to a permanent stop.

The police arrived on the scene and arrested the trio. They charged Chuck with attempted murder and weapons possession, then sent him to hospital to be treated for his critical injuries. Joe and Ron were hauled away to face charges of auto theft and criminal mischief. We don't know what happened to the bouncer, but it's likely people will think twice before messing with him again.

NOT A READ-NECK

In 2014, "Cole" stood accused of shooting and killing a man in Kansas. Prosecutors said that, after murdering the man, Cole drove the body to another county and dumped it in a ditch. The body was found the next morning by hunters.

The case would soon be coming to trial, but the *Great Bend Tribune* reported that Cole was worried his tattoo might prejudice the jury.

The tattoo consisted of the word *murder*, written in large, open capital letters on the front of his neck. The letters were the full height of his neck and ran from below his left ear to below his right ear.

The word was in mirror writing—*redrum*—but a person would still have to be half-blind to miss it. Cole's lawyer said the inscription would be "extremely damaging if seen by a jury."

Cole and his lawyer requested that the suspect be allowed to have access to a professional tattoo artist who could remove or modify the huge inscription. The prosecution had no objections—they were confident they had a strong case, whatever was written on the defendant's face.

We can't help wondering what change Cole intended to make. How exactly do you transform *murder* into something less incriminating? Do you try to pass as an illiterate who loves his mom and change it to *mudder*? Or do you attempt to win over the *Lord of the Rings* fans on the jury with *Mordor*? Perhaps adding letters might work, transforming *murder* to *lemur derby* (whatever that is, it sure sounds cute). Or do you just add *of crows* around the back of the neck?

We'll never know—because the tattoo changes couldn't be made. Under Kansas law, licensed tattoo artists are not allowed to work outside their own establishment, and the sheriff's department wasn't going to give Cole a day pass so he could get some fresh ink. The lawyers decided that a turtleneck would be sufficient to hide Cole's tattoo in the courtroom.

Cole finally got his court date. He claimed self-defense, and he wore a turtleneck sweater to hide the correct answer. It didn't help. After two days' deliberation, the jury found him guilty. In April 2015, after a series of heartrending statements by the victim's family, Cole was sentenced to life imprisonment, with no parole for twenty-five years, for the crime of first-degree Mordor.

ON THE WRONG FOOT

In Waco, Texas, in 2015, five biker gangs had gathered at a restaurant, according to the *Santa Fe New Mexican*. Bikers are sensitive about the perception that they are all engaged in criminal activity. Police claimed that this Waco meeting was about bikers trying to settle differences over "turf," but one gang spokesman said that was untrue—they were just discussing motorbike laws and intellectual property issues, such as club logo trademarks.

The trademarks included those of the Bandidos and the Cossacks. There had been previous issues between the groups, including an earlier incident at a steakhouse where two men using the Bandidos insignia were involved in stabbing two other men wearing the Cossack label.

Arriving at the current meeting, some members had a difference of opinion about parking. During a thoughtful discourse on the subject, one rider ran over the foot of another.

This incident led to a wider disagreement in which many members offered their insight and analysis. Police arrived to mediate in this exploration of alternative viewpoints. When the discussion was over, nine gang members were dead and eighteen were injured.

Police confiscated around fifty weapons—mostly firearms and knives—from those who had attended the candid exchange of opinions and gunfire.

One of the bikers, a club vice president who was also a long-haul trucker, said that the motorcycle enthusiasts had only gathered to talk about legislative issues. He said that his group, the Boozefighters Motorcycle Club, organized charity events and family gatherings and was not a criminal gang.

When asked what had happened inside the restaurant, he declined to comment, saying that his highest priority was "not getting shot."

Around 170 bikers were charged with engaging in organized crime.

A police spokesperson said that the investigation was being hampered by witnesses who "are not being honest with us."

THE GETAWAY

NATURAL-BORN GRILLERS

In the suburbs of Dublin, a man owed money to a drug gang. It seems that the gang bosses had decided to make an example of him in December 2021, and they sent out two ruthless hit men to kill him.

According to Ireland's *Sunday World*, the assassins found their target and shot him. Unfortunately, it wasn't actually the man they were looking for, but a mechanic who lived in the neighborhood and was nearly thirty years older. (Fortunately, the mechanic didn't die and was rushed to hospital.)

But that was just their first mistake.

The assassins were unusually determined to cover their tracks. They had parked a car to use in their getaway, and after fleeing the scene in a van, they pulled up next to the car and switched vehicles.

Before leaving, they threw their weapons into the van. One of the gunmen doused the van in gasoline, then set fire to it. He was careless with the gasoline and set fire to himself, too. After they'd extinguished the flames on the burning hit man, the two got into the new car, a small black hatchback, and sped away.

Far from hiding their escape, their actions had drawn attention to it. The smoky blaze attracted the notice of everyone in the area, and neighbors called to report a fire.

Meanwhile, the men drove to their next location. They were still determined to "cover their tracks," so they switched vehicles again, this time to a silver hatchback that had been left waiting for them. As one man started the new getaway vehicle, the other repeated the previous routine, dousing their old car in gasoline. This time, he was even more careless splashing the jerry can around, and when he lit the car, he ignited a fireball that engulfed him.

The hit man—who was now more of a hot man—tried to run for the new getaway car, but he was disoriented and ran for the wrong vehicle, pulling desperately on its locked door. He finally ran for the silver hatchback, and the would-be killers made their escape.

The police checked hospitals for suspicious burn victims, but the criminals still have not been caught—which is the only aspect of their crime that can be considered "successful." One police source commented, "We have rarely if ever seen such a chain of complete incompetence linked to a planned assassination."

STICKUPS "R" US

"Aaron" liked fast food restaurants—not eating at them, but robbing them. He carried out many raids in the late 1990s. His modus operandi was to climb onto the roof and cut his way into the restaurant from above. He would then wait until the first workers entered the restaurant, rob it, and leave.

According to the *San Francisco Chronicle*, his method has earned him the nickname "Roofman," and he is thought to have robbed dozens of restaurants across the USA using this odd method.

You may wonder: Why cut a hole in the roof? Why not just walk in through the door? Because Aaron was an idiot, that's why. Which is also why he was caught and thrown in prison on a forty-five-year sentence. But in this case, that's just the start of the story.

Aaron was sent to Brown Creek Correctional Institution in Polkton, North Carolina. Nobody had ever escaped from the facility, but Aaron saw that as a challenge. In June 2004, when he was just four years into his sentence, he arranged a bold method for breaking out. He intended to leave by hanging under a truck, but he knew the undersides of trucks might be inspected. To avoid being spotted, he built a false platform resembling a truck undercarriage and managed to slip it under one of the vehicles. He escaped hidden between the platform and the real truck undercarriage as it left the prison.

It was, in its way, an impressive escape, and since he would be facing at least another forty years of prison if he were recaptured, you might expect that he would keep running, getting as far away as he could—Mexico, perhaps, or Chile.

Instead, he hitchhiked a short distance to Charlotte, North Carolina, and stayed there. That was strange.

Stranger still was his choice of a hideout. He made a home at the back of a Toys "R" Us store, cutting out a hidey-hole behind a bicycle display. Incredibly, he stayed hidden there for months without anyone finding him.

At night, he would ride bicycles around the store, or—going back to his Roofman persona—climb up onto the roof of the store and race toy cars around.

In the daytime, he went out like any normal citizen. He even got himself a girlfriend, "Grace." She was a few years older than Aaron, and she was charmed by him. He seemed well dressed, well spoken, and polite. She introduced him to the members of her church, and they were impressed, too.

Grace's church had a program for needy families, and Aaron volunteered to be a part of it. He generously donated toys to the needy kids. It's not hard to guess where the toys came from.

Grace and her church friends wanted to know more about her new boyfriend, but there were things he couldn't talk about. He told them he had a secret government job.

Aaron gave his girlfriend diamond earrings and other expensive gifts. It's not certain how he got them, although theft seems a likely guess. He gave gifts to her three children, too. Grace was delighted with her beau.

The creativity Aaron put into his audacious lies didn't seem to extend to his other life choices. It never crossed Aaron's mind to leave his toy-store home and find a safer place to live, although it seems obvious that, if he were discovered there, the police would get involved and he would be on his way back to the lockup. But Aaron stayed put.

It's not as if life at Toys "R" Us was comfortable. In fact, his lodgings weren't much better than the prison he had left—his living space was cramped, and he was eating mostly snacks and baby food he'd stolen from the store. There wasn't much to do at night, so he watched movies on DVD.

As Christmas approached, the toy store became busier. Staff were starting to get suspicious about the quantity of items going missing at the store, but Aaron still wouldn't leave. Instead, he extended his secret hideout, burrowing right through the wall and into a vacant electronics store next door. He set up a second cubbyhole there, under a stairwell. He painted his backup lair and decorated it with posters and action figures. He was thirty-three, but this looked like a prison escape by a ten-year-old.

However, Aaron wasn't so innocent, and he certainly hadn't given up on crime. On one occasion, he robbed a pawnshop and stole a gun. And when he needed to get some dental work done—perhaps it was all that Toys "R" Us candy he was eating—he burned down the dentist's office afterward. It's likely that he wanted to destroy any dental records that might be used against him—although it's also possible he had a grudge against the dentist.

Aaron planned still bigger crimes. He was preparing to carry out a robbery of a local store. Here, too, he seemed to suffer from a failure of imagination, because, in a city of 800,000 people, the store he picked to rob was the Toys "R" Us he was living in.

He carried out his master plan on Boxing Day, holding up the store at gunpoint. He got some cash, but the robbery didn't go well—two employees escaped and called police. The cops came for Aaron, and he escaped through his secret tunnel. Although he wasn't caught on-site, there were enough clues left behind in his criminal clubhouse that police were able to make further investigations. Members of the church identified pictures of Aaron, and police realized they were dealing with the same man who had escaped from prison the previous June.

The police talked to Aaron's girlfriend. Poor Grace was devastated when she discovered that the new love of her life was an escaped convict and robber. At first, she wouldn't believe it, but when they showed her the evidence, she was convinced.

But the police still hadn't got hold of Aaron, and they thought that his relationship with Grace might be a way to catch him. They persuaded her to help. Grace invited Aaron to a birthday party. When he showed up to the party—"Sur-*prise!*"—the police were waiting to take him into custody.

After he was back in jail, Aaron apologized to Grace for all the deceptions. She didn't know what to make of it all. She said, "I don't hate him. I'm disappointed and confused. I don't know whether to smack him or hug him." (We suggest option three: avoid him.)

Aaron also talked to his mother, in Sacramento. She wasn't impressed by her son's antics or his attitude. She commented, "He doesn't seem super-embarrassed about the notoriety. I know I would be."

PRISON BREAKS

"Jared," a twenty-three-year-old man from Maine, hated the idea of being in prison. He had been charged with trafficking and possession of drugs, and if convicted, he faced up to thirty-five years behind bars.

While waiting for his trial, Jared was held in the county jail, according to the *Portland Press Herald*. One day, during recreation period, Jared seized his moment. He ran, scaled a fence, and scrambled through two rows of barbed wire. Along the way, his pants and underwear got caught on the barbs, but every moment was critical, so he left them behind.

He kept running. He made it to the roof. Then he jumped—about a twenty-five-foot fall. As he landed, he fractured both feet.

Jared staggered on and stole an SUV. He drove toward his ex-girlfriend's house, intending to ask for her help in making a getaway.

Unfortunately, he crashed the vehicle not far from the jail. But there was no way he was stopping after he'd come this far. He kept driving. The police were following him by now. The car had a flat tire, so the police engaged in a low-speed chase.

Jared reached the ex-girlfriend's driveway and managed to crash the SUV a second time. (She might have been glad to be out of the relationship.) He was then arrested and taken to the hospital.

Unfortunately for Jared, his attempt to avoid jail time landed him additional charges of escape, which is a felony punishable by up to five years in prison. He was also charged with unauthorized use of property and violation of condition of release. He heard these charges via teleconference while in his hospital bed.

He also had to be moved from the county jail to the state prison so that he could have access to the medical services he needed to treat his many injuries.

PLAY DEAD

There's a snake called the hog-nosed snake that looks formidable but is harmless to humans. When the snake is threatened and can't get away, it tries a few tricks. First, it will coil up, hiding its head, and strike at the enemy with its tail. If that bluff doesn't work, the snake will roll on its back and pretend to be dead. If you put the snake on its front, it will roll around again, as if to say, "No, honestly, I'm quite definitely dead."

A thief in India used a similarly inept strategy, hoping to avoid arrest.

"Adri" was an old criminal who had built up a gang of young thieves. He called his gang "The Devil's Angels"—a name he'd lifted from a 1967 movie. He lured in impoverished young members, giving them gifts of mobile phones and tablets. One of these suckers was "Raju," a twenty-year-old. Adri sent him out on many burglaries.

According to the *Hindustan Times*, in April 2018, Adri, Raju, and another gang member broke into an apartment in Delhi a few minutes after they had seen the owners leave to go shopping.

Adri and the other gang member waited outside, while Raju went in to inspect the apartment. This was Adri's usual practice—he didn't like risks, so he'd let the kids do the crimes while he stayed safe.

Unfortunately for the crooks, the neighbors were also aware the homeowners had gone out, and they were puzzled by the sounds from the apartment. They went to investigate. The two men lurking outside the apartment ran for it, leaving their young comrade Raju behind.

Raju was unable to escape—a group of angry neighbors was gathering outside the door. Instead, he locked the door and stayed in the apartment.

Meanwhile, the neighbors called the owners, who confirmed that there should be nobody home. Whoever was in there was a thief.

Raju ran to the balcony to see if he could jump out. More neighbors were gathering there, and they were in a mean mood. Escape through that route was impossible.

The police soon appeared on the scene. They called for Raju to come out. He refused. The police kept asking. They warned Raju that, if he didn't unlock the door, they would have to force their way in. Raju didn't trust them and was afraid of being killed by the mob. He stayed put.

It was then that Raju hit on a scheme as bold as it was idiotic: he would pretend to be dead.

He banged his head against a wall, then smashed some crockery against his face to simulate what he hoped would appear to be a mortal injury.

The door burst open. The police rushed in. They found Raju lying under the dining table with his eyes tightly closed.

It's not clear exactly what deception Raju had in mind. He had been talking to the police minutes earlier, and he was the only person in the apartment. What was supposed to have happened here to bring about his demise? An attack by ghosts? A tragic accident while plate-spinning? He hadn't quite thought this through.

We also don't know exactly what he expected to happen when his poor corpse was discovered. Perhaps he thought the police would shake their heads at the waste of human life and leave his china-riddled body unguarded on the street or in an ambulance—whereupon he would make a quick getaway.

Of course, it wasn't going to work. As a cadaver, Raju was a complete failure. When the police pulled him out from under the table, his twitches made it perfectly obvious that he was alive and awake, even if he was sporting pieces of crockery on his face and clenching his eyes closed.

Still, he maintained his "I'm dead" pose as police shook him and asked him questions.

Finally, the officers told Raju that they really were police, not people pretending, and they would make sure he was safe from the crowd outside.

That did the trick. Raju opened his eyes and returned to the world of the living, allowing the officers to take him into custody.

However, Adri and the other treacherous gang members who had left him behind might have wished Raju's fake death had been real, because once Raju was in police hands, he found he had a receptive audience. He informed on the rest of the gang. Thanks to Raju's information, police arrested eight gang members—and two others who had received the stolen goods.

SCAMMERS

A DOUBLE SCAMMY

"Charles" was a middle-aged gentleman living in Farmington, New Mexico. Despite his respectable appearance, he was desperate for money and decided to con it out of his neighbors.

He made friends with a local couple at a basketball game, according to the *Albuquerque Journal*. He explained to them that he had just sold a valuable parcel of land, but the sale couldn't go through because someone had a lien on the land, and he also had to pay property taxes. The sympathetic couple lent him $1,700 to help out.

But Charles soon needed more. A month later, he returned to the couple and explained that there were further problems with the deal. The couple gave him more money. When he needed even more a few months later, he went to them again, and again they paid. Soon, they'd lent him $7,500. Charles assured them they needn't worry—once the money for the land deal arrived, he'd pay them back, along with an extra thousand for their kindness.

This couple weren't the only people paying Charles. He was spinning similar tales all over the area. To some, he gave the same story of a land deal. He told others he had a sick wife and needed to pay for her medical expenses. He was a good talker and appeared respectable. People heard his story and were moved. They wanted to help. In total, he scammed more than $86,000 from kindhearted people in his community.

But why did Charles need this money in the first place?

It was because he had received an email from a man in Nigeria, offering him the sum of $18 million for his assistance in withdrawing money from a bank.

That's right, Charles had fallen for the classic Nigerian email scam. Millions are promised, but first the dupe must send thousands to

Africa, to cover taxes, legal fees, bribes, and other fictional expenses. Every time the Nigerian scammer asked Charles for more money, Charles made up a new story to con the funds from his friends and neighbors.

Things came to a head when Charles finally ran out of money. Bankruptcy proceedings revealed the truth, and Charles was convicted of fraud, while the Nigerian scammers moved on to their next victim.

EXCUSES, EXCUSES

"Bill" was working for a private college in Calgary, Alberta, when he had a genius idea. The students all paid fees to the school. What if he could get them to pay their tuition fees directly to him? Instead of depositing the funds into the school's bank account, he would put them in his own. He'd be rich.

Bill managed to divert the tuition and enrollment fees of twenty-six students into his own bank account. According to the *Calgary Herald*, he collected over $14,000.

But in February 2019, he ran into a predictable problem. The students he'd bilked at the school were told their tuition hadn't been received. They said they'd already paid it to Bill. It didn't take Sherlock Holmes to solve the mystery.

The students didn't lose out, but the school had to eat the costs. They reported Bill's activities to the police, and the police took the fraudster in. Bill admitted his crimes. He was charged with theft over $5,000.

But when the court date rolled around for his sentencing in October 2021, Bill was a no-show. He said he couldn't make it because his mother had just died.

The judge wasn't happy, but set a new date in November, and told Bill he'd better show up.

Again, Bill didn't appear—at least, not in person. He talked to the judge from his iPhone. His excuse this time was that he was stuck in Toronto and couldn't get a flight for his court appearance.

The judge gave Bill a few more days to show up in court.

And again, Bill didn't appear. At that point, the judge didn't want to hear any more excuses and issued a warrant for Bill's arrest.

We don't know what excuse he would have given. Maybe "The dog ate my arrest warrant."

MONEY PYTHON

A woman in Africa took the theft of academic fees to a higher and more ridiculous level, as Nigeria's *Premium Times* reported in 2019.

"Faith" worked in an office for the Nigeria's National Examinations Council. Her office collected the fees paid by students who wanted to take exams. As a cashier, Faith took care of the money and made sure it was correctly deposited.

An auditor arrived to carry out a routine check of the books. Faith was worried about his arrival. She went to his hotel room and gave him an envelope of cash—the equivalent of around $140. She said it was a "gift" from her boss. She encouraged the auditor to accept the gift and go home, no questions asked.

The auditor was nervous, and he did go home, taking the money with him, but he immediately reported the bribe to his superiors. His bosses could see there was something bad going on here and carried out a detailed analysis of the council's accounts.

They discovered a huge shortfall. Around 36 million naira was missing—that's roughly US$100,000.

They called Faith in and asked if she could explain the missing money. Indeed, she could. She said that a snake had eaten it. There were a few problems with this theory, though. The sheer volume of paper the snake must have eaten would have been enormous—the missing money would have comprised at least 36,000 banknotes. And how did the snake get into the locked safe where the money was kept?

Faith offered other theories. She told investigators that a mermaid had sometimes appeared to her in her bedroom and attacked her. She also claimed that her housemaid was a witch. Perhaps one these supernatural events might be linked to the missing money.

Later, perhaps worrying that her story might have seemed incoherent, she tried to tie the elements together. She asserted that her witch-housemaid and her evil accomplices had been stealing the money spiritually. They summoned a magic snake that crawled into the office to steal the money from the vault. Now the story made sense.

Then, on further reconsideration, she claimed she had never said anything about a snake, and that higher-ups had stolen the money and put the blame on her.

Subsequent investigation showed that the same amount missing from the examination board had appeared in Faith's bank account. Faith assured them it was merely a coincidence. She explained that she liked to buy lottery scratch cards, and she had had some lucky wins.

The authorities did not accept any of her explanations and began legal action. When we last checked, Faith and a male colleague had been charged with fraud, misappropriation of funds, and criminal breach of trust.

On Twitter, Nigeria's Economic and Financial Crimes Commission commented that it would show no mercy to the "snake" that swallowed the money.

THESE AREN'T THE DROIDS
WE'RE LOOKING FOR

In 1977, America was going crazy for robots. *Star Wars* had just been released, and everyone loved the film's droids, R2-D2 and C-3PO.

When would technology like that be appearing in our homes?

"Right now," according to one inventor, "Carson." The *New York Times* reported that his company, Quasar Industries (nothing to do with the company that made TVs), claimed it had just completed a "domestic robot." This house robot looked like a cone with a round metal head. It was a little over five feet tall, with two flexible arms. Publicity photos showed it vacuuming the floor and turning storybook pages for a small child.

Carson demonstrated his robot live, too. It could speak, and it could understand simple instructions.

The robot was just a prototype, but they would be produced in quantity soon, claimed Carson. Consumers would be able to buy one for $4,000—which at the time, was the price of a low-end car. Starting in 1979, the company would produce 125 robots a day.

The announcement was a media sensation. Articles about the new invention appeared in the world's press and were included in encyclopedia yearbooks.

But computer experts were skeptical, to put it mildly. MIT professor Marvin Minsky had been working on computers and robotics for years. He said, "I don't think there's a ghost of a chance a mad scientist could come up with this."

Another scientist said the robot was "a preposterous fraud," adding that the "state of the art is nowhere near this—not in voice recognition, vision recognition or motion."

Carson was indignant. "What happens if I sell a thousand robots and they don't work? I'll be in jail. I'll be sued to high heaven. I tell you I've got the finished robot to prove our claims. I've got the goods."

Carson added, "They put Marconi down. They put Newton down. Every major scientist has been put down. To everyone who has put us down, I say, 'Just wait and see, buddy.'"

People waited, and they did see. And Carson didn't "have the goods." No robots came rolling off the production line in 1979, because the robot was a fake. Some models contained a human operator, while others were remotely controlled. The whole thing seems to have been an attempt to drum up investment for a device that was far beyond the capabilities of the time.

But although his robot was exposed as a fake, Carson was slippery enough to avoid jail. If he had found any investors, they didn't sue him when the robot was debunked. And when investigators pointed out the use of remote controls, Carson and his executives were evasive, saying that some of the features of the promotional droid had been intended only as "entertainment for the public."

Carson dodged a legal bullet. And the rest of us will have to wait a little longer for a domestic robot.

BEATING THE HIGH COST OF LOVING

Internet dating has offered new possibilities for the scammer. Take the case of "Candy," a lonely Australian widow who ventured into the world of online dating at the age of fifty-eight, whose story was reported in Adelaide's *Advertiser* newspaper in 2017.

On one site, Candy met "Stewart," a British doctor. He was charming and funny. He was also kind—he dedicated much of his time to volunteer work in Africa, where he was working on a synthetic form of animal feed that would help fight world hunger. As noble as his pursuits were, his career choice left him with little income, and most of his money was tied up in his account back home.

Candy wanted to show her new flame that she could bring something to the table, too. She happily handed over her savings—in a relationship, what's mine is yours.

But then Stewart ran into more trouble and needed more money. Candy didn't have any more to give, so she got creative.

She regularly attended a dance class, and one of the other women there had a wealthy husband, "Christopher." Candy approached him for a handout. She didn't tell Christopher about the doctor's work—perhaps she didn't want to reveal too much about her private life. Instead, she claimed she needed money to pay for own late husband's hospital and funeral bills and asked Christopher for a loan. Christopher gave her the money, and she passed it on to the doctor, who was grateful for the donation.

When Stewart needed more, Candy went to Christopher again. Over the next few months, Christopher loaned her more than $25,000 Australian (around US$20,000).

Eventually, Christopher started to get suspicious, and Candy soon received a visit from the police. She admitted the truth: she had been scamming Christopher so she could send money to her doctor boyfriend, Stewart.

Of course, it didn't take much investigation to reveal that Stewart didn't exist—Candy was simply funneling money to another scammer in Africa. It was a classic "romance scam."

Candy eventually sold her house to repay the stolen money. "Stewart" wasn't so generous and disappeared from the picture.

If you ever find yourself dating online, try some tricks to make sure the person you're talking to really is who they say they are—maybe ask for a picture of them holding up a sign that says, "I'm an impoverished British doctor who's figured out the secret to curing world hunger."

RANDOM ACTS OF CRIMENESS

NOT-SO-SMOOTH OPERATOR

People make calls to 911 for the strangest reasons. But you can expect the emergency operator to do their job properly . . . usually.

"Sophia" was a 911 operator in Houston, Texas. According to the *Houston Chronicle*, she had a unique way of fielding calls. When a call came through to her line, she would pick up and say nothing. Regardless of what the person on the other end was saying, she would then hang up. If coworkers looked in her direction, she was seen to be answering calls quickly. She looked like she was working. She probably figured that, if it was so important, the caller could phone back and be patched through to a more communicative operator in the big call center.

Obviously, when you're dealing with life-and-death situations, this is a bad way to do your job. Between 2015 and 2016, the forty-four-year-old operator received calls from people in the midst of armed robberies, medical emergencies, and even from police officers needing emergency help.

One man phoned to report a holdup and shooting at a convenience store. He ran from the store and phoned 911. Sophia answered the call. The caller tried to explain what was happening. Sophia hung up on him.

It may seem strange that she could get away with this behavior, but the call center where she worked handled more than three million calls a year.

Sophia's bosses only discovered her behavior when they carried out a routine check of emergency call data. It seemed that Sophia had a high number of very short phone calls—less than twenty seconds. A few short calls might be explained by technical problems or callers misdialing the emergency number, but it didn't make sense that so many of these calls were Sophia's. They took a closer look at her calls and discovered a few where she had replied to the caller. When a security guard called to report dangerous drag racing on the highway, she told him she didn't have time for it and hung up. Her bosses finally realized what was going on—that she had hung up on thousands of emergency callers, and endangered lives.

When police asked why she had ignored so many calls, she told them she "did not want to talk to anyone at that time."

She was charged with interference with emergency telephone calls. In court, her lawyer admitted she was "a poor-performing worker" but said she was "going through a hard time in her life." Sophia was found guilty. She could have been sentenced to a year in jail, but instead was given ten days in jail and eighteen months' probation.

SHOOTING HIS MOUTH OFF

We don't recommend that you ever hire a hit man, but if you do feel the need, make sure you choose carefully.

"Vince," aged thirty, was one of the owners of a gas station and convenience store on the outskirts of a small city in Louisiana. The other owner was his business partner, "Les." It's common for grudges to build between business partners, and when you're sitting behind the counter of a lonely store near a highway, there's plenty of time to let those grudges fester and grow. Perhaps that's what happened here. What we know for sure is that Vince wanted Les dead.

Vince contacted a mysterious figure, "Spike," who he figured would be a good assassin. Spike came to Vince's place of business, and Vince set out his expectations. He wanted Les dead and was willing to pay for it. Spike listened carefully, then went searching for Les. He found the intended victim, but instead of killing him, Spike warned Les that Vince was trying to kill him. Spike then went to the police and told them everything Vince had said.

According to a report on ABC affiliate WGNO-TV, the police carried out a detailed investigation and gathered evidence of the conspiracy. We're guessing the information-gathering was mostly chatting with Spike and taking notes. They then issued a warrant to arrest Vince.

When Vince heard he was a wanted man, he turned himself in—the whole case doesn't seem to have been a big strain on police resources.

Vince was booked and charged with solicitation of murder. The penalty for this crime in Louisiana is a minimum of five years in prison.

LOOKING FOR HITS ON THE WEB

"Megan" had been in a relationship with a guy, but then he dumped her. She wasn't going to take that sort of disrespect, so she went online to find someone who could bump off her ex.

It doesn't seem so unusual a story, but Megan and her ex-boyfriend were both fourteen years old.

According to ABC News, Megan found a site called Rent-a-Hitman and posted a request for a hired killer. She posted pictures of her ex, described which buses he took to and from school, and the places he normally hung out—all the information a killer might need to identify and kill her former boyfriend.

Megan didn't realize that Rent-a-Hitman isn't real. The site was created as a joke, originally to measure "hits" on webpages, and later as a spoof assassin site. But with a domain name like that, they sometimes get serious requests for assassins, and when that happens, the site administrators forward the requests to the police. Some reports have led to people being charged or convicted.

Megan was one of the lucky winners. She was arrested and placed in juvenile detention.

COP SHOP SHOPLIFTERS

Someone broke into the police station and stole the toilet last week. Detectives still don't have anything to go on."

Breaking into a police station sounds like a joke, but it's also a real—and really dumb—crime. And it happens more often than you might think.

Canadians are normally law-abiding, but when they crack, the police station is sometimes a target. In April 2022, CTV News reported on a thirty-eight-year-old thief in a small Ontario town. He apparently held a grudge against the cops, so he thought he'd break into their workplace. He tried to enter through an employee entrance. He had no luck there, so instead he vented his rage against The Man by cutting the internet lines going into the building. It did cause a disruption to police communications, as well as disconnecting a business next door. The Man then charged him with breach of probation, attempted breaking and entering, and mischief under $5,000. That showed 'em.

In July 2018, in London, Ontario, the police Twitter account reported on a forty-two-year-old vandal who went on a destructive nighttime spree. He smashed the window of one store, then repeatedly hit the door of another. (Door hitting doesn't seem like a satisfying way to release your pent-up anger, but who are we to judge?) His next stop was the police station. He used a bicycle chain to strike the glass door of the station. The glass eventually broke, and he made his way inside. Of course, by that time, the police were waiting for him. They ordered him to drop the chain. When he refused, they shot him with a Taser. He was charged with breaking and entering with intent, possession of a weapon, and mischief under $5,000.

A twenty-seven-year-old woman in West Wyoming (a borough of Pennsylvania) had a different motivation for her 2019 police station break-in, according to NBC News. She'd been arrested the previous year and had fallen in love with the arresting officer. He had no interest in her, but it didn't stop her from sending him a barrage of suggestive messages on social media. She also used to call 911 in the hope of hearing his voice. One night, she smashed the station's glass doors with a cigarette butt receptacle—pure class!—and went rummaging through the station's filing cabinets to remove her own files . . . and perhaps to find more information about the cop of her dreams. The whole thing was caught on camera, and she was later caught in person, facing charges that included burglary, vandalism, and harassment.

In Malawi, locals weren't impressed with their police force when a robber broke into the police station and stole guns while the officers were present. According to the website *Malawi24*, the twenty-five-year-old thief entered the station early one morning in February 2022 and lifted a rifle, with eleven rounds of ammunition, from the counter. The thief also took two mobile phones belonging to officers—the phones were plugged in, charging at the outlet.

The officer on duty said he only caught a glimpse of a hand taking the rifle. He called for help, but said the thief was too fast and escaped. It didn't sound too convincing, and the public demanded changes to the way the police operated. One citizen asked if anyone was safe in a country where a twenty-four-hour police station could be so easily robbed.

The thief was found two months later and arrested for the crime. The officers on duty faced charges of negligence.

But these crimes can also happen in countries where the police have a good reputation. Stuff.co.nz reported one example. In Wellington, New Zealand, a thirty-nine-year-old burglar was walking down a city street. The date was April 25, 2019—Anzac Day, a holiday in New Zealand

and Australia. The criminal spotted an open garage door at the police station. He crept in, broke down an interior door, and entered an area where weapons were kept. The country had recently passed tough new gun laws, and the police station had an exhibit of some of the weapons that were unacceptable. The burglar stole those—twenty-six guns in total—and made a successful escape. New Zealanders were outraged that such a thing was possible, and questions were raised in the country's parliament. Police were deeply embarrassed—and highly motivated to catch the thief. Their efforts paid off. Most of the weapons were eventually recovered. The thief was caught and jailed for two years and three months.

NO-GOOD BAD GUYS

JUST DESSERTS

A successful robbery requires planning—but the devil is in the details. Consider this example reported in the *Des Moines Tribune* back in 1959.

It seems two New York thieves were preparing for a lucrative job. The thieves, who were also brothers, were going to steal the payroll of a local garage owned by the Fifth Avenue Coach Company.

They knew payday was coming up. The payroll was around $3,000, and the cash was kept in a box. The brothers needed to hit the garage at just the right time—while the money was on the premises, but before anyone had been paid. Then they could walk away with the lot.

They didn't want to risk their car registration being recognized, so they stole a car and used that to drive to the garage. They both had guns.

They entered the garage. The timing was perfect. Two mechanics were sitting there, and nearby was a cardboard box. The mechanics were shocked and surprised as the brothers pulled out their guns, grabbed the box, and left the premises.

The thieves ran back to their car and made a fast getaway—perhaps a little too fast. As they sped along the highway, driving an unfamiliar vehicle, they sideswiped several other cars. The collisions brought their drive to an end. The police arrested the thieves and took them in.

Inside the car, the police found an automatic pistol, a revolver, and a cardboard box. Inside the box was not $3,000 in cash, but a treat the mechanics were hoping to enjoy at lunch: a custard pie.

HANDS UP—I HAVE A BOTTLE

The really inept robbers don't work for long. For some, their career is over in a few hours, like the fellow behind this sorry crime spree reported in the *Amarillo Globe Times*.

"Vito" was twenty-three years old and lived in Fresno, California. In March 1973, he hit the streets for a day of profitable crime.

First stop: to pick up a fistful of easy cash from the convenience store. Vito walked in. He didn't have a gun, and figured he didn't need one. With the right attitude, any weapon would do. Vito grabbed a bottle and waved it toward the clerk. "I want cash and I want it now."

The clerk ignored him, so Vito tried again. The clerk was unimpressed by Vito and his bottle. He continued to ignore him.

Vito threw the bottle in the direction of the clerk, then ran out of the store. His first robbery was a failure.

Vito changed strategy. Who needs money from convenience stores, when you can just take what you need from random people on the street? Vito spotted a guy in a nearby alley. He walked up to the man and demanded five dollars.

The man wouldn't pay. He said if Vito wanted money, he'd have to fight for it.

Vito was ready to follow through. He fought the stranger. He lost. Badly.

Vito staggered away, covered in blood—mostly his own. He found some water in a nearby yard and washed his face. The homeowner came out—a kind lady. She was concerned for Vito and invited him inside to clean himself up properly.

Vito went into the house and treated his wounds. It was a nice place, and he thought he wouldn't mind staying a while. So, when the lady who owned the house asked him if he would please leave now, he simply refused.

The woman was alarmed and left her house, leaving Vito alone there.

Some minutes later, Vito heard police sirens approaching. But he'd counted on this—all he had to do was hide. If the cops can't find you, they can't catch you.

Vito figured the cops would be looking for him inside the house, so he would foil them by going out onto the street and sliding underneath a car. He could watch the cops investigate the house, then slide back inside when they were done.

Unfortunately, the police quickly spotted the criminal hiding under the car and dragged him out.

Vito was charged with robbery and battery. And if incompetence were a crime, they'd have thrown the book at him.

HARSH JUDGMENT

Psychiatrists talk about the Dunning-Kruger effect. It means that, if you're bad at something, you may be so bad at it that you can't see how bad you are. In fact, if you're inept enough, you may think you're pretty good.

"Dalton" was a hard-core burglar in England who thought he was good at his chosen career. The *Daily Mail* reported that, in February 2018, he left his home on the outskirts of London and drove eighty-five miles to a little village, not far from Stratford-on-Avon.

He had carefully chosen his target house—an expensive home on a quiet, country road. The house sat on three acres of land and wasn't visible from the road.

He broke into the house and started hunting around for valuables. But either he didn't realize the house was occupied, or he thought he was being much quieter than he was. The couple who lived in the house heard his movements and checked their dining room, where they discovered Dalton in mid-theft.

Dalton ran, grabbing the keys to their car on his way out. He reached the driveway and jumped into their expensive Porsche SUV. One of the homeowners tried to grab the keys from him as he ran past, then tried to smash the vehicle window once he was inside, but Dalton floored it and sped away.

The couple immediately reported the break-in. Automated cameras on the motorway soon picked up the license plate as Dalton raced by. Police were alerted and moved in to catch the thief. Dalton was now being followed by police cars and a police helicopter.

For the next twenty-five minutes, Dalton led the police on a high-speed chase, traveling at speeds of more than 115 miles per hour. Finally, he was surrounded and forced to a stop. Police officers approached the car, but Dalton refused to open his car doors. The officers had to break into the vehicle to drag him out. Dalton was arrested and taken away. He tested positive for cocaine. He was charged with burglary, theft, and dangerous driving.

In court, the judge reviewed Dalton's long criminal record. At forty-six, he had many convictions, including numerous domestic burglaries. Dalton thought of himself as a "professional" burglar, but the judge offered a fresh perspective of Dalton's thieving abilities. He said, "It is amazing that with thirty-one convictions for 115 offenses, it has not dawned on you that you're not very good at crime."

With that criticism ringing in his ears, Dalton was led away to serve a six-year sentence.

KEEP ON SUCKIN'

"Jordan" was a car thief with more determination than skill. He had his larcenous eye on a certain truck in Abbotsford, British Columbia. In late 2018, he broke into the truck to steal it. He pulled out the ignition wires so he could hot-wire the vehicle, but the engine wouldn't turn over. Finally, frustrated, Jordan had to leave the truck where it was. It was a real shame.

Jordan went off to practice his hot-wiring abilities. According to the *Abbotsford News*, he returned to the truck a few months later. The owner had fixed the damage from Jordan's previous break-in, so the thief decided to take another crack at it. He broke into the truck, pulled out the wires, connected them . . . but still he couldn't start the engine. The failure was maddening, but nothing could be done. For a second time, Jordan had to give up.

But this thief was no quitter. He just needed more practice to hit that next level. A few months later, he felt ready. He was calm. He was confident. He was ready for another attempt. He stood before the truck once again. It had been repaired and looked as good as ever. Third time's the charm, surely. This time, the prize would be his.

Jordan broke into the truck. He applied his new leveled-up hot-wiring abilities. And, once again, nothing happened. The engine wouldn't start. He couldn't drive the truck away. Another disappointment.

We can't be sure what happened next, but Jordan seemed determined to get that truck, so it is likely that he returned for a fourth crack a few weeks later. When he did, in August 2019, he found a handwritten note on the truck window. It was written by the truck's angry owner. It read:

Dear Thief: No fob = No engine start. You suck at stealing this truck. After three attempts in ten months, probably time to learn a new skill as you can't even properly steal a truck. You've cost me $1,200 in lost use and deductibles and fees for others.

He signed off: "Quit trying to steal my truck. You suck at it!"

The letter was printed in the *Abbotsford News* and made a laughing-stock of the thief.

It all seems to have been the last straw for Jordan. As far as we know, he hasn't touched the truck since then. Jordan was never caught by police. We hope this inept car thief took the owner's excellent suggestion and changed to a more useful career.

THERE'S ALWAYS ANOTHER BUS

"Kevin" was fresh out of prison on an early release. According to the *Scottish Sun*, he'd been handed his release papers and a travel voucher with his name on it, covering the cost of his trip home.

He left the prison building, HMP Grampian, and walked to the bus stop, where he waited for the bus. The bus was some time in coming and the wait made Kevin impatient. Finally, he figured he'd skip the bus and take a taxi.

Literally, *take* a taxi.

He found the cab at a nearby gas station. The driver had left his vehicle at the pump while he went inside to pay for fuel. Kevin jumped into the vehicle and drove away.

He wasn't a careful driver. By the time he arrived at his destination in Aberdeen, one of the taxi's windows was broken, the wing mirrors were damaged, and the car had many other dents and scratches.

Kevin abandoned the vehicle and walked to the house of his ex-girlfriend. This was another legal problem for him—there were issues between them, and one of the conditions of his bail was that he had to stay away from her.

He visited the ex and talked with her, then he left. He didn't want to go back to the battered taxi, so he stole her car on the way out.

In the meantime, police found the cab. Kevin had left his prison travel voucher, which had his name on it, inside.

Later, they also found the girlfriend's stolen car, parked on another street. Kevin had forgotten some papers there, too—his prison release documents.

The police caught up with Kevin himself the next day, as he was riding a bicycle. And yes, the bicycle was stolen.

One of Kevin's representatives said he had since had a "shift in his thinking" and wanted an opportunity to "sort himself out." But others pointed out that this didn't seem likely, given the crime spree he'd been on. He had only been out of prison for twenty minutes before stealing that taxi.

One lawyer said Kevin's string of crimes was "absolutely insane," and was "some of the most inept and unsophisticated criminal behavior I have ever seen." And that was the lawyer defending him.

In court, Kevin pleaded guilty to the six charges against him—two thefts of a vehicle, driving without a license, driving without insurance, theft of a bike, and breaching bail conditions. He was sent back to prison to serve another ten months of his original sentence, plus 123 days for the new crimes.

If you can't do the time, don't do the crime. And if you *can* do the time, and they finally let you out, you can surely wait a few more minutes for the next bus.

WORST BURGLAR ON FACEBOOK

"Cameron," a thirty-five-year-old car thief, tried to steal a van in Manchester, England. He was interrupted in mid-crime and ran off. And, like a few other thieves we've looked at, he forgot his ID and mobile phone.

Usually, this is the cue for the owner to contact police and for the criminal to be arrested, but the owner of the van, "Michael," was furious about the break-in and wanted to let Cameron know exactly what he thought of him. While this might not be an approach the police would recommend, it was an embarrassing outcome for Cameron.

According to the *Sun* newspaper, Michael used the phone to log onto Cameron's Facebook account. He changed Cameron's job title to "dosser" (British slang for a worthless vagrant) and added a few comments in Cameron's name. "Am I a crackhead? Yes. Do I leave my phone in people's vans I'm trying to jack? Yes I did."

Cameron was livid when he saw the posts. In his expletive-filled reply, he demanded to know who had taken his phone, adding, "It's on when I find you."

Michael responded by changing Cameron's Facebook password, so Cameron could no longer access his own account, then taunting him more. Cameron's contacts were entertained by the exchange and mocked their thieving Facebook friend.

A DIST-INK-TIVE FACE

Twenty-year-old "Gabriel" saw himself as a tough guy. He dressed and posed like the gang member he was. Colorado's *Pueblo Chieftain* reported that, over his upper lip, in place of a mustache, he had a tattoo with the words *East Side*—his gang's name. Below his lower lip, where a hipster might grow a soul patch, he had a triangular tattoo with a stylized number thirteen. He lived in Pueblo County, Colorado, an area with a sky-high rate of violent crime.

You wouldn't think a guy like that would be drawn to Elvis Presley—perhaps his tough exterior hid a penchant for flamboyant bell-bottoms and sequins? Whatever the reason, in May 2010, Gabriel and his gangland chums decided to rob the home of a local Elvis impersonator.

Gabriel put on a mask and joined his gang as they carried out a home invasion of the impersonator's residence. But, although the mask obscured most of Gabriel's face, his mouth and the text around it were all clearly visible.

Shortly after the robbery, Gabriel was busted and sent to jail on unrelated drug changes.

While he was locked up, police were busy gathering information and clues relating to the home invasion. One eyewitness described a man with writing on his face, and the police reaction seems to have been, "Oh, *that* guy—the one with the goofy looking East Side mustache tattoo." So, while Gabriel was languishing in prison on his drug offenses, he suddenly found himself facing new charges for robbing the Elvis impersonator. "Thank you. Thank you very much. And now it's time for 'Jailhouse Rock.'"

It proved to be a useful arrest for law enforcement. A few months later, the *Pueblo Chieftain* reported that, despite having had his gang's name tattooed on his face, Gabriel was not averse to snitching on its members. He testified against another gang member, telling how the two of them had been walking by a gang-controlled garage in 2009 when they heard a party going on. His friend fired seven shots randomly through the door, killing one man. As a result of Gabriel's testimony, the killer was charged with murder and attempted murder and given a life sentence, plus one hundred years.

It sounds like Gabriel made a deal with the police. But if he enters witness protection and doesn't want to be tracked down, he should really do something about those tattoos.

FOR YOU, NO CHARGE

In 1987, "Ralph" and "Doug" were having problems with their Cadillac. The car needed a new battery, but these two didn't want to pay for one. As they cruised the streets of San Jose, Ralph spotted an auto parts store. A suitable battery stood on display in the window, just steps from the entrance. They came up with a plan to steal the battery.

According to a UPI news story, they parked their Cadillac at a gas station across the road from the auto parts store. Ralph went into the store first and talked to the salesperson to distract him. Then Doug crept in, picked up the battery, and ran for it.

The two men had arranged to rendezvous back at the gas station. On close inspection, they noticed that their new battery was lighter than usual. Was it some modern technology? Ralph opened it up and looked inside. He spotted a problem: it was dry. Obviously, it needed to be topped up with water. So, they set to work filling it up.

It didn't seem to occur to the thieves that Doug, who'd fled the store with the battery, was now standing directly across the road from the scene of the crime, in easy view of the salesperson he'd just robbed. As Ralph and Doug were putting the new battery in place, police cars showed up at the gas station.

The two men were arrested, and the stolen battery was returned to the auto parts store, whose assistant manager was mystified by the theft. The "battery" the pair had stolen was just a display piece—an empty case with cardboard inside. "We have to drain it out now because all the cardboard is soaked," he complained.

The battery might not have been charged, but Ralph and Doug were—one of the dumber criminal duos to operate in San Jose.

A comment by one of the police officers sums up this case, and perhaps most of the crimes in this book: "We don't catch the brilliant ones."

ACKNOWLEDGMENTS

I'd like to give special thanks to my daughters Zoë McKenzie and Marina McKenzie for all their work in finding and researching many of the stories in this book.

I would also like to thank Dr. Thorsten Heitzmann for his advice and help in translation, and Professor Robert Gellately at Florida State University for his invaluable assistance with the story of the German imposter Schilling.

Duncan McKenzie
Oakville, Ontario